Yalla Niclas *The camera's mirror reflects the photographer's vision.*

EXAKTA

P H O T O G R A P H Y

A manual of the Exakta-Exa single-lens

Reflex Camera System

BY JACOB DESCHIN

Author of "35mm Photography"

CAMERA CRAFT PUBLISHING COMPANY • 95 MINNA STREET • SAN FRANCISCO 5, CALIFORNIA
THE FOUNTAIN PRESS, 46 47 CHANCERY LANE, LONDON WC 2

Contents

                    5

LIST OF CONTRIBUTORS OF PHOTOGRAPHS

Preface

The first Kine Exakta reached this country from the Ihagee Camera Works in Germany early in 1937. In a period when, as now, the current trend was 35mm photography, the new camera came as an original contribution in a field dominated by rangefinder miniatures. Not that the principle was unique. The Ihagee company itself had placed on the market four years earlier a so-called "vest-pocket" size Exakta, which took 1⅝x2¼-inch pictures. But the concept was different, incorporating in an attractive, compact format, a number of advanced features built on precision lines, the new design standard which even then was beginning to affect the entire photographic industry.

In many respects—quick interchangeability of lenses, a condenser type ground glass for increasing image brilliance, a range of twenty-nine shutter speeds, etc.—the latest IIa model, the fifth in the line, remains unchanged from the first. Important, relatively recent innovations, which many feel have given the single-lens reflex field a new lift in popular favor, are the pentaprism, which interchanges with the reflex hood for eye-level focusing, and the automatic preset-diaphragm lens. In addition, a simplified version of the big camera, the Exa, with some of the Exakta's basic features, though considerably less complex, was introduced a few years ago.

This book is about the Exakta Light-Meter IIa and VX and the Exa, a detailed manual on how the cameras and their accessories work, and their many applications in a wide range of activity from the amateur's recreations to the specialized demands of the professional and the scientist. Julius Weber has contributed an authoritative, comprehensive and practical chapter on the Exakta's uses in medical, dental and scientific work, and in another chapter Lynwood M. Chace has done a similar service for nature photography with an Exakta. To these, to others who have supplied essential data and inspiring illustrations, and in particular to Wolf Wirgin, whose suggestions and guidance in the preparation of this book have been invaluable, the author acknowledges his debt and offers grateful thanks.

Jacob Deschin
Smithtown, New York

NOTE: *Because of the frequent reference to details of the Exakta or Exa camera in this manual, the reader is urgently advised to have his camera handy while reading the book. Thus he will be able to check descriptions and comments by immediate examination of the camera and make the most of what the book can offer him in practical help and advice.*

8

1
The Exa

2 *The Exakta Light-Meter IIa*

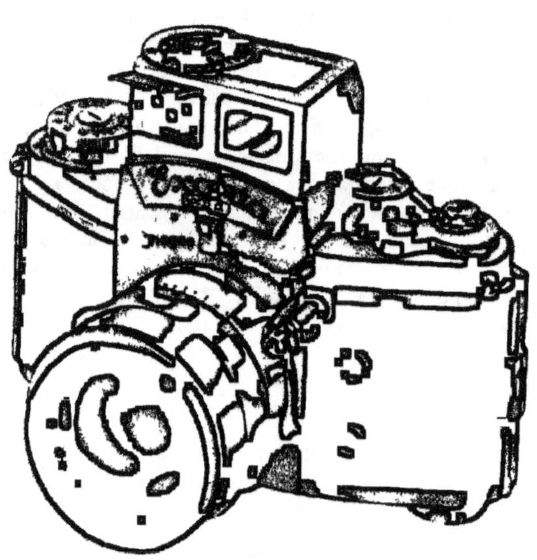

The Reflex Way—Two Versions

Picture subjects are viewed and focused in the Exakta and the Exa cameras by means of the mirror reflex principle: the lens projects an image of the subject onto the mirror, which, being set at an angle, in turn reflects the image up to the ground glass in the camera hood, where it is studied for interest and composition, and focused for sharpness. Because of the action of the lens, the picture in the mirror is upside down and reversed from left to right. When reflected to the ground glass, the image is seen right side up again but still reversed laterally. When the shutter is released, the mirror automatically swings up against the ground glass to permit the image to come through to the film plane. The mirror is reset when the lever or knob is wound for the next exposure.

The principle basically is the same for the two finder devices used on the Exakta and the Exa—the conventional reflex hood (Fig 3) and the pentaprism (Figs 7, 8, 9)—but the latter goes a few steps further. One, it shows the image both right side up and correct as to right and left, two, it is designed for eye-level focusing and viewing, a particularly valuable feature when taking pictures in a vertical format; three, both eyes are used wide open, instead of squinting with one as with other camera types—one for the finder, the other to watch the subject directly; four, the subject is seen exactly the same size in the finder as it is in life.

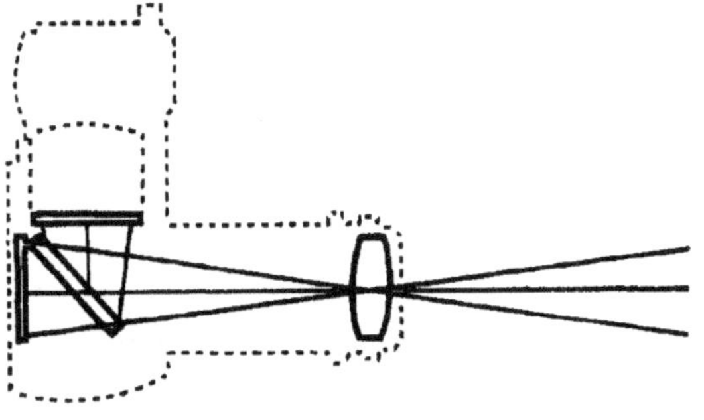

The diagram illustrates the principle of the mirror reflex camera, the practical application of which is demonstrated on the opposite page The angled mirror gathers the image and reflects it up to the ground glass above, where it is studied by the photographer.

4

The subject appears reversed from left to right when viewed on the ground glass in the camera hood. Actually, it is only an upside-down mirror reflection (picture below) seen right side up

5

Because a lens projects an image into the camera upside down, this is the way it looks on the reflex mirror. The mirror is set at a critically placed angle to receive the full image and to reflect it up to the ground glass At the instant of pressing the shutter release button, the mirror moves up by spring action swiftly out of the way (to rest flat just under the ground glass) and the image is recorded on the film just as it appeared in the mirror

6

When the developed negative is printed, emulsion side toward the printing paper the subject is shown correctly as to right and left.

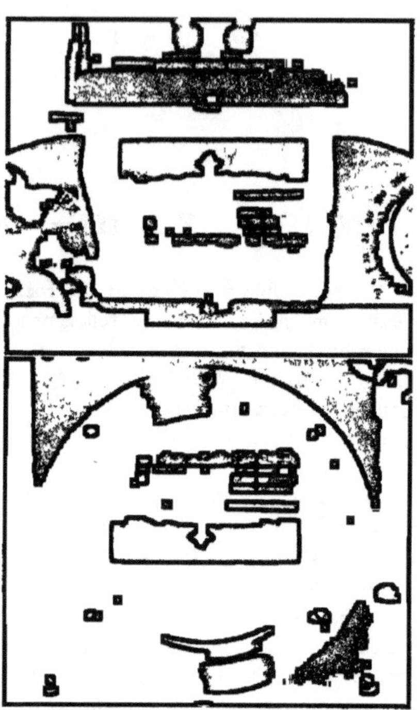

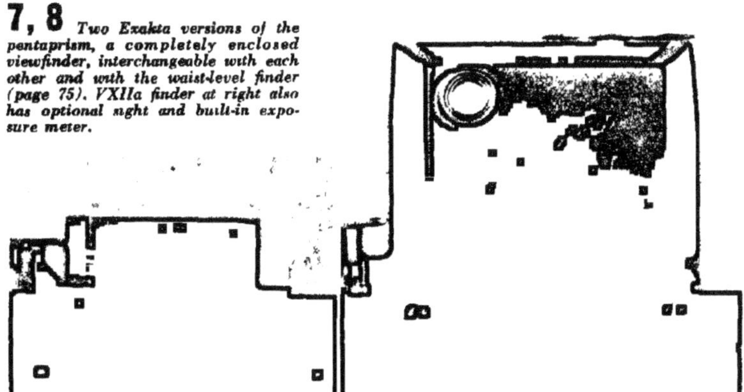

7, 8 *Two Exakta versions of the pentaprism, a completely enclosed viewfinder, interchangeable with each other and with the waist-level finder (page 75). VXIIa finder at right also has optional sight and built-in exposure meter.*

Reflex vs. Pentaprism

All of these are wonderful advantages and have done much to promote the wider use of the single-lens reflex camera type However, increased operating convenience has been achieved at the expense of some versatility (see Figs. 122-126) of the regular reflex hood, including such possibilities, for example, as the low angle and the overhead shot Therefore, although many subjects are best handled with the Pentaprism, accessibility of both finders will provide the photographer with a more complete battery of viewing and focusing facilities. Since both finders are instantly interchangeable on either the Exakta or the Exa, switching from one to the other is a simple matter

Handling routines, as well as fuller design details, are covered in Chap. 6

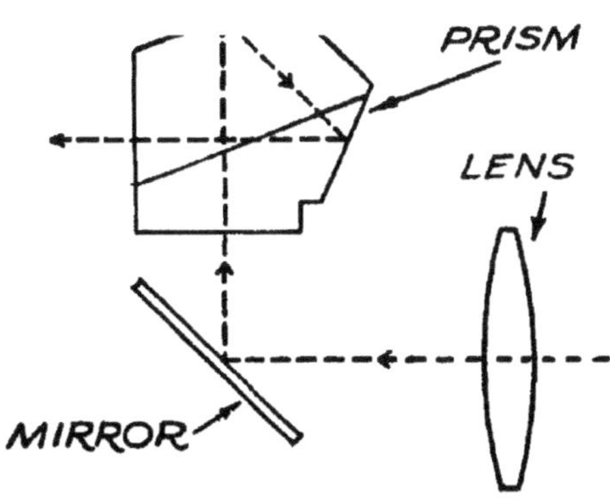

In the pentaprism, as in the reflex finder (Fig. 3), the image is intercepted by the angled mirror and sent up to the finder, but the viewing and focusing arrangement is radically different The arrows show the course of the image as it travels from lens to mirror, to prism and, via the eyepiece, to the photographer's eye.

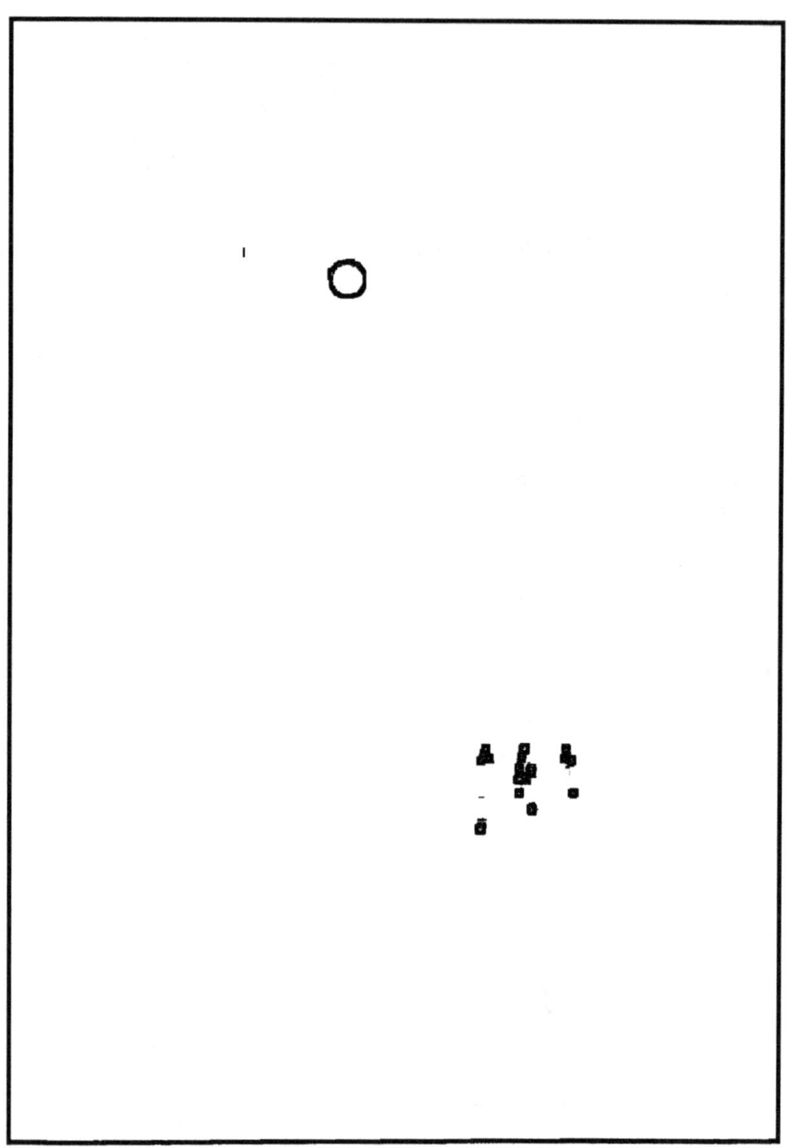

10

Yella Niclas. *A moonlight scene that looks and is real because it was shot "straight" A 1/5 second exposure on medium-speed film with the Biotar f/2 wide open, plus careful processing did the trick*

The Two Cameras-An Introduction

This chapter is by way of introduction to the working parts of the two cameras that are, in the main, the subject of this book, the Exakta VXIIa and the Exa 35mm single-lens reflex cameras Primarily, the purpose is identification. Illustrations and captions to this end appear on pages 15, 16 and 17 for the VXIIa, on 19, 20 and 21 for the Exa. How the various parts perform in actual practice will be described in detail as we go along in the book.

The Exakta VXIIa, like its predecessors in the line, uses standard 35mm miniature film, has provision for interchanging lenses ranging widely from 24mm focal length to 1000mm, and is equipped with a focal-plane shutter that offers 29 automatic speed settings from as long as 12 seconds to as short as 1/1000th of a second.

Because the subject is viewed, as well as focused, directly through the lens that takes the picture, the camera is free of the parallax problem which exists when the focusing-viewing function is separate from the lens. Parallax is the phenomenon of disparity between the limits of the subject as seen in the finder and the image that comes through the lens. It is caused by the fact that the finder device is located at another point on the camera than the lens, usually above it.

For many, and in particular for those who are interested in working close to the subject, this feature is the single-lens reflex camera's chief attraction. For this reason, it is much favored by nature photographers, technical and research workers, in the medical and other specialized fields, as well as by the amateur, whose interests are legion.

Wide Choice of Lenses

The ease of interchanging lenses (and auxiliary accessories) on the Exakta simply by flipping a lever and giving the lens a short turn on the bayonet mount, has inspired the production of an endless variety of lenses for the Exakta, so that a photographer can switch in a matter of moments from a minute subject extremely close up to a mountainous one at a great distance, and get acceptably large images in both instances.

The variety of opportunities made possible by this plentiful choice is discussed in the chapter on lenses. But mention should be made here of the

(Continued on page 18)

11

The front view.

12, 13

Top and bottom views

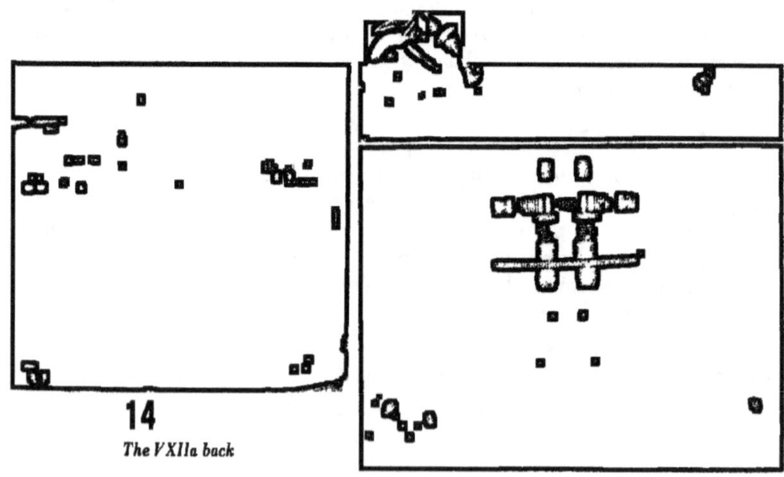

14

The VXIIa back

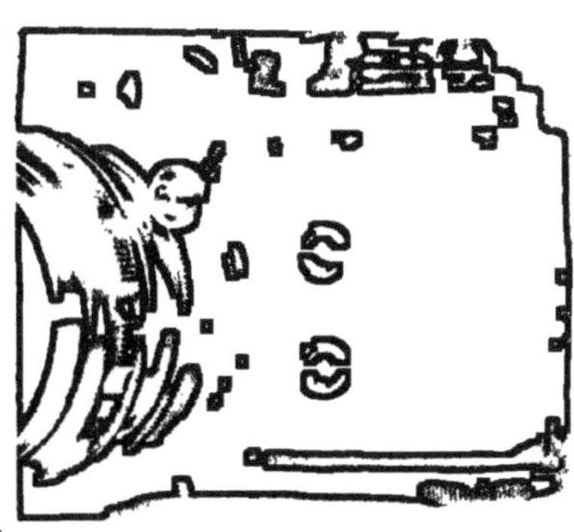

15

The right-hand, front side of the VXIIa shows the electronic (X) flash socket (top) F bulb socket below Alongside the lens, top to bottom, are the shutter release lock over the camera body release, hidden by the automatic-diaphragm control (with cable release socket) in front of the body release, and the lens-change lever Just under the VXIIa emblem is the catch for releasing the finder so it can be lifted out

16

The left side shows the M flash socket and the pin (partially extended) which holds the back attached to the camera To remove the back the pin is pulled all the way out of the hinge Adjacent (extreme left) is a lug for attaching a carrying strap

17

Left to right, exposure counter window (which is set by turning the small arrow-marked disk above it); film rewind release button; the lever for simultaneously advancing the film and winding the shutter; and the fast-speed shutter-setting knob (outer ring is lifted and turned to set the desired speed)

18, 19

Two views of the slow-speed knob; left, face of the VX knob, showing automatic time exposure setting (1/5th to 12 seconds) and—in light numbers—delayed-action time exposure settings from 1/5th to 6 seconds. The tiny window at extreme left shows the "speedom eter" that revolves as the film is advanced or rewound Right, the IIa knob, showing film type and speed indicator for black-and-white and color film.

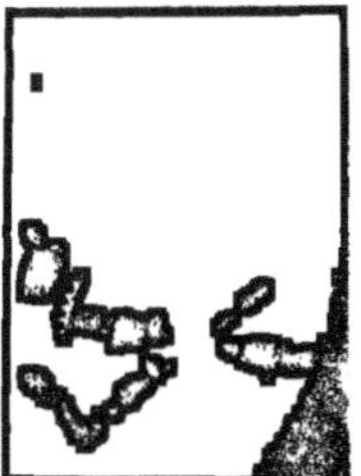

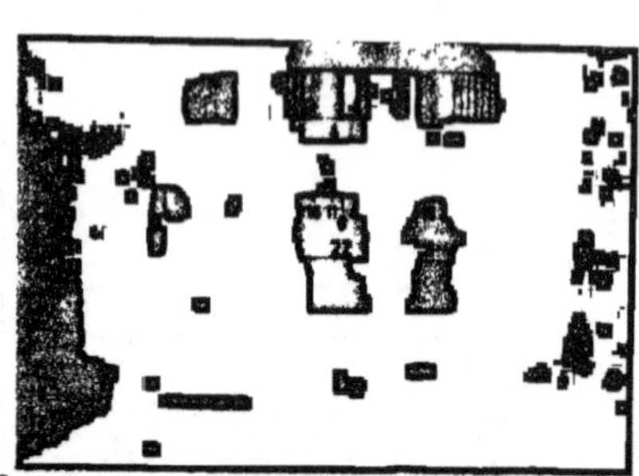

20

The Auto-Quinon 55mm f/1 9 on the IIa, with lever release at left for operating the automatic-diaphragm control Principal scales of figures, from bottom to top, are the lens aperture ring with click stops, the depth-of-field scale, and the distance scale, in feet. Knurled ring at front is for focusing

21

Facing bottom of camera right hand knob is depressed at center as shown for rewinding the exposed roll into the original cassette (unless the spool-to-spool method, Fig 88 is used) while depressing the rewind release button (Fig 17 The partially extended shaft operates a built-in knife for cutting off partially exposed rolls (Fig 88).

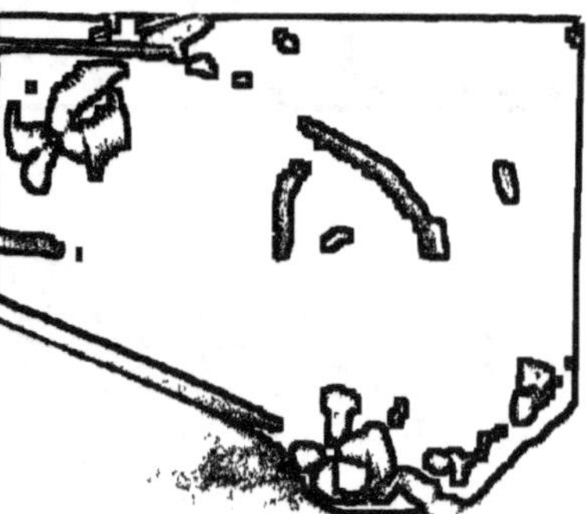

22

The locking device for the I X and IIa camera back When the knob is pulled out and given a short turn, the lock is released and the back can be opened To lock the camera the back is closed and the knob is given a short turn when it will spring into the camera body, shutting it up tightly At left is the tripod socket and camera leveling foot The interior of the Exakta is covered on page 45

23

The eyepieces of the Light-Meter pentaprism viewing and focusing finder (Fig. 8) on the VXIIa The finder is interchangeable with the regular focusing hood (Fig. 33) or pentaprism At right is the film-indicator knob.

automatic-diaphragm control on some Exakta lenses, such as the 58mm Biotar f/2 (for the Exakta) and the 50mm f/3 5 Meyer Auto-Primotar (for the Exa), which permits viewing with the lens wide open until an instant before the exposure, when the lens is closed down automatically for the exposure The necessity for viewing a darkened ground glass caused by stopping down the lens has been a drawback of the reflex camera until the innovation of the new idea several years ago.

Reference is also deserved for the pentaprism finder, the design and virtues of which are discussed in Chapter One Other conveniences that contribute to the efficiency and flexibility of the Exakta are cassette-to-cassette loading (Fig. 84); the built-in film knife for cutting off partially exposed rolls for processing; full flash and electronic flash synchronization facility, etc.

Exakta Features in the Exa

The Exa is a simplified version of the Exakta Although it lacks the many refinements of the latter, it does incorporate some of the more important features, including the automatic diaphragm lens, lens interchangeability and facility for using the hooded finder or Pentaprism. The lens mount is identical with the lens mount of the Exakta. Its shutter is not the focal-plane type but a slightly curved (drum-type) metal capping device with speeds from 1/25th to 1/150th of a second, plus bulb for time exposures.

The "Dry Run"

Owners of new cameras fall generally into two classes, those who are so eager to get going that they only half-read the instructions before they start using the camera (sometimes with disastrous results) and that class of over-diffident novices who are in such awe of the instrument that they find it hard to get started at all.

On the theory that, following a minimum do-this-then-this briefing, a quick acquaintance with the camera's operation through actual use of the parts, will satisfy the first group and benefit the other, pages 24 and 25 list step-by-step instructions for a "dry run" (no film in the camera) with the Exakta and the Exa. Only the worst case of camera stage fright will survive this harmless and invigorating exercise. As for the eager-beaver, the cold plunge should serve to calm the initial ardor sufficiently to permit a more patient consideration of the camera's features.

18

24

The front view

25, 26

Top and back views

27

The bottom view

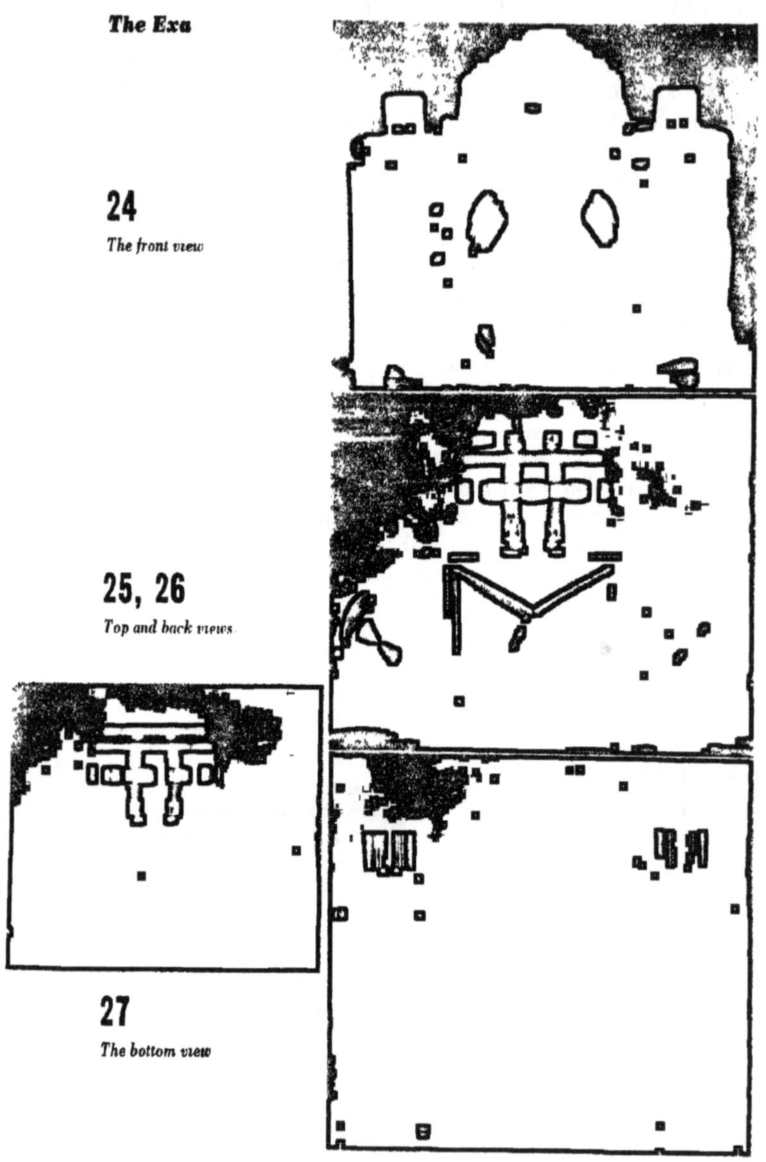

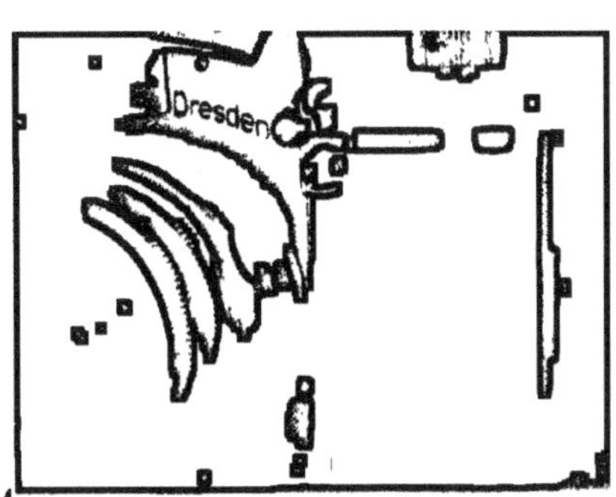

28

The right-hand side of the Exa Just under the Exa emblem is the catch for releasing the finder so it can be lifted out. Back of the lens is the body shutter release, lower down the lens-change lever. Near the top is one of the strap lugs, at the side the camera back lock

29

The two flash sockets at the camera s left The green F is for flash lamps, the red for electronic (X) flash use

30

The shutter-speed slot with the setting lever, offering a choice of 1/25th to 1/150th or bulb (time exposures) The knob is for rewinding the film into the original cartridge

31

The simultaneous film-advance and shutter-wind knob The exposure counter and counter-setting ring Above is the rewind release button, which is held down while turning the rewind knob (Fig. 30).

20

32

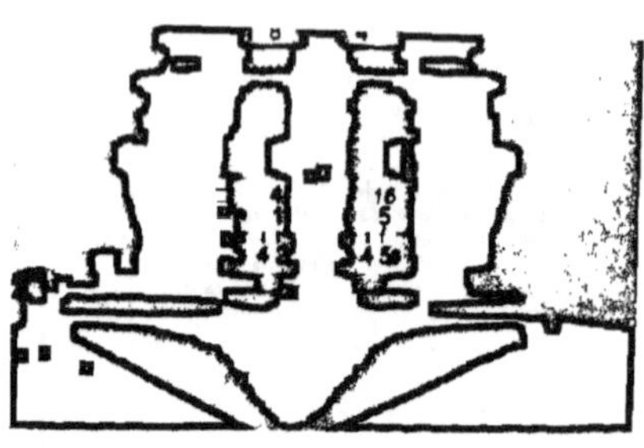

One of the desirable lenses for the Exa is the Meritar 50mm f/2.9, camera body release at left. Rows of figures from top to bottom are lens aperture ring, distance scale (red row in feet, black in meters), depth-of field scale Large knurled ring is for focusing

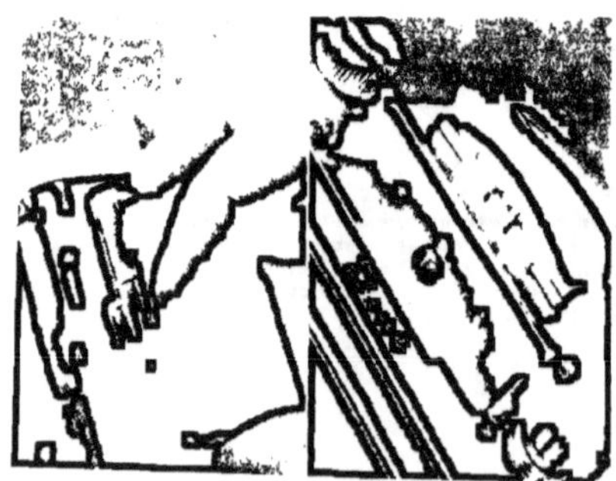

33

The reflex focusing hood, showing all essential parts side and back walls in position; peepsight at back for eye-level viewing through uncovered frame at front, condenser ground glass at the base, magnifier in position, tiny lever at upper right for swinging the magnifier up or back to rest position against the back of the front wall.

34

Note the novel body design for assuring light-tightness for the Exa. The back is permanently hinged and is locked by snap-action The tripod socket in the center is flush with the bottom of the camera The interior is covered on page 48

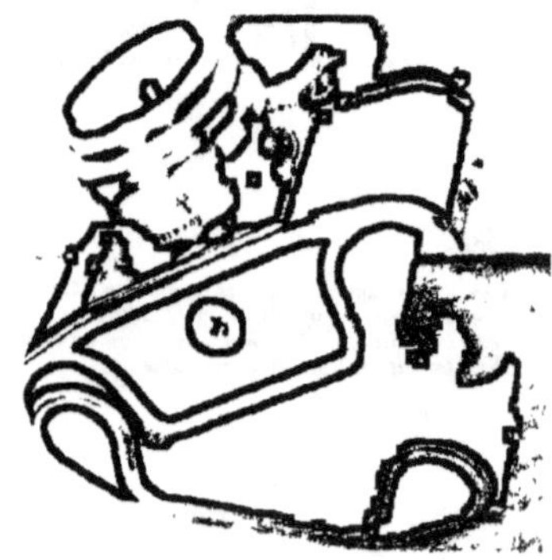

35

The finger-nail catch of the camera lock is pushed down to release the lock and open the camera.

36

The closed reflex hood is opened by pushing in the catch at the back.

Earlier 35mm Exakta Models

In many basic respects, the 35mm Exakta remains unchanged from the first model introduced in the United States early in 1937, when the writer, through his monthly photography department in Scientific American, made the first public announcement of the new-type miniature in the April, 1937 issue. Describing the camera as a single-lens reflex "using 35mm film, which can be focused at either eye or waist level with provision for easy interchangeability of lenses of various speeds and focal lengths," he continued:

"This most recent advance in miniature camera design has been named the Kine-Exakta, sister of the Ihagee Exakta ($1\frac{5}{8}$x$2\frac{1}{4}$-inch single-lens reflex camera), made by the Ihagee Camera Works of Dresden, Germany, which has gained such a fine reputation for itself in the vest-pocket field. Shaped like the regular Exakta and having about the same dimensions, the Kine-Exakta is equipped with a focal-plane shutter permitting speeds ranging from 12 seconds to 1/1000th of a second, as well as delayed action allowing practically the same speeds except in the lower bracket, where the longest possible automatic timing is 6 seconds." The writer then went on to list the features that have since become widely familiar and which are discussed in detail here

The Models I, II and V

The first batch of the Model I to reach this country had a round magnifier instead of the rectangular one which has since succeeded it, and the magnifier was exposed (see Fig. 37). The reflex hood was permanently attached to the camera and the camera back was removable. There was only one set of flash contacts and the shutter was locked when the hood was in closed position Manufacture of this model was discontinued in 1946

When distribution of 35mm Exaktas was resumed in 1949 with Model II, the principal change was the introduction of a protective cover for the magnifier.

Within a year, Model II was replaced by Model V, sometimes referred to as the Varex. Exakta cameras marked Varex and lenses marked Jena B, T or S are made for sale outside the United States, particularly Europe, and are not handled in the United States. The Exakta V, which also lasted only a year, introduced some notable advances, which were greatly expanded in 1951 in the Model VX and several years later in the model IIa, which are the subject of this book. Model V incorporated two pairs of flash contacts, one marked V for regular flash, the other E for electronic flash. The reflex hood was made removable to permit interchange with the prismatic eye-level focusing finder. Principal external differences between the V and the current IIa include, on the latter, the film speed indicator, film transport signal, new film counter which counts exposures after they are made, a new slow-speed knob, and a new-type camera back lock, plus the new light-meter and viewfinder device.

37 *The Exakta I*   **38** *The Exakta II*

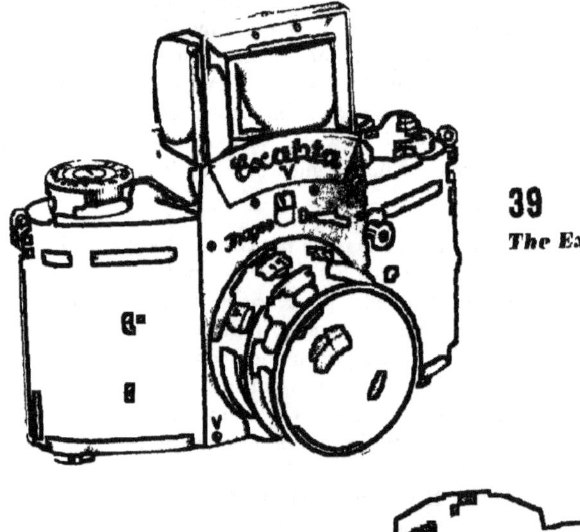

39

The Exakta V

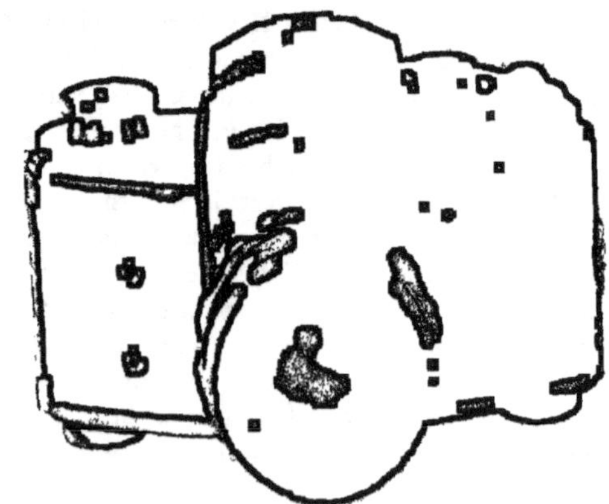

40

The Exakta VX

'DRY RUN" FOR THE EXAKTA VXIIa

(Consult Figs. 15 to 23 if in doubt as to names and functions of parts.)

1   With the camera in picture-taking position, open the viewing-focusing hood by depressing the button at the base of the hood. All four sides of the hood will simultaneously spring into place.

2   Wind the film-shutter lever all the way around to the other side of the speed knob. The lever will then return to its original position by itself, but brake the return swing with thumb. This lever action winds the shutter, transports the film, and sets the mirror.

3   Set the fast shutter speed knob Select one of the numbered speeds (fractions of a second). Lift the knob and turn it in the direction of the arrow until the selected number is opposite the red dot; let the knob drop into place For the purpose of this exercise, we will ignore the slow-speed knob on the other side of the finder, as well as several other details.

4   Set the lens stop. Grip the aperture ring; push it down and hold it down while turning it until the desired lens stop is opposite the red arrow on the black front of the lens barrel It will then click into place. (The reference here is to the Biotar lens. See page 32 for other lenses with automatic diaphragm control.)

5   Pull the automatic-diaphragm lever of the automatic Biotar all the way over to open the lens wide for focusing. (When the shutter is released, the lens will close down automatically to the preset opening).

6   Holding the camera at waist level, or the pentaprism finder at eye-level, study the ground glass image Locate the selected subject on the ground glass. Focus by turning the knurled distance focusing ring until the image looks sharp.

7   When ready to take the picture, press the shutter release button.

8   To take another picture of the same subject, at the same lens opening and shutter speed, repeat steps 2, 5, 6 and 7.

'DRY RUN" FOR THE EXA

(Consult Figs. 28 to 36 if in doubt as to names and functions of parts.)

1 With the camera in picture-taking position, open the viewing-focusing hood
by depressing the button at the base of the hood. All four sides of the hood
will simultaneously spring into place.

2 Turn the film-shutter winding knob at the right in the direction of the
arrow and past the slight resistance point. This action winds the shutter,
transports the film and sets the mirror.

3 Set the shutter by pushing the speed-selector lever at the right to the desired
speed number (fractions of a second).

Set the lens stop by turning the lens-aperture ring until the desired lens
opening number clicks into place opposite the long red line in the middle
of the adjacent depth-of-field scale

5 Push the automatic-diaphragm lever of the Primotar down until it stops.
This action will open the lens wide for viewing and focusing convenience.
(When the shutter is released, the lens will close down automatically to
the preset opening).

6 Holding the camera at waist level, or the pentaprism finder at eye-level,
study the ground glass in the hood. Frame the selected subject, and focus
by turning the distance ring at the front of the lens mount until the image
looks sharp

7 When ready to take the picture, press the shutter release button

To take another picture of the same subject at the same lens opening and
shutter speed, repeat steps 2, 6 and 7. For the purpose of this exercise,
several details are ignored.

Now that he has had his constitutional and has acquired at least a bowing acquaintance with the identity and performance of the parts that constitute the Exakta VXIIa and the Exa, as well as an appreciation of the picture-taking advantages offered by the single-lens reflex system, the reader is invited to go into the matter in fuller detail.

The sequence of topics is planned to treat first things first and in such fashion that the reader is made aware of relationships between the functions of the various elements involved in the photographic process as it concerns the two cameras in question. Thus, since the camera is a recording medium and, in consequence, the sole reason for using it is to expose film which thereafter becomes the basis for making a photograph, first consideration is given to lens, shutter and available film emulsions, the essential trio of the exposure phenomenon.

Control of the subject image proper then follows logically in practical discussion and explanation of viewing and focusing facilities and methods, and suggestions for handling the cameras most efficiently and conveniently. The steps involved are described and illustrated as fully as space permits, the aim being comprehension and usefulness

41, 42, 43

Morris H. Jaffe

The brief picture story on the opposite page of a remarkably friendly encounter between "Mr Scratch," an exceptionally gifted white rabbit and a wayward turtle, is an excellent illustration of how the Exakta's reflex finder can be used to advantage The low angle demanded by the subject was handled with ease and convenience and, because the subjects were seen directly through the lens, the necessary close views were no problem Aside from the unusual interest of the pictures as pictures, the reader's attention is called to the excellently rendered detail and general technical quality.

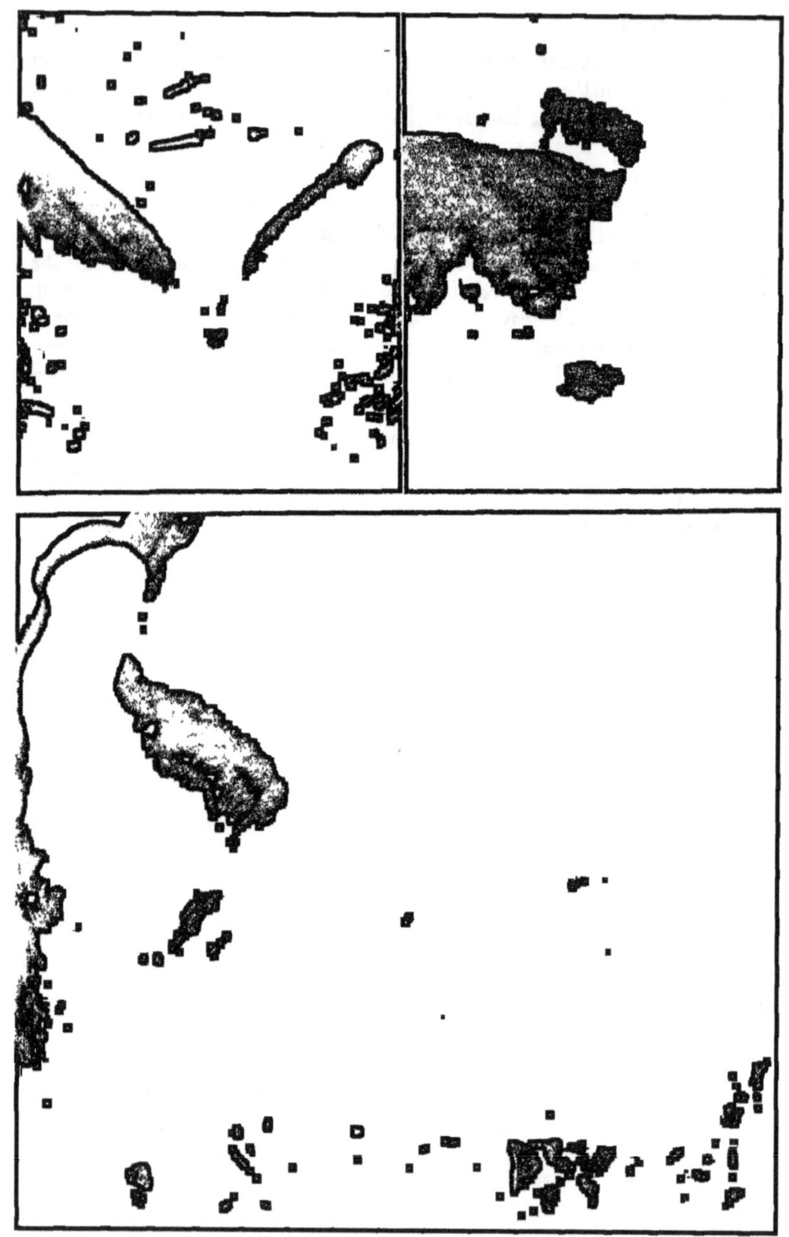

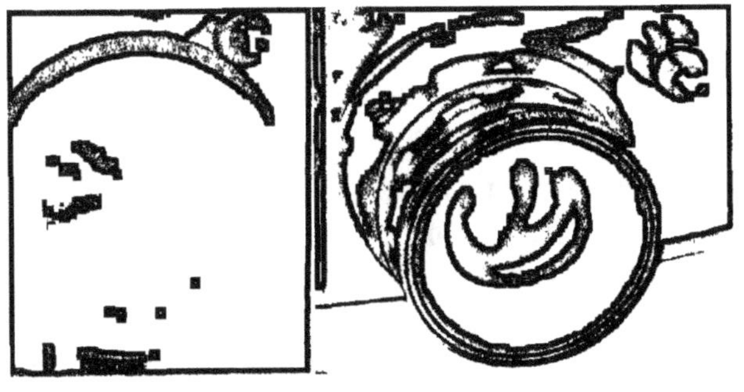

H   H   R   E   E

The Basic Lenses

All lenses have certain features in common, though the variants are many
and significant (see Chapter 8). The lenses with which the Exakta IIa and
the Exa come normally equipped will therefore serve as a starting point in
examining the various phases of the lens as a working tool in picture-taking.

Basically, the lens is a carefully made and assembled group of glass elements mounted in a metal barrel and worked by a group of controls to receive
the light rays reflected from the subject being photographed, to resolve these
rays in the form of an image of the subject, and to project that image onto
film at the back of the camera. How much of the subject is received by the
lens and the brightness of the image that reaches the film are the two principal
factors involved. The area covered is determined by the so-called *focal length*
of the particular lens in use, the brightness of the image at the film plane is
a function of the diameter of the lens aperture or opening, or diaphragm, as
it is variously called.

Because lenses consist of several elements, some separated by air spaces,
light reflections entering through the lens tend to bounce from one glass
surface to another, causing some light loss and a slight veiling of the image
because of flare and light scatter. These hazards are greatly minimized by the
modern process of lens coating, which is done at the factory by treating the
lens surface to a vapor bath of a white powder—magnesium fluoride, a salt
which coats a lens surface so effectively that the coating becomes almost as
hard as the lens and as durable. The coating is applied in a high vacuum, in

which the magnesium fluoride rises in a warm vapor cloud which comes to rest in an even film over the surfaces of the lenses.

Although, by comparison with an uncoated lens (most lenses are coated these days, however) the lens achieves about 25 percent increase in lens speed as a result of the coating, this benefit is negligible, particularly in the light of the coating's more important advantages. Because the coating reduces reflection between the glass surfaces, there is an increase in light transmission, elimination of light scatter and flare, and in consequence better image clarity and contrast. It is especially beneficial in color photography, where the colors reproduce with improved brilliance and with higher color fidelity.

The serial number identifies one particular lens, and serves therefore as a means of record. If the lens is lost or stolen, this number is the means by which it may be traced and ownership established. It is suggested that the owner register this number, as well as the serial number of the camera itself, with the importer of Exakta equipment, and take out a floater insurance policy, giving both numbers.

Focal Length, Lens Speed

The maximum opening designates the "speed" of the lens, which is stated as a fraction of the focal length (the distance from the front of the lens to the plane of the film when the lens has been focused on a very distant object, usually referred to as the infinity point) Because the f/2 is a larger fraction,

46, 47 *Setting the lens aperture on the Biotar. Push down the ring (left) and turn it until the wanted opening is opposite the arrow on the barrel. Then let the ring slip into the notch at that point (right).*

it is said to be a "faster" lens than the f/2.8. The 2/58 on the Biotar is read as maximum opening f/2, and focal length 58mm (millimetres). The speed of the lens, or the size of the lens diameter at full opening, is therefore 58—2, or 29mm (1-9/64 inches). The Auto-Primotar figures are of course read the same way except that the figure 1.3.5 is used to indicate the maximum opening.

The focal length of the basic or "normal" lens (which establishes the area of the field it covers from a given point) is determined by the diagonal of the camera film frame, which is 44mm in the case of the 35mm frame of the Exakta and the Exa It is standard practice, however, slightly to exceed this limit for the basic lens; in the Auto-Primotar it is 50mm, covering an angle of 47°; the Biotar's 58mm, being longer, covers 40° (see Chapter 8).

The light image that enters the lens is controlled by a graduated series of lens diameters called apertures or stops. Like the maximum opening, these are stated in fractions of the focal length and are shown at spaced intervals on the aperture ring of the lens. On the Biotar the scale is at the front of the mount. on other lenses on a ring near the back and which is set by turning the ring until the selected aperture clicks into place opposite the index on the adjacent depth-of-field scale (this and the distance scale are treated in Chapter 6); on the Biotar the aperture is set by pushing down the ring and turning it (Figs 46, 47) until the selected opening clicks into place opposite the red arrow on the black front of the lens mount.

Lens Openings

The variation in opening is achieved by means of an iris diaphragm between the lens elements, a device consisting of a group of thin blades. As the aperture ring is turned, the blades move simultaneously toward or away from the center of the lens, and thus are made to form a hole or opening of a specific size, or f/stop corresponding to the figures on the aperture ring.

Since the numbers represent fractions, the number becomes larger as the size of the lens opening is reduced. Smaller apertures (larger numbers) admit one-half as much light as the preceding aperture; successively larger apertures (smaller numbers) double the amount of light entering the lens.

These differences are related to exposure time (Chapter 7). The shutter is adjusted to remain open for twice the time when the light is halved, for only half the time when the admitted light is doubled. For example, if the shutter speed at f/8 is 1/50th of a second, it will be 1/25th for the smaller stop of f/11, and the other way around.

The aperture scale on the Biotar reads: 2, 2.8, 4, 5.6, 8, 11, 16. The dots between the numbers represent half-stops. The relative sizes of the openings are shown in Figs. 48-58.

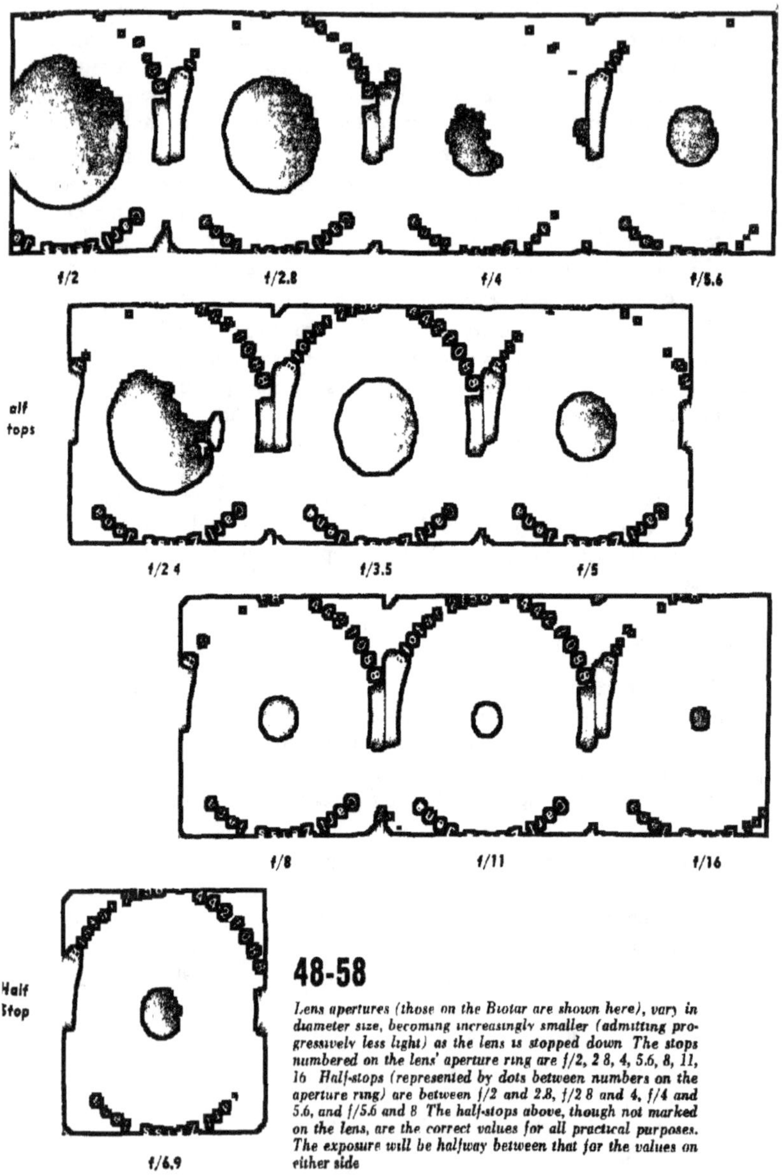

48-58

Lens apertures (those on the Biotar are shown here), vary in diameter size, becoming increasingly smaller (admitting progressively less light) as the lens is stopped down The stops numbered on the lens' aperture ring are f/2, 2 8, 4, 5.6, 8, 11, 16 Half-stops (represented by dots between numbers on the aperture ring) are between f/2 and 2.8, f/2 8 and 4, f/4 and 5.6, and f/5.6 and 8 The half-stops above, though not marked on the lens, are the correct values for all practical purposes. The exposure will be halfway between that for the values on either side

31

Intermediate stops are possible on other Exakta lenses too, simply by setting the lens halfway between the click stops.

The basic Exakta and the Exa lenses have an additional feature, the automatic-diaphragm mechanism which is one of the most remarkable of modern advances in equipment technology. Until the advent of this convenience, closing down the lens diaphragm has caused a darkening of the image seen in the ground glass. With the automatic device, which is an integral part of the two lenses, the lens is preset for the desired aperture as usual, but remains wide open for viewing and focusing. An instant before the exposure is made, the lens closes down to the preset opening

The Automatic Biotar

Here is the way it works on the Exakta's Automatic Biotar. Set the desired lens aperture as described above. Advance the knurled lever on the bottom of the lens to set the spring mechanism. This will open the lens to its fullest aperture for viewing and focusing ease at the maximum available light.When you press the plunger, the lens will be closed to the preset aperture an instant before the shutter is released, taking the picture Since the plunger on the lens serves only to close down the lens, press firmly all the way to make sure the rear of the plunger pushes in the camera body release button far enough to trip the shutter.

If the user encounters difficulty in this connection, the trouble may lie in the length of the plunger. This may be adjusted (Fig 59). Remove the lens from the camera, and insert a small screw driver in the notch at the rear end of the plunger. Turn it toward you to lengthen it, away from you to shorten it. In addition to improved contact between the lens release and the shutter release, the adjustment also offers control of the time lapse between the closing down of the diaphragm and the release of the camera shutter.

In order to study the ground glass at wide aperture for another picture, the lever has to be advanced again The preset aperture, however, is left untouched unless a different opening is wanted.

The Automatic Xenon

The new Automatic Xenon f/1.9 lens, with white depth-of-field indicator band, may be set for manual or automatic operation. For automatic, turn the chromed part of the knob to line up the two black dots with the red dot on the black part of the knob. For manual, line up the red dots on both parts of the knob Select the lens opening by moving the lever until the desired aperture appears in the cutout part of the mount just under the white dot. The

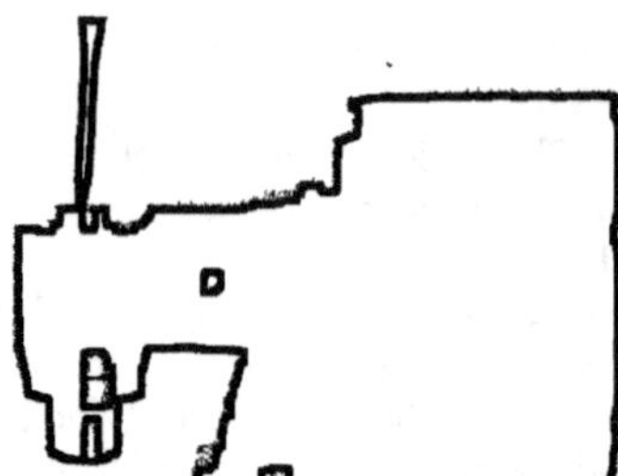

59
Adjusting the length of the Biotar plunger

white dot is also the distance indicator Focusing is done by turning the large knurled knob The white-band depth-of-field indicator shows the in-focus area in white, the unsharp zone in red. For release, press the chome knob as far as it will go, thus automatically closing down the diaphragm to the preselected opening.

The Steinheil Automatic

The Steinheil automatic lenses have a knob at the side of the lens mount for converting to manual operation when desired When pushed in, the operation is automatic; for manual settings, the knob is pulled out For automatic operation, preset the required stop by turning the base knurled ring until the aperture clicks into place. Focusing and viewing is at full aperture. When the release lever is pushed down, the diaphragm closes down automatically to the preset stop, then reopens to full aperture when you let go the lever. When changing from manual to automatic, push the release lever down once to reopen the diaphragm to full aperture. If the shutter is cocked, you can avoid actual release by moving the lens slightly out of its bayonet mount (use the bayonet mount lever).

The Primotar Automatic

The Meyer Primotar lens is set for automatic operation by turning the ring above the aperture setting ring until the *red dot* is opposite the red triangles The desired aperture is then selected, using the *red dot* as the automatic index. For manual settings, use the *black dot* index. When plunger is pressed, the lens closes down automatically to the preset opening, then reopens automatically to full aperture. When using the slow-speed knob, a special locking cable release is employed to avoid camera movement during the exposure and to keep the diaphragm setting constant.

The Bayonet Mount

The convenient bayonet lens mount on the Exakta and the Exa permits quick and easy removal or attachment of lenses To remove the lens from the camera, simply press the lens locking lever (Fig. 60) to disengage the pin that locks the lens on the barrel, and give the lens a quarter turn counter-clockwise. Slots on the rear of the lens barrel will disengage corresponding slots in the lens flange on the camera, and permit removal of the lens by simply lifting it off. To attach a lens, locate the red dot on the rear of the lens or, in the case of the automatic-diaphragm lenses, the plunger, and line up the dot with the red dot on the camera flange (Fig. 61). When the lens is well seated inside the flange, give the lens a quarter turn clockwise; it will click securely in place.

Care of Lenses

Since lenses are easily scratched or otherwise damaged, they should be handled carefully during use and well protected when stored. Hazards include resting the lens on rough surfaces (particularly those lenses whose rear elements protrude slightly from the lens barrel) and using abrasives or other harsh cleaning agents. Use protective lens caps on front and rear ends of lenses not in use. When interchanging lenses, use a soft cloth or similar surface on which to rest lenses

Dirt, lint, mist will settle on the lens surface in spite of precautions, but fingerprints can be avoided. Take a look at the lens occasionally, at a slight angle. If you observe dust or lint, a gentle dry blow will usually get rid of it. If not, a camel's hair brush will. For mist and fingerprint smudges, breathe gently on the glass, and wipe off the moisture with a clean soft leather chamois, clean lens tissue, or a much used, well washed linen handkerchief

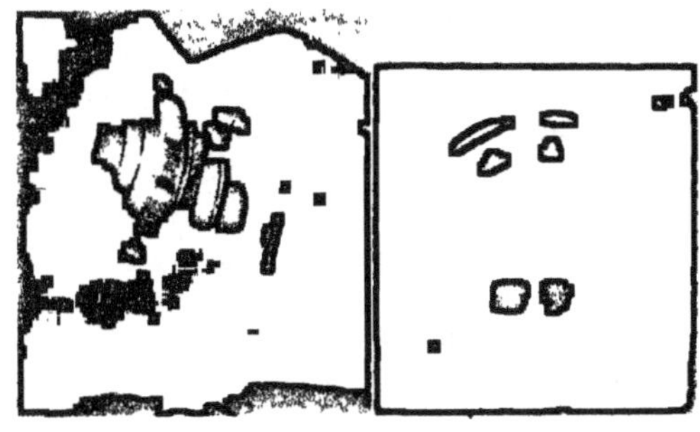

60

Removing the lens from the camera.

61

Lining up the red dots on lens barrel and camera lens flange.

Working the Shutters

The lens openings described in the last chapter control the brightness of the image projected into the camera. To set the moment when that image is to strike the film itself is the function of the camera shutter, which also controls the length of time the film is to be exposed to the light. By means of an automatic mechanism, the shutter opens when a button is pushed and, at the end of the present exposure interval, automatically closes again.

Lens openings and shutter timings (or so-called speeds) vary, and the relation between the two constitutes the general basis of what is broadly called *exposure* in photography. If the shutter speed has allowed enough time relative to the size of the lens opening, a picture will result. If the timing is too long, the picture will be overexposed, if too short it will be underexposed, causing difficulties in printing the picture in either case

Shutter speeds are stated in fractions of a second, though for space economy on camera speed dials they are indicated as whole numbers, the addition of the prefix symbol 1/ being assumed. Thus, 50, 100, etc mean 1/50th, 1/100th of a second Which of the several speeds to use for which lens openings depends on several factors, the first being the light sensitivity of the film in the camera (Chapter 5).

Light Volume is the Key

Of the other factors, only the primary one will be mentioned at this point, namely, the amount of light admitted by the lens opening in use. Relatively, the more light admitted, the shorter, or quicker, the shutter timing; for less admitted light, the shutter should be set for a longer duration Thus, for a lens opening of say f/8, the required shutter speed may be 1/25, 1/150 or even 1/1000. The reasons for these and other exposure variables, as well as aids in determining the correct exposure for a particular subject are covered in Chapter 7.

Although the automatic split-second shutter speeds will take care of most situations, there will be occasions when longer timings will be needed. There is provision for these on both the Exakta IIa and the Exa. The shutter is wound, or set, on the IIa by turning a lever, on the Exa by turning a knob.

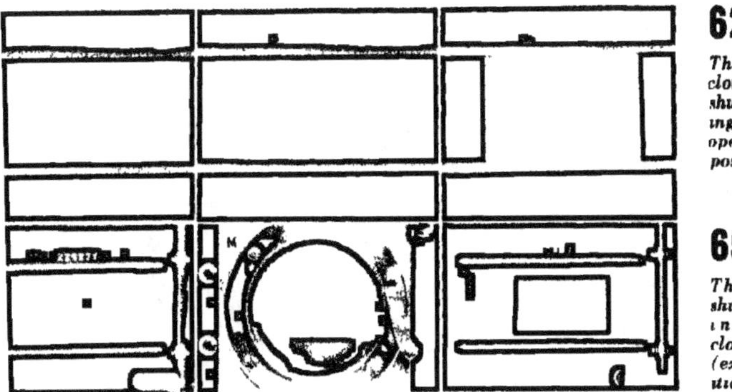

62-64

The VX and IIa cloth focal-plane shutter in closing, closed and open (exposure) position

65-67

The Exa metal shutter curtain in closing, closed and open (exposure) position

The shutters on both cameras are designed to prevent double exposures. After releasing the shutter for one picture, it has to be rewound for the next one.

The Exakta IIa Shutter

The Exakta shutter system consists of five inter-related elements: the focal-plane (so-called because it is positioned immediately in front of the plane at which the film lies) two-curtain cloth shutter; the knob for setting fast (instantaneous) shutter speeds; the shutter-and-film winding lever; the slow-speed and delayed-action release knob, and the shutter release button at the front of the camera. A hinged guard is provided for the button to prevent accidental release and, in consequence, a spoiled film. An exposure cannot be made until this guard has been swung aside. An oversize release knob is available for screwing into the cable release socket. It is especially useful when wearing gloves. Incorporated in the shutter mechanism are built-in flash synchronization contacts for use when shooting with either regular flash lamps or electronic flash (Chapter 11)

The shutter curtain is, of course, the heart of the system. To study its action, open the camera back and watch the curtain in the picture window (Figs. 62-64) The action of the shutter during exposure is explained so clearly in the literature of the camera's importer, the Exakta Camera Company, that it would be difficult to improve upon, so we quote:

> *The curtain that you see covering the picture area is actually only one-half the shutter. Your shutter is made up of two cloth curtains, which move from left to right on rollers during the exposure. One curtain uncovers the picture area, the other covers it. The curtain that you see covering the picture area is the second one. The first one is rolled up on a roller to the right of the picture area.*

36

68-70 *(at left)*

Fast Speeds. *To set the fast shutter speed knob: 1. wind the lever all the way, 2, lift the outer ring (top left); 3, turn the ring in either direction until the desired shutter speed is opposite the red dot (left center, set for 1/100), 4, let the ring drop into place*

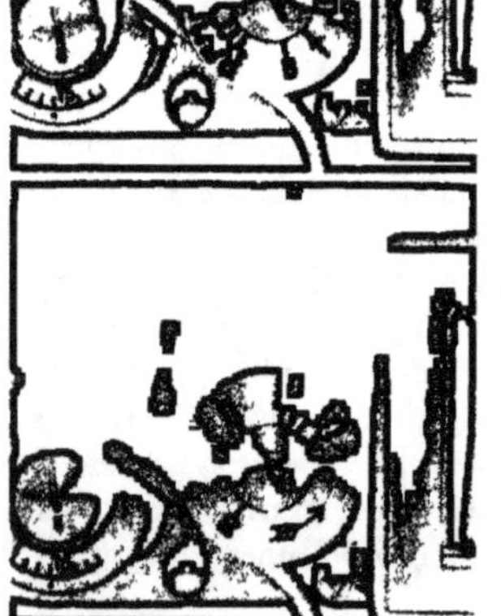

71-73 *(at right)*

Slow Speeds and Delayed Action. *To set the slow-speed knob 1, follow fast-speed routine but set that knob at T or B on the dial (above); 2, wind the slow knob firmly until a definite resistance is felt, 3, lift the outer ring (top right) and turn it to one of the black figures (1/5th of a second to 12 full seconds), 4, let the ring drop into place. (Center right shows setting for 12 seconds.) To set the slow knob for delayed release repeat the above, but use the red number scale. Lower right shows setting for 6 seconds.*

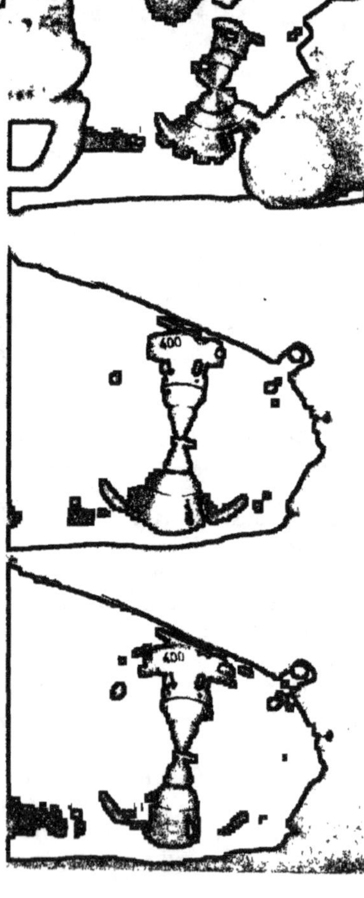

*Now wind the transport lever (Figs. 74-76) and set the fast knob
(Figs. 68-70) on the slowest speed on the dial, 25. If you watch the
shutter curtains during this action you will see that the second curtain
is pulled to the left of the picture area where it winds up on a roller
and the first curtain is pulled in the same direction and comes to a
stop covering the picture area. Note that the picture area is never
uncovered during the shutter-cocking action.*

*When you press the shutter release of your Exakta, the first cur-
tain begins to travel to the right, uncovering the picture area so that
light strikes the film. At a specific instant later, the second curtain
starts traveling to the right and covers the picture area.*

*The first shutter curtain travels at a rapid speed. The second
shutter curtain travels at a speed of about 25 percent that of the first
These speeds are constant. The exposure is made by the light that is
admitted through the gap or space between the back end of the first
curtain and the front end of the second.*

*Different exposure times are achieved by variations in the size of
the slit between the two curtains. The width of the space between
the two curtains determines the amount of light admitted to the film.
so it controls exposure.*

Operating the Lever

The winding lever on the Exakta and the knob on the Exa perform four
tasks simultaneously: cocking the shutter; bringing fresh film into the picture frame; advancing the exposure counter to the next number on the
counter scale (a device for keeping tabs on the number of frames exposed,
and how many are still left on the roll); and setting the mirror for focusing
and viewing the next picture (Chapter 6). The recommended method of
operating the lever is explained in Figs. 74-76. The lever must be wound *fully*,
until a definite stop is felt. Unless the lever is wound *all the way* around to
the back of the fast-speed knob (it will start swinging back of its own accord),
the shutter cannot be released.

The Fast-Speed Knob

The Exakta's fast-speed knob can be set for any one of seven split-second
speeds—25, 50, 100, 150, 250, 500, 1,000—as well as for time (T) and bulb (B)
exposures (Figs. 68-70). After winding the lever, pull up the dial ring and
turn it to left or right in the direction of the arrow until the wanted speed is
opposite the red indicator dot. The spring-controlled knob will then drop
neatly into place, flush with the fixed center of the knob. The speeds should
be set after cocking the shutter.

The B setting is also for time exposures, usually for relatively brief intervals. Repeat as for T, but keep the plunger depressed for the duration of the exposure. When you let go, the shutter closes. If fairly long exposures are wanted, as when using the B setting on the Exa, which does not have provision for T, buy the type of cable release that has a plunger lock on it. This will keep the release down until the plunger is unlocked. For time exposures, the camera of course should be placed on a firm support, such as a table or, preferably, attached to a sturdy tripod. When shooting from a tripod or other support, the cable is useful for instantaneous exposures, too.

Double Exposure With the IIa

Although the Exakta IIa is designed to prevent accidental double exposure, this facility is available when needed. After making an exposure, you can get one, two or more additional images on the same frame of film (for trick or experimental effects, for example) Here is the method. *Do not wind the lever,* for this would advance the next film frame, but simply turn the fast-speed knob counter-clockwise (Fig 77) until it comes to a dead stop. The

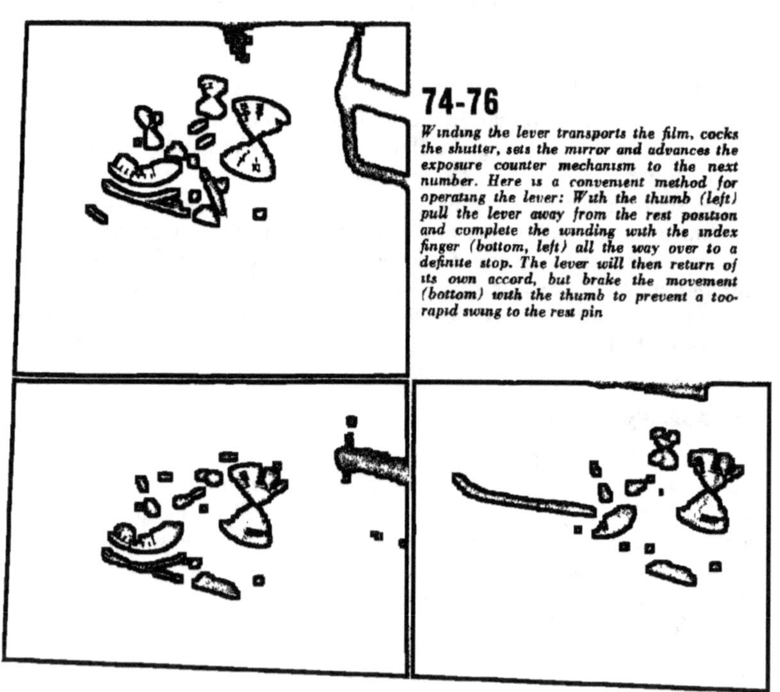

74-76

Winding the lever transports the film, cocks the shutter, sets the mirror and advances the exposure counter mechanism to the next number. Here is a convenient method for operating the lever: With the thumb (left) pull the lever away from the rest position and complete the winding with the index finger (bottom, left) all the way over to a definite stop. The lever will then return of its own accord, but brake the movement (bottom) with the thumb to prevent a too-rapid swing to the rest pin

strong spring will keep pulling the other way, so you will have to brake the counter movement with the thumb all the way until you hear a click The action will re-cock the shutter, which is then released in the usual way. Repeat for successive exposures on the same film. Incidentally, the knob can be turned easier if the finder is removed.

The Slow-Speed Knob

This is a unique feature, permitting accurately measured time exposures for intervals of 1/5 to 12 full seconds. There are two scales· the black numbers are for straight time exposures for the times indicated; the red numbers are delayed-release exposures. The black figures are 1/5 and 1/2 of a second, 1, 2, 4, 6, 8, 10 and 12 seconds (the black dots between 2 and 4 and between 4 and 6 are for 3 and 5 seconds respectively), the red figures are 1/5, 1, and 2, 4 and 6 seconds (the red dots between 2 and 4, and between 4 and 6 are for 3 and 5 seconds respectively). The interval of 1/2 second on the black scale, but not on the red, provides an additional speed which can be used regardless of whether the delay release is needed.

The winding knob is rotated by a strong spring, therefore calls for much heavier winding than the lever wind. The required amount of winding varies with the speed setting The 1/5 exposure takes just a nudge on the wheel, whereas an exposure of say 9 or 12 seconds will take a much longer turn. The key is in the release of the tensioning of the strong spring that does the job of timing. After a 1/5 exposure, for example, the spring has to unwind a smaller amount than after an exposure at one of the longer intervals. Therefore, if the previous exposure was say 12 seconds, the knob will have to be wound the longest to restore the spring's power to full strength. After the click of the shutter is heard, the continuing sound is that of the unwinding spring

The Slow-Speed Sequence

To assure results every time, the required operating sequence should be followed to the letter. The penalty for not doing so may be damage to the shutter. Six steps are involved, in this order:

1. Since the fast and slow shutter mechanisms are interlocked, it is necessary first to wind the lever as usual.

2. Set the fast knob on T or B.

3. Wind the slow knob *all the way* and with firmness until a definite stop is felt.

4. Lift the dial ring and turn it either to right or left to select the time interval.

5. For straight time exposures, line up the selected black number with the

red dot on the center post (Fig. 72). For delayed-action release, line up the dot with one of the red figures (Fig. 73). Let the ring drop into place at that point.

6. Press the shutter release to start the exposure.

To make a second exposure at the same speed, wind the lever and the slow knob, and release; for a different speed, add steps 4 and 5

The Delayed-Action Release

When the red scale is used, there is a lapse of just 13 seconds between the time the shutter button is pressed and the shutter curtain opens to begin the preset exposure period.

The delay mechanism may also be applied to the fast knob speeds, in this manner: 1, wind the lever; 2, set the desired speed on the fast speed knob; 3, wind the slow knob; 4, set on any red speed; 5, push the shutter release. Note that the difference between this and the normal slow-speed sequence is that the fast knob is set for a specific exposure time instead of on T or B.

In addition to the popular use of the device, permitting the photographer to get into the picture after establishing the picture area, focusing the lens and releasing the shutter, it is invaluable for copy work, photomicrography, etc. Another use for the timer is in providing a 13-second delay before exposure to allow the camera to stop moderate shake due to handling. This is particularly valuable when using long telephoto lenses on inadequate supports.

77, 78

To take a double exposure on the Exakta, do not wind the lever for the second shot; just turn the fast knob counterclockwise until it stops (below) and press the release button again For time or bulb exposures, set the camera on a tripod or other steady support, and expose with a cable release (right) screwed into the socket on the camera release button or, as shown, on the plunger.

The Exa Shutter

The components of Exa shutter operation are the simplified metal curtain shutter; the shutter-and-film winding knob; the shutter-speed setting lever; and the shutter release button at the front of the camera. When equipped with the hooded reflex finder, the hood must be in open position (push the button at the bottom, rear). The Exa shutter also has built-in contacts for flash synchronization of regular flash lamps or electronic flash (Chapter 11).

The action of the shutter is illustrated in Figs. 65-67. The upper end of the shutter fits into a light-tight groove at the bottom end of the mirror. When the shutter is cocked by winding the knob (at the same time advancing the film, counting the exposure and setting the mirror), the mirror pushes the shutter down into a shallow pocket at the base of the camera. When the shutter is released, the mirror swings up to lie just under the ground glass and is followed immediately by the shutter curtain. The interval between these two actions constitutes the period of exposure.

The Exa shutter has four speeds—25, 50, 100, 150—and provision for bulb (time) exposures, all of which are lined up alongside a slot in which a lever is moved forward or back to line up with the selected speed Operation of the Exa shutter is simplicity itself: just wind the knob and press the release button. To change speeds between shots, just push the lever forward or back as needed The speeds can be set either before or after cocking the shutter.

79   *Yolla Niclas*

The photographer caught the quality of mystery in this picture of turbulent sea in one of its strangest moods. It was taken in New England at about 6 o'clock one summer day just as the "eye" of a hurricane was dying out The lens aperture was f/8, the shutter speed 1/150 (short enough adequately to stop the motion of the waves) and film of medium speed was used.

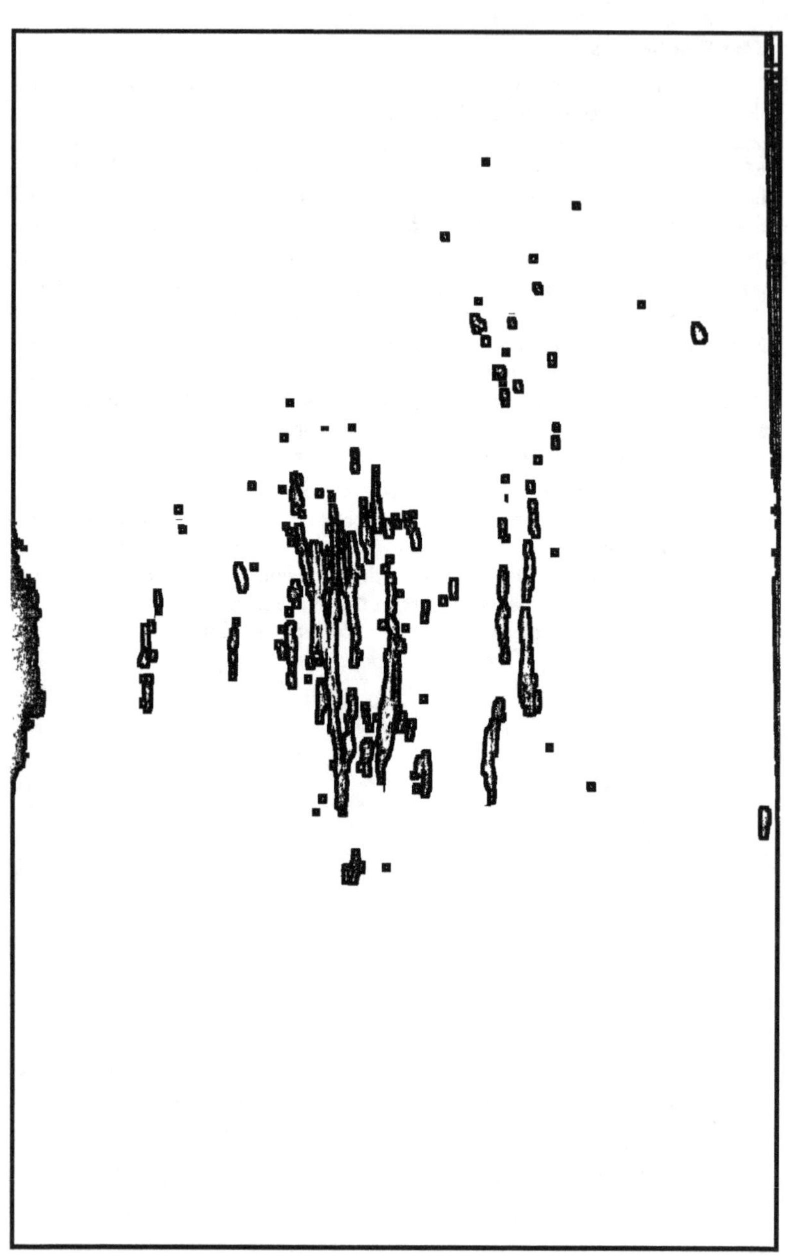

Loading the Cameras, the Film They Take, the Filter Controls

The Exakta and the Exa picture gate (Figs. 82 and 91) delivers an image just 24x36mm, or approximately 1x1½ inches, on sections of film successively brought into the picture frame by the film transport lever on the Exakta, the winding knob on the Exa The image actually seen in the ground glass viewer is 23x35mm, or ½mm smaller on all four sides, a slight precaution against viewing error.

The cameras use a variety of standard 35mm film material in ready-to-load, light-tight cartridges containing either 20 or 36 exposures (a list of available films appears on page 53) Illustrated instructions for loading the cartridge in the camera, and for unloading it when the roll has been exposed, are given on the next three pages.

The Exakta has a film reminder engraved near the base of the slow speed knob (Fig. 19), which is set for the type and speed, ASA of the film in the camera, with indicators for black-and-white and color, (C in red, C in black, for tungsten and daylight color, respectively). NC in red and NC in black for color negative film for artificial and daylight respectively. After loading the film, turn the ring until the setting is opposite the engraved triangle.

At the same time, an automatic exposure counter on the VX or IIa is set by turning the small knurled dial in the direction of the arrow until the figure 1 appears opposite a red dot. A similar device on the Exa is set by turning a knurled dics. Near the base of the VX or IIa slow knob is a window showing the "speedometer" which revolves continuously when film is advanced or rewound. This serves as assurance that the film is moving properly in the camera. Another check in this connection is the notch on the pivot of the transport lever, which will revolve as film is wound on the spool, or unwound.

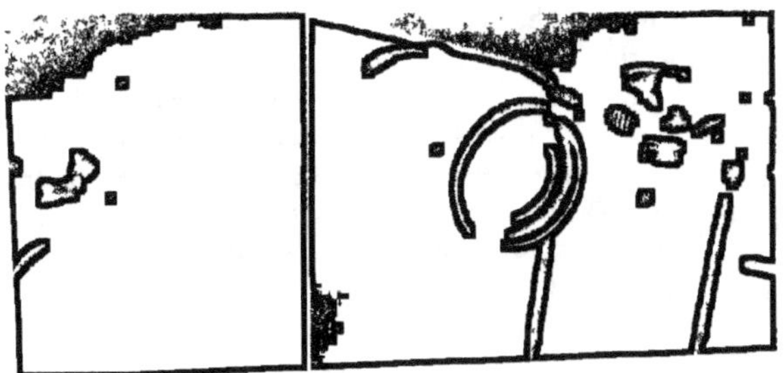

80, 81

Left, how take-up spool engages notch in camera so film can be advanced as lever is turned. Right, film cartridge is loaded in similar way so it can be rewound when exposed.

Loading the Exakta VX and IIa

Open the back of the camera (Fig. 85). The interior (Fig. 82) reveals two film troughs, the one at the left for the film take-up spool, the other for loading the full cartridge. Adjacent to the left is a shaft with sprocket wheels at each end. These sprockets engage the perforations at the edges of the film, thus pulling the film toward the take-up spool for the film length measured by the transporting lever. Left of the other trough is the built-in film knife (Fig. 88) for cutting off partially exposed film while the camera is still closed. Between the two troughs is the film gate or frame, showing the focal-plane shutter. Above and below this gate are the tracks which help to keep the film moving evenly through the camera.

The camera's interior and the back cover are hinged by means of a retaining pin which is simply pulled out (Fig. 89) so the back can be removed for convenience in loading. The rectangular plate in the middle of the back cover is a spring-suspended film pressure plate, which presses the film gently against the back of the film gate to make certain the film is lying perfectly flat The two knobs at the bottom are the rewind knob (Fig 87) and the camera lock.

Loading Suggestions

To load the camera, release the lock (Fig. 85) by pulling out the knob and giving it a short turn in either direction, and open the back. Some prefer to remove the lens while loading so the camera may be put down more safely. In such cases, use lens caps to cover the lens front and rear. If loading outdoors, better wrap the lens temporarily in a clean handkerchief and put it in an empty coat pocket or an empty compartment of a gadget bag. Also, even though the film because of bits of torn film in the camera, the user is advised to check the inside of the camera for dirt particles each time the camera is reloaded. Occasional cleaning with a soft brush is good camera housekeeping.

To avoid the possibility of "railroad tracks" (parallel scratches on the back of the film due to dust or dirt on the pressure plate) or jamming of film because of bits of torn film in the camera, the user is advised to check the inside of the camera for dirt particles each time the camera is reloaded. Occasional cleaning with a soft brush is good camera housekeeping.

The Exakta VX and IIa offer two types of film loading, by attaching the free end of the film to the take-up spool (Fig. 80), or using for this purpose an empty film cartridge (Fig. 84). The advantage of the latter is that the exposed roll can be unloaded without having to rewind it into the original cartridge. The routine of loading and unloading is described on the next two pages.

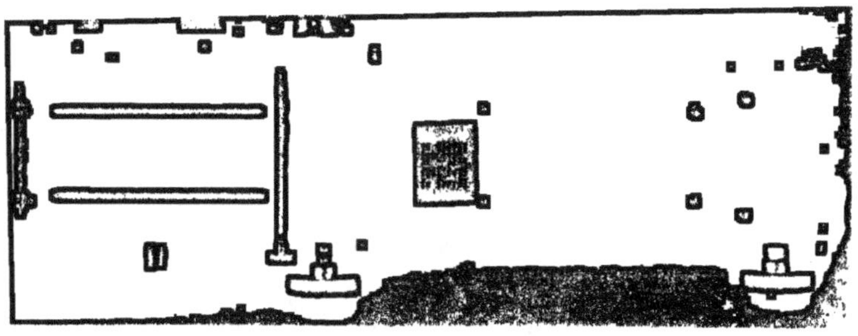

82

The VX interior and back cover (page 45)
The IIa is similar

83, 84

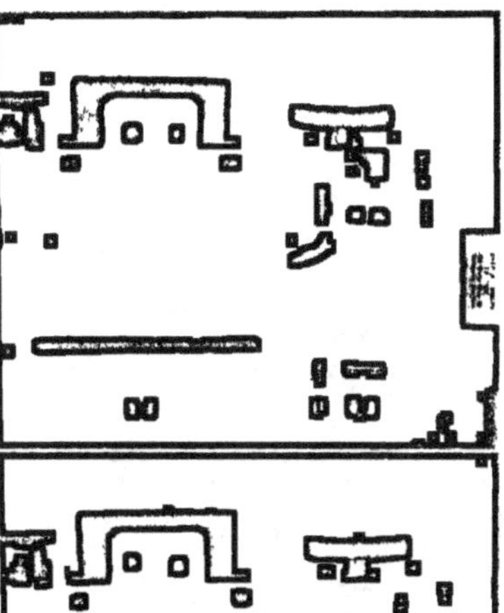

*Before loading, make sure the rewind knob
is pulled all the way out, as shown above
Insert the leader end of the film securely
under the spring clip of the take-up spool
Fit the take-up spool in the left trough so
that it engages the notch (Fig 80) provided
for it, and place the cartridge in the other
trough Check to see that the film edge is
flush with the flange of the spool, that it is
lined up with the film track, and that the
film perforations have engaged the sprockets
Holding the rewind knob by the **outside
ring**, push it flush with the bottom of the
camera (**be careful not to push in the center of the knob**). Check again to see that the
perforations are engaged Close the camera
(Fig 86) by holding camera body and cover
together in one hand and giving the lock a
short turn with the other The knob will
spring flush with the camera body, locking
it securely. The same routine applies to cartridge-to-cartridge loading (Fig 84) except
for the loading of the take-up cartridge,
which is described on page 54 Set counter
(first make two blank exposures to dispose
of the fogged leader, and set the shutter
again) and film guide and check that film is
moving (page 45)*

85, 86

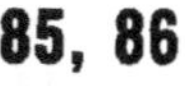

*The camera back is opened by pulling out
this lock knob and giving it a slight turn to
keep it extended To close, hold camera and
back together, turn the knob, it will spring
closed.*

Unloading the VX and IIa

87

After all the exposures have been made, the exposed film must be returned to the original light-tight cartridge for unloading. Depress center part of rewind knob, and turn outside ring while holding down rewind button, as shown. The turning indicators (page 45) will stop turning when winding is complete. An accessory rewind lever is available that fits under the rewind knob ring. The take-up cartridge, being light-tight itself, may be unloaded without rewinding.

88, 89

*In cartridge-to-cartridge unloading, cut end of film away from original cartridge **before** (otherwise last two frames will be fogged) opening back, using the built-in knife. Simply loosen knob at bottom and pull; the hooked blade will catch edge of film and make neat slice as knife is drawn down. The knife is primarily useful in cutting off part of a roll. This may be done in daylight with the cartridge take-up, but the regular take-up spool, being unprotected, has to be unloaded in the darkroom of course. When through, push knife into camera and screw it in again. Fig. 92. The hinge pin that joins the camera body and back cover. It is pulled out to separate the two. At bottom is the rewind knob in rest position; for rewinding, the prongs are pushed forward into the cartridge.*

90

If you have not watched the counter you may find at the end of the roll that the lever will balk. Do not force it; just depress the rewind button and keep it depressed while turning the lever, which will then move along normally.

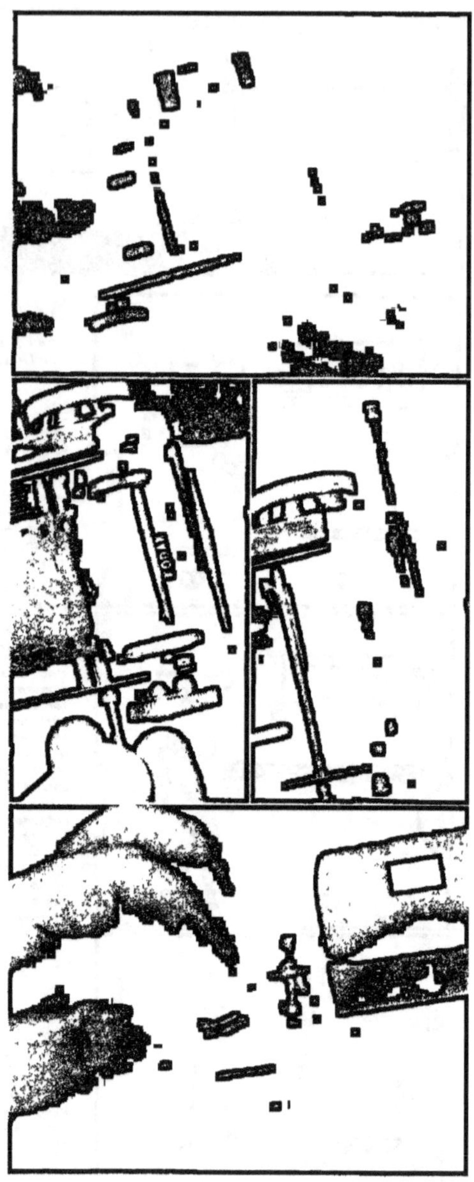

Loading the Exa

Open the camera. Press down the finger-nail catch on the side and swing
away the cover. The interior (Fig. 91) reveals two troughs, the one at the left
for loading the cartridge, that at the right for the take-up spool Both have
the same split-shaft knobs for gripping the crosspieces on the inside of the
spools, the wind knob to advance the film in taking pictures, the rewind knob
to get the film back into the cartridge for unloading when the roll has been
exposed. The troughs have open ends, which facilitate both loading and
removal of film. Adjacent to the take-up trough is a shaft with sprocket teeth
at each end to take the perforations on the two sides of the film and thus to
pull the film along, frame by frame, for successive exposures as the knob is
turned. Between the troughs is the film gate, which frames the portion of
the film to be exposed. Above and below this gate are the tracks which help
to keep the film moving evenly through the camera.

The Exa Back

The back, which is permanently hinged to the camera body, is a novel
design, with "wings" at the sides to close up the troughs when the camera is
shut. The edge of the back slides into grooves at the base of the camera to
make it perfectly light-tight.

The inside of the back has spring clips at each side to keep the ends of
both film cartridge and take-up spool from moving even slightly out of place
when the back is closed. Between the two pairs of clips is a rectangular panel
which is a spring-suspended film pressure plate, which presses against the back
of the film at the film plane to make certain it is lying perfectly flat

Some Cautions

Loading instructions are described on the opposite page. Set the camera
down on a clean, soft surface. Some prefer to remove the lens, in which case
it is desirable, if loading outdoors, to wrap the lens in a handkerchief and to
place it in an empty compartment in a gadget bag or an empty coat pocket,
or use lens caps to cover the lens front and rear. Incidentally, though film
cartridges are designed to be light-tight, it is a sensible precaution to load the
camera in a shady place or with your back to the sun.

To make sure the film is moving when the winding knob is turned, check
the rewind knob occasionally. It should be turning in the opposite direction
to the arrow as the film is unrolled. Sometimes the film is a bit loose, especially
at the beginning of the roll. Turn the knob clockwise to tighten it gently.

The Choice of Film

Film is distinguished from other film principally by its speed, or relative

91

Interior view of the Exa and its hinged cover.

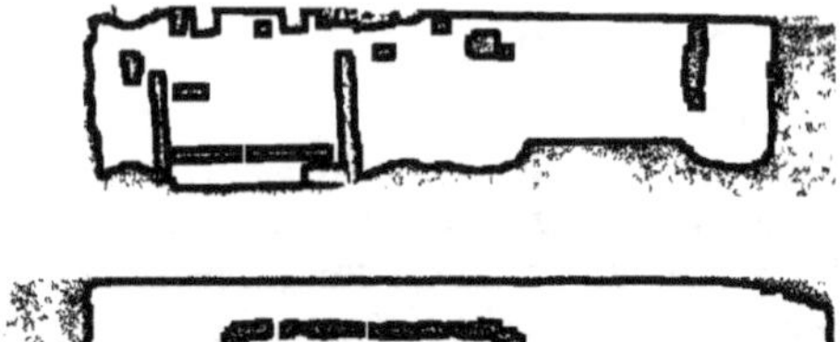

92

The hinged back is opened by releasing the spring catch. Pull out about four inches of film and attach the end under the spring clip of the take-up spool in the manner shown (this is the emulsion side) The edge of the film must rest against the flange of the spool

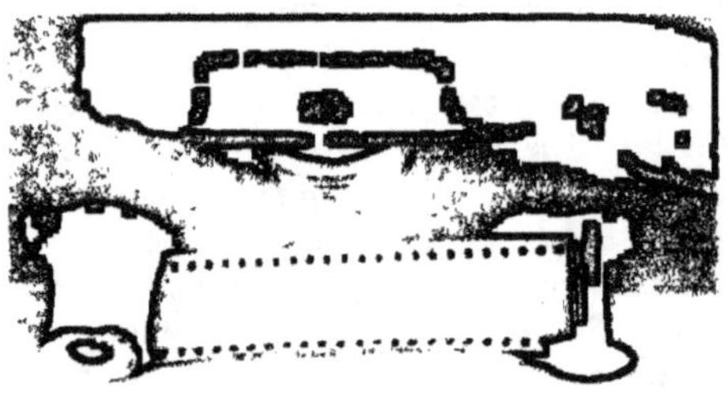

93

With the film emulsion side turned toward the lens, insert the cartridge and the take-up spool so that both engage the split shafts of the respective knobs (rewind and wind knobs at left and right, respectively) Note that both rows of sprocket teeth engage the perforations and that the film is lined up with the tracks Wrap the film securely around the shaft of the take-up spool. Close the back, which will snap shut

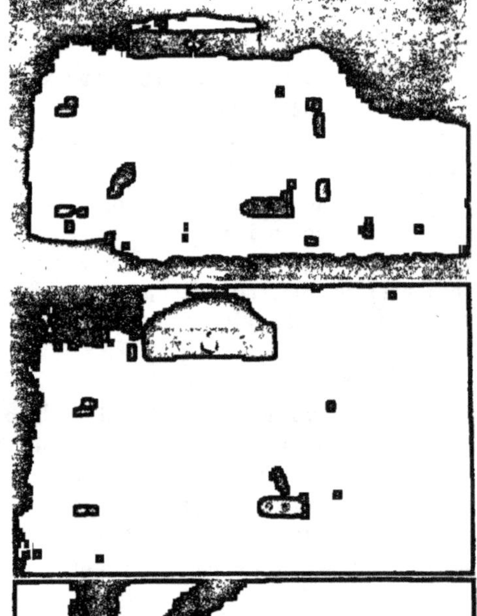

94

Open reflex hood by pressing button at back (shutter will not work unless hood is open). To dispose of film fogged during loading, wind shutter and release Repeat Wind again. Now set counter to the first number. Camera is open to show direction of film wind

95

Unloading the Exa. When roll has been exposed, rewind into cartridge by holding down the rewind release button while turning the rewind knob in the direction of the arrow When the other knob stops turning, the film has been returned to the cartridge. Open the camera and remove the cartridge. Before inserting a fresh film, trip toward you the small lever near the rewind button

The Film Speed Ratings

Experience has shown that for optimum quality, the manufacturers' exposure indexes on the opposite page, which incorporate a "safety cushion" to allow for variations in equipment and methods and for slight miscalculations, must be increased by two to two and one-half times, and in some cases even higher. But these higher indexes are usable only if the photographer has established a personal figure by actual test and carefully measures every exposure.

Shoot a few exposures, at the indicated index, and over and under, then develop the results and make enlargements. The most satisfactory picture will then indicate the figure that is "right" for you. Incidentally, a higher index may be used for flatly lighted subjects than those lit from the side or with normal distribution of light and shade. These variants must therefore be taken into consideration in rating a film for different uses.

The "correct" index rating is also dependent on proper development in the appropriate solution. For thin emulsions, select one of the high-definition developers, which are designed to exploit the image sharpness characteristic of these films. Accurate pairing of time and temperature is mandatory for best results. The new approach in developing fast films is to use the highest practicable index in making the exposure and to develop normally, rather than to use a slower index and "push" in development for a higher rating

To sum up, quality negatives depend on a correct working relationship between a particular film material and the particular developer in which it is processed after exposure.

Color and Special Film

The references thus far have concerned only black-and-white films. Color film is another major classification (see list on page 136), one in fact that is being used in increasingly greater volume by amateurs, professionals and specialists. The recent introduction of color emulsions that are three times to as high as ten and sixteen times faster than the traditional color speed limit has accelerated interest in color photography perceptibly The exposure index is for daylight, tungsten or flash, depending on the color balance in the film (see Chapter 10). Films for special uses are listed on page 122.

Film Packaging

The various 35mm films are packaged in a standard light-tight cartridge

LIST OF AVAILABLE BLACK-AND-WHITE 35mm FILMS

Black-and-White Films	Exposure Indexes		(4) *Packaging*
	Day	Tungsten	

(1) *Thin-Emulsion (Moderate Speed) Films*

Adox KB-14	20	16	20, 36-exp cart., 50-ft bulk
Adox KB-17	40	32	20, 36-exp cart., 50-ft bulk
Agfa Isopan F	32	25	20, 36 cart.
Agfa Isopan FF	16	12	20, 36 cart
Gevaert Microgran 27	32	20	20, 36 cart., 100-ft bulk, 36-exp. cart., daylight refills
Ilford Pan-F	25	16	36 cart 36-exp darkroom refills; 30-ft., 100-ft. bulk
Kodak Panatomic-X	25	20	20, 36 cart., 27½-ft., 50-ft., 100-ft bulk
Perutz Pergrano 14	20	16	20, 36 cart., 50-ft., 100-ft bulk
Perutz Perpantic 17	40	32	20, 36 cart., 50-ft., 100-ft bulk

(2) *General-Purpose Films (Medium Speed)*

Adox KB-21	80	64	
Agfa Isopan ISS	80	64	
Gevaert Gevapan 30	64	50	same as for above films by the same manufacturer
Ilford FP3	64	50	
Kodak Plus-X	80	64	
Perutz Peromnia	100	64	

(3) *High-Speed Films*

(7) Agfa Record	650		same as for above films by same manufacturer
(6) Agfa Isopan Ultra	200	320	
Ansco Super Hypan	(7)500	400	20, 36-exp cart., 27½-ft., 100-ft. bulk
Gevaert Gevapan 33	125	100	
Gevaert Gevapan 36	250	160	same as for above films by same manufacturer
Ilford HP3	200	160	
Ilford HPS	400	320	
(6) Perutz Peromnia 25	250	320	

(1) *Thin emulsion films are characterized by exceptionally high image resolution (resulting in fine detail and in consequence sharper picture) extremely fine grain (smooth tones) and long-scale (subtle differentiation between adjacent tonal areas) gradation By contrast with the faster emulsions they are thinner hence the class name, and therefore have the advantage over the thicker fast emulsions in yielding better definition Exposure must be fairly on the button and development in special high definition developers must be carefully timed to assure the optimum performance in fine grain and image sharpness*

(2) *As the group title implies these films will serve the widest range of uses under a variety of lighting conditions, with exceptional latitude in exposure and development In fact most photographers do very well with a film picked from this list turning to the top or bottom group for special applications*

(3) *These films are intended for use principally under conditions of low illumination and in situations where, even in fair or good light small stops and/or high shutter speeds are demanded Properly rated (see opposite page), effective speed considerably beyond the official figures can be attained with normal development*

(4) *Bulk film is economical, but only if the photographer uses enough of the same kind of film to make it worth while Otherwise, he is better off buying films in the convenient ready load daylight cartridges*

(5) *This is the fastest 35mm film available The maker's basic rating is given here, but the usual recommendation is to increase the speed to 1,600 for best results*

(6) *These films are exceptions to the usual rule that the rating is lower when the film is exposed by artificial light This is due to favoring the yellow-red sensitivity of the emulsion in manufacture, suppressing the blue*

(7) *These are exposure indexes with the ASA safety factor (see page opposite) eliminated, in anticipation of a revision of the American Standard of exposure indexes which was well on its way to acceptance as this book was going to press*

containing a strip of film measured out at the factory to supply enough material for 20 or 36 exposures of 1x1½ inches each. The cartridge consists of a spool to which one end of the film is securely attached (so it can be rewound in the camera), a protective metal or plastic apron with a light-trapped opening through which the film is advanced in the camera, and protective caps at both ends that are taken off (in the darkroom) to remove the film for processing.

The list indicates which films are available in 20 or 36-exposure rolls and which in both sizes. There is also a 27½-foot load, which has five loadings, tongued and notched at 36-exposure intervals ready for loading in a cartridge or cassette in the darkroom. The 28-foot Anscochrome "Easy Loader," with film enclosed, and tongued and notched for eight 20-exposure rolls, is a clever device that permits loading in daylight. Another special film package is the Gevaert 36-exposure daylight refill A long black paper leader permits loading a cartridge or cassette in daylight.

Some of the special-use films are supplied only in bulk rolls of 100 feet. Such rolls in 50-foot lengths as well as 100, are also available for the other films, for 36-exposure loadings of 9 and 18 rolls, respectively Advantages of bulk-loading are economy, a saving of up to two-thirds the cost of ready-loaded units, and the choice of shorter lengths than those provided in the ready-loaded cartridges.

However, Exakta photographers who prefer the convenience of the latter, in spite of the higher cost compared with bulk-loading, are offered a similar advantage in the use of the built-in film knife (Fig. 88) for cutting off part of a roll, and re-attaching the unexposed balance to the take-up spool for later shooting in the usual manner (see p 46).

Bulk Loading

Loading from bulk rolls of 35mm film is done in the darkroom by means of a small winding device or a light-tight daylight loading unit; one example of the latter is provided with a frame counter—so many revolutions, so many frames. Bulk film must be shaped at one end to provide for insertion in the film spool, and a properly cut tongue at the other end for attaching to the take-up spool. Both jobs are accomplished neatly with a template device designed for the purpose. The tongue must be attached firmly to the shaft of the loading spool so that the film does not come loose when rewinding after exposure of the roll.

The film may be loaded into empty cartridges, which may be obtained from camera stores or photofinishers, if you do not have some yourself. Make sure the cartridges are not bent and that the covers fit snugly. Loading from bulk should be done carefully. Handle the film by the edges, work in a

dust-free, dark place and load slowly to the capacity of the spool. If you wind
on too much of the film, or too fast or too tightly you may get stress marks
for your pains in the form of tree-like black lines on the negatives.

Film Characteristics

The first question a photographer asks about his film is, "What is its
speed?" The second one might well be, "Do I need it, or instead one slower
or faster?" Actually, speed is valuable only when there is a real use for it,
a burden and a misuse when a slower film will do the job, and do it better.
The speed of a film is an index to other qualities in the film. It is important
for its own sake, regardless of the other factors, only when high sensitivity
is required to cope with the particular situation (see Chapter 7).

Incidentally, photographers are advised not to take the rated speeds at
their face value, since they are only guides, but to make a series of exposure
tests and to establish their own speeds Because of variations in equipment
efficiency, processing and preferences as to negative quality, one man's speed
may be different from another's

Aside from speed, film has six principal characteristics, all of which
should be carefully weighed against speed in deciding on the most suitable
choice for a given phase of work. In making this evaluation, it is helpful to
keep in mind that the type of processing will also influence the choice.

1. *Graininess,* or the total appearance of the silver particles that form the
image upon development, a factor determined by the nature of the film and
by development; a grainy image shows mottle, a fine-grain image shows an
even silver deposit.

2. *Contrast,* a quality of the film, but which is also controllable by exposure and development; a low-contrast film has a softer gradation (the differences between tones are more gradual), a longer scale (more tones) than
a high-contrast film, but the latter has finer grain.

3. *Resolution,* or the relative ability of a film to record fine detail. Generally, the slower the film, the higher the resolution.

4. *Latitude,* or the capacity of the film to be overexposed or underexposed
(or overdeveloped or under), yet retain satisfactory printing quality. Fast
films generally have more latitude than do slow films.

5. *Acutance,* also known as edge or contour sharpness of adjoining tone
values, the ability of a film to yield a sharply defined image. Differs from fine
grain, which a film may possess yet lack the quality of high acutance, a
characteristic generally associated with the new thin-emulsion films (see
page 52).

6. *Color sensitivity*   All 35mm black-and-white emulsions available in this country are in the panchromatic-sensitized class (sensitive to all colors), but they vary from film to film in their relative response to daylight and artificial light, generally (with the exceptions noted on page 53) being rated higher in daylight.

The current tendency, inspired by the journalistic approach of "available-light" photography, is toward the higher speeds, but most photographic requirements are fully met by the medium-speed film, which is the happy compromise of the several factors involved, offering adequate general purpose speed, satisfactory grain and contrast, acceptable resolution, and reasonable latitude.

Moreover, if latitude is not over-exploited and exposure and development receive proper attention, these medium-speed films can often be made to yield results that are fairly comparable with those obtained with the high-speed and moderate speed films.

The moderate speed films have the finest grain and best resolution, but are more contrasty than those in the other two categories, and have the lowest exposure and development latitude   That is, both must be fairly accurate. The fine grain pattern and tonal contrast inherent in these films will be useful where full detail must be reproduced in the final print.

The high-speed category, which was in its heyday at the time this was being written, is characterized by soft gradation (a desirable quality where contrasty subjects are involved, for example, and for portraiture) shows less tendency than do slower films for highlights to block up in development, and offers considerable latitude. Where speed is essential, these qualities go far to console the photographer in the matter of relatively coarser grain.

Infrared, Regular and High Speed

Although distinguished from any other film on the market, by the fact that it is sensitive to infrared rays, which are beyond human vision, infrared film has in common with o·her films a sensitivity to blue-violet light as well In order to achieve the infrared effect, therefore, it is necessary to use a filter (Wratten No 25A) to eliminate the blue.

The combination of infrared film and the red filter is slow, on a sunny summer day, nearby landscapes and architecture may be photographed at $f/4.5$ and 1/25th, distant scenes at $f/8$ and 1/25th. Since the infrared rays do not affect the meter an exposure meter cannot be used. The focus of the infrared rays is different from that observed by the eye, after focusing, therefore, the lens should be moved forward slightly (¼ of 1% of the lens' focal length) The film may also be used indoors by photoflood illumination and with a

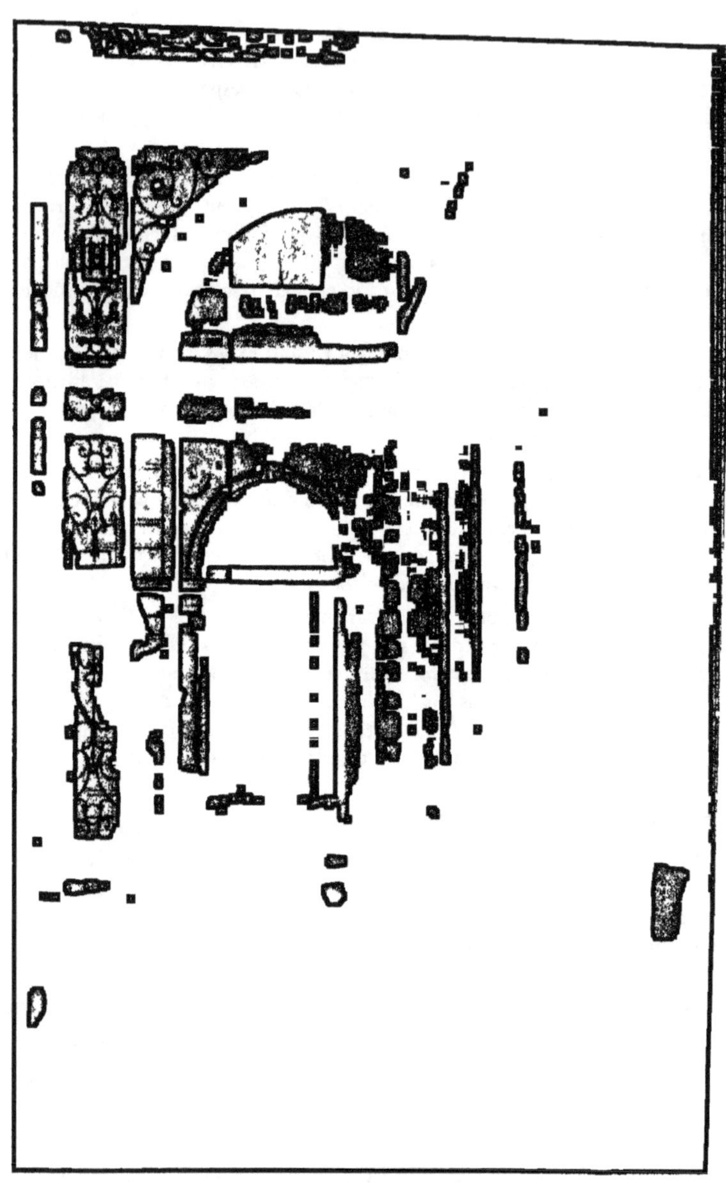

97 *Morning chat at the Continental in Paris. Medium speed film was adequate for the range of values in this subject.*

Wratten A, G or F filter. The exposure for a dark-colored subject illuminated by two No. 1 photofloods in efficient reflectors at 3 feet from the subject is f/11 at 1/2 second; at 5 feet, f/8 at 1/2 second.

An available-light version of the film is marketed as Kodak High-Speed Infrared Film, which is said to be ten times faster than the regular product. A number of experimental exposures under colored lights were made with and without a filter, including a ¼-second darkroom shot of a print in a developing tray by the light of a S-55-X safelight The outdoor exposure index for this film was rated at 200 ASA.

Infrared film penetrates haze in taking distant scenes, sets off white clouds dramatically against black skies Because of the reflection of infrared light in the chlorophyll in foliage, trees, grass and other plants with green foliage appear as white or very light tones in the print. Infrared pictures of sunny summer skies often resemble moonlight effects.

Infrared also has important technical uses, such as the detection of erasures and forgeries in questionable documents, and in several phases of medical work (Chapter 13). The film may also be exposed by flash, using the General Electric 5R "black" bulb (Chapter 11).

Other films in the special class are used principally for close-up work and copying (Chapter 9). The Kodak Direct Positive Pan Film (see list on page 122) has practical possibilities for the Visual Education field, providing black-and-white slide positives by reversal processing. A medium-speed film, it should be particularly useful for the teacher and lecturer who prefers black-and-white slides for certain subjects rather than color.

Filters Change Film Response

The colored (usually) piece of glass or colored gelatin between glass known as a filter is brought into use in photography whenever it is known that a film will not give a satisfactory or a desired special result by itself. Primarily, a filter separates colors (or their translation into various tones of gray) 1, to achieve contrast similar to that seen by the human eye; 2, to heighten, sometimes to exaggerate contrast for the sake of a particular effect. It is also employed to penetrate atmosphere that the unaided film emulsion would otherwise render hazily, softening or even hiding detail, and it has other corrective uses. One class of filters has to do principally with color (Chapter 10).

How a Filter Works

A filter works because of its ability to alter the balance of light values that it allows to come through to the film. This ability lies in its color, which varies both in hue and in intensity. Placed over the lens, it serves as a kind of

FILTERS FOR MINIATURE BLACK-AND-WHITE FILM

Effect	*Filter to use*	Kodak Exposure Factor*		Ansco Exposure Factor*	
		Day.	Tung	Day.	Tung
Natural contrast between clouds and blue sky; to control strong sand and snow reflections in bright sun For tone improvement generally	Light Yellow	1.5	1.5	1.5	1 5
	Medium Yellow (K-2)	2	2	2	2
More contrast, darker sky; penetration of distant haze; helps reveal wood grain in furniture.	Orange (G)	3	2	3	2
Improve texture in nearby green foliage, better tone values in portraits, indoors and outdoors, for copying (see Chap. 9).	Light Green (X-1)	4	3	4	3
	Medium Green (X-2)	5	3	5	4
Greater contrast than yellow or orange filters. Dramatic white clouds against dark sky For dark wood furniture by artificial light. Also for use with infrared film (see text) ***	Red (A, No 25)	8	4	8	5
To add haze in distant scene for effect, texture rendition in dark blue; copying (see Chap. 9).	Blue (C-5)	5	10	6	10
To reduce reflections; darken sky	Polarizing screen· Neutral	2 5	2.5	2 5	2.5
	Yellow	6	—	6	—
To minimize atmospheric haze in distant scenes, for scientific detection	Ultraviolet	none	none	none	none
To cut down light volume without affecting contrast or color	Neutral density	**		**	

*These factors are for Ansco and Kodak films For other films see instructions packed with film

**The filter factor for neutral density filters varies with the density of the filter It can be determined by dividing 100 by the percentage transmission of the filter Thus if the percentage transmission is 20% the factor would be 5

***See exposure instructions packed with Infrared film

brake or control of the variously colored light rays that bid for entrance through the lens. Its action is selective. Depending on the filter in use, it will "hold back" or absorb certain rays of the spectrum and transmit others to the film.

Thus, the yellow filter will absorb some blue and transmit red and green as well as its own color. The color absorbed to a greater or a lesser degree, depending on the depth of the filter color, will appear darker in the print than it would have looked without the filter. By contrast, the colors transmitted will appear lighter. This is the familiar example of the white clouds that "come out" as compared with the unfiltered image with a blank white sky in which the clouds are lost in white paper. The principle is the basis for filtered effects in general: the rays of the filter's color pass through to the film, but others are partially or wholly absorbed by the filter.

Filters vary in the depth of the color. Some are light, some medium, some dark, the color in the medium, for example, being deeper than in the light one. The deeper the color, the greater the effect; that is, there is more contrast between the tones. In addition to contrast, this density difference is related also to exposure, since the filter necessarily cuts out some of the total light. The loss is made up in estimating exposure by means of a multiplier called a filter factor, which is usually indicated as 1½X, 2X, etc, indicating the normal exposure is to be multiplied by this figure. The compensation can be made in any one of three ways: in the case of a 2X filter, for example, by doubling the exposure time, by opening the lens one stop, or by using a lower film rating Thus, for a 2X filter, a situation which calls for an exposure of 1/50th at f/11 on a ASA 100 film without a filter, may be exposed at 1/25th and f/11, at 1/50th and f/8, or by reducing the film rating to 50, which of course will give the same result as the second method except that meter readings can be made directly.

The Filter Factor

The factor depends on the set of conditions under which the exposure is made, and involves the filter proper, the film used and the nature of the illumination. With a given filter, some films may require higher or lower factors than others Because artificial light sources generally contain less of the blue, to which film is more sensitive than sunlight, pictures taken by artificial light will call for a different factor for any given filter than the day-light figure. Filter factors vary with film of different makes even in the same sensitivity class The manufacturer's recommendation should be consulted

Exposure has to be fairly right as too high a factor may not give the desired effect. A comparatively lower factor, within the latitude of the film, will give a stronger effect than the higher one As in the case of film speeds, therefore, the photographer is advised to make tests to find the factor number best suited to his standards. Tables of filter factors are not the last word, only guides.

Filter Variety

The most popular filter color is yellow, the medium density of which is most used because it gives the average correction needed in general photography. For moderate correction, where it is desired to restrain the blue only just

A yellow filter gave tone to the sky, which would have been a disturbing paper-white without the filter. Incidentally, Harold Feinstein made this shot just as the sergeant called his name for assignment to Korea.

enough in order, for example, to retain atmospheric quality, or where short exposures must be used, the light yellow is often preferred.

In addition to the yellows, filters are available in several other colors for various requirements. The greens, light and medium, bring out flesh tones, improve the rendering of green foliage. The medium green is particularly useful in minimizing chalkiness in indoor photography by artificial light. The orange or light red filter will give darker sky tones than the yellows, or may be used for other subjects, as in photographing the grain of wood, or to bring a subject away from a background to the color of which the film is unduly sensitive, or with infrared film.

A little used filter is the light blue, which is found valuable by the pictorialist and other workers in photographing misty scenes. Because of the blueness in the atmosphere, the filter will help in reproducing the foggy effect in the negatives. Another use for the blue filter is in clearing up detail in outdoor shadows, which are strong in blue

To counteract the presence of ultraviolet rays, which, like infrared rays, though invisible to the eye, create atmospheric haze in aerial, mountain and other distant scenes, ultraviolet filters are used. They cut through the haze and result in improved clarity of detail. Although red and orange filters will do the work too, the advantages of the UV filters are that the factor is lower and the color is not affected. The filters are also employed in the examination of altered documents and other materials.

The neutral density filter has come into prominence with the introduction of the very high-speed films. As its name indicates, it has no effect on the film, but merely reduces the amount of the light coming through the lens Thus, the Kodak ND-3 and similar neutral density filters are offered to cope with the problem of using high-speed films in bright light outdoors. The filter has the effect of cutting down the lens aperture by three stops, thus allowing a quick adaptation from indoor to outdoor photography.

Filter Do's and Don'ts

A filter should not be used unless there is a valid need for it. Most pictures in general photography are in fact taken without filters. There are instances too where a filter normally would be used but because of the color of the outdoor light, it should be dispensed with. In the early morning or late afternoon, for example, no filter is needed to get good sky tones as there is enough yellow in the general illumination to provide the filtering effect.

The filter is most useful when the sky is clear, less so when it is covered by a mist since there is less blue to hold back. The sky near the sun is less blue than elsewhere, therefore less affected by filter action. Watch out for the common error of using an orange or red filter when shooting a dark

subject against the sky, in which case, since both record dark, the two will
merge and the subject will not be recorded. Use a yellow filter in that case
instead. No filter will have any effect on a gray overcast sky.

Polarizing Screen

A special type of light control device, not really a filter but usually classified as such, is the polarizing screen, the main function of which for general
purposes is to minimize or eliminate light glare and reflection in photography.
It may also be used to darken blue skies, particularly in color photography,
because it will do so without affecting other colors in the scene.

For maximum effect, the angle of the camera should be about 35 degrees
from the plane of the reflecting surface At other camera angles the screen
is less effective and at 90 degrees it has no effect at all Setting the polarizer
short of the full effect will often be found more satisfactory, giving sparkle and
life instead of the dull picture that may result when reflections are eliminated.

Light-polarizing filters come in two types, Neutral and Yellow. The
Neutral is used for color and black-and-white film, the Yellow only for
black-and-white. The effects of the Neutral filter include darkening the sky
without distorting other color values; eliminating unwanted reflections from
water, polished wood, windows and other non-metallic surfaces. The Yellow
is a combination of the ordinary yellow filter and the standard polarizing
filter. It darkens the sky, as normally, but in addition, the polarizing action
will give an even darker sky and offer the other advantages of this screen. The
filter factor for the Neutral filter is about $2\frac{1}{2}$ times, for the Yellow about 6.

In use, the polarizer is placed over the Exakta lens like a filter and is
rotated until the desired effect is seen. The camera's reflex system therefore
has an advantage in this respect as compared with other cameras where the
effect is seen first by the eye, and the screen then placed over the lens.

Filter Mounts

Filters come in mounts either for screwing onto a lens mount in which
threads have been provided for this purpose, or for clipping onto the lens
mount. The series type of combination attachments, which also take a lens
hood is especially popular. The attachment is a device in which filters as well
as other accessories are securely held by means of rings. Once the basic unit
is acquired, the additional items are added as need dictates. Filters are made
in various sizes, are usually measured in millimeters (mm) for accuracy and
fit outside lens-mount diameters of different sizes. The Series V sizes are
19mm to 30mm; the Series VI, 31.5mm to 42mm; the VII, 42.5mm to 50mm.

a direct optical sports finder, which gives the normal-lens angle of view; and a built-in photoelectric exposure meter

The meter is designed for use in ordinary light conditions, but is quickly converted for low-illumination levels simply by lifting the meter's baffle cover The meter is set for the ASA speed of the film in use, and aimed at the subject. A white needle swings across a black field and stops. The outer ring is then turned until the black triangle is positioned opposite the same white or black wedge as the needle indicator. Apertures and speeds are then read off from adjoining aperture and shutter speed scales at the bottom

When working in poor light, the baffle is lifted, thus increasing the meter's sensitivity about 32 times, and the red triangle is used instead of the black. The meter may of course be used as an ordinary exposure meter when one of the other viewfinders is mounted on the camera.

The optical finder will be handy in following action, sports, children at play, and other quickly moving subjects. In such cases, the subject will be prefocused by setting the distance scale, or by focusing through the pentaprism

An inexpensive leather-type extension hood is available which fits over the reflex hood and blocks out light, it is particularly useful for outdoor photography.

The Prism Finder

The pentaprism (see Chap 1 for basic differences between this and the hooded finder) is a compact viewing-focusing device which incorporates as its name indicates a five-sided prism It is exclusively an eye-level finder and is therefore more convenient to use than the hooded reflex for taking pictures at that level either horizontally or vertically

Only one part of the pentaprism is removable — the ¼-inch (at center) ground glass, which is interchangeable for special work with other focusing glasses (see Chap. 9). The glass is held in place by two small springs on each

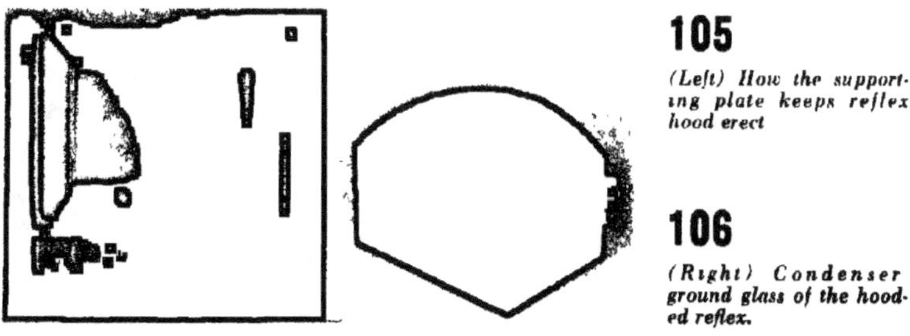

105

(*Left*) *How the supporting plate keeps reflex hood erect*

106

(*Right*) *Condenser ground glass of the hooded reflex.*

side. The unit consists of the prism locked in a frame and a magnifying glass which forms the eyepiece at the back of the finder. Correction glasses can be inserted to accommodate individual differences in vision. An accessory eyepiece hood is available for persons who wear glasses. The image is picked up by the camera mirror, reflected through the ground glass to the prism and then to the eye, with the result that it is brightened, enlarged to life-size and shows the subject correct as to right and left.

An advantage of the prism finder, especially in shooting sports and other action subjects, is that both eyes may be kept open. Thus, as the camera is panned, the free eye can follow the subject movement without restriction. Moreover, because the image is unreversed as in the case of the hooded reflex, the camera may be moved in the same direction as the subject.

A prism attachment is available for the hooded finder which works like the pentaprism. It fits over the open hood and is quickly lifted if not wanted.

The Distance Scales

The ground glass image is focused on the Exakta IIa and the Exa by turning a ring on the barrel of the lens. When the lens has been turned as far back as it will go it is focused on infinity; when it is turned as far forward as it will go, it is focused on the nearest limit of the lens' focusing range. (See Chap 8 for table of metric equivalents in feet and inches).

The focused distance is indicated by the figure opposite the index on the lens scale. The reading immediately adjacent to the index will be in meters in the case of both lenses, the scale just above it in feet.

The Biotar distance scale reads:

Meters	Inf.	15	8	5	4	3	2.5	2	1.7	1.5	1.3	1.1
Feet	Inf	50	26	16	13	10	8	6.6	5.6	5	4.3	3.6

Meters	1	09	0.8	0.7	0.65	0.6	0.55	0.5
Feet	33	3	26	2.3	2.15		1.8	1.65

107-108

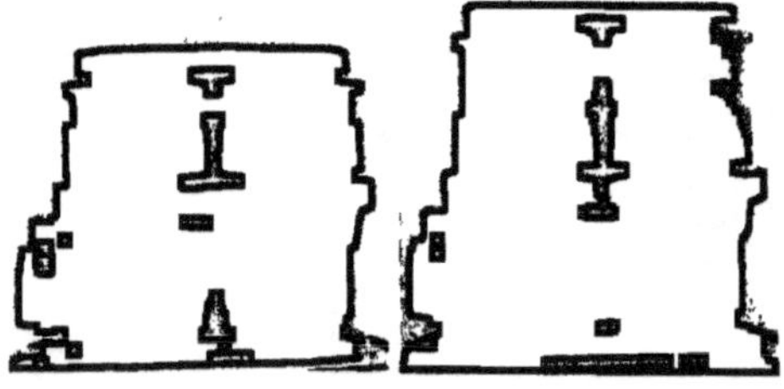

Lens movement in focusing when large knurled ring on Biotar is turned, the barrel moves from infinity position (left) forward for closer subjects (right).

The distance scale is automatically operated as the lens is focused, but may also be used independently of the ground glass, by manual setting based on visual estimate when ground glass focusing is not feasible. In addition to focusing, it serves the auxiliary purpose of providing depth-of-field information (see below).

Focusing the Ground Glass Image

The bright image made possible by the condenser and the prism in the finders of the Exakta VX, IIa and the Exa makes focusing with these cameras remarkably easy. But when this basic facility is further improved by the wide-open diaphragm focusing and viewing provided in the automatic lenses (Chap. 3) the subject lighting has to be dark indeed to make focusing the chore it would be without these benefits.

Even so, however, the photographer who has never used a ground glass is in for some practice in recognizing when the image is really sharp. When using the waist-level reflex viewfinder he can help along his initial efforts by using the magnifier A few trials and the trick will be his. Focus until the image appears to be sharp, then focus in either direction two or three times until, by comparison, you know that you have achieved sharp focus.

To help you in focusing, pick a sharp line in the subject, a cross-lighted straight object, like a tree, a doorway, a dominant texture pattern, or the line of a dress or collar It is easier to focus such a point than the less defined general area.

The VX and IIa Rangefinder

Rangefinder and ground glass are combined in the coupled Zeiss Split-Image Rangefinder and Focusing Viewfinder (Fig. 176) in a special glass that interchanges in the Pentaprism finder with other glasses for a wide variety of focusing requirements (Chap. 9). The Zeiss device is a plano-convex condenser with a ground glass base in the center of which is a circle containing two bright half-circle prisms, the rangefinder elements The prisms split the image. When out of focus, the two portions of the image are separated laterally. The focusing ring is turned to bring the two in line and, in consequence, into sharp focus.

The rangefinder shows only a small though a brightened portion of the image. The full picture is seen in the ground glass, which is simultaneously focused and may be used for this purpose independently or in conjunction with the rangefinder, as a check, one on the other The rangefinder cannot be used at lens stops smaller than f/5.6. The Zeiss device is useful for general as well

109-113

*Front, rear and top views of the Exakta IIa
Light Meter Viewfinder, which includes the
pentaprism, optical finder, and a built-in meter
(Right), rangefinder in ground glass*

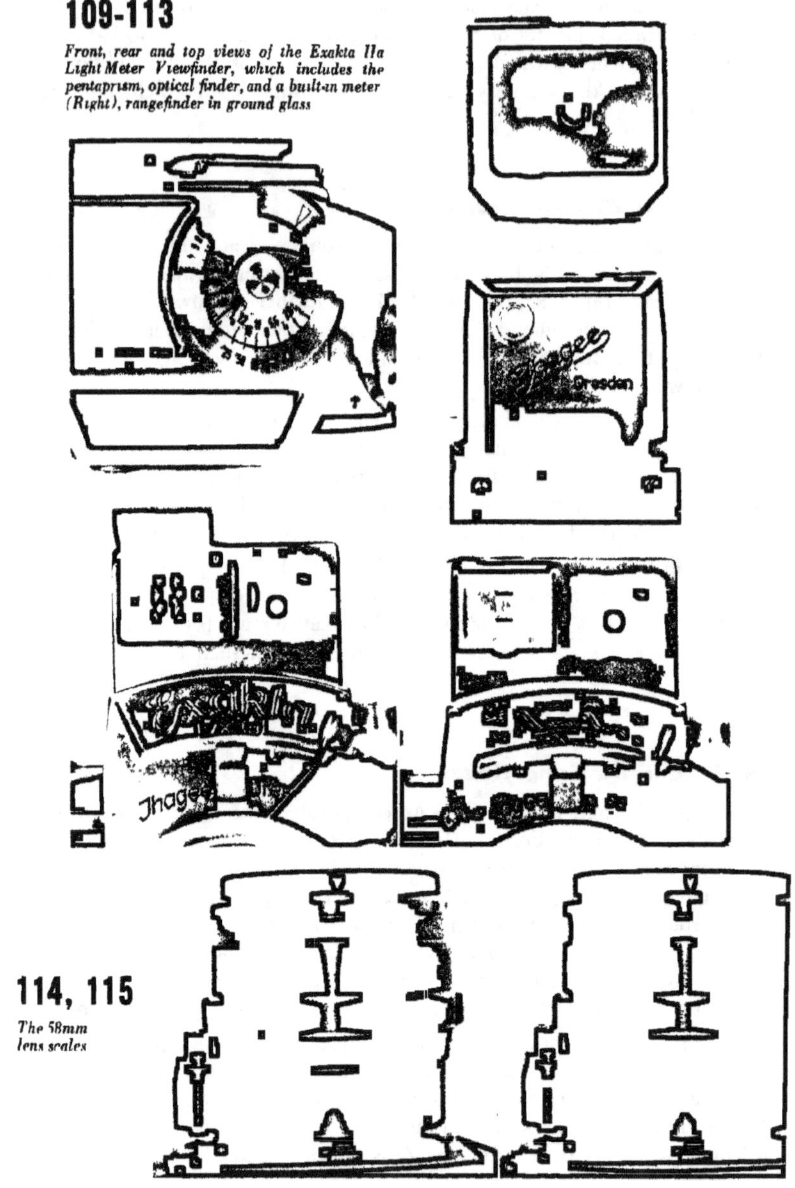

114, 115

*The 58mm
lens scales*

as close-up photography, particularly, because of the bright prism image, in poor lighting.

The Field of Sharp Focus

In photography you focus on a single object, or plane, and presumably only that plane is sharp Actually, other planes or objects in front of and behind the focused point are also sharp How much is sharp from nearest the camera to the far limit is called the *depth of field* This area of acceptable sharpness depends on several factors.

(Continued on page 73)

116
Fons Iannelli.
Using a 75mm lens
a close-up view at
the medium aper
ture of f/8 gave the
photographer the
result he wanted to
point up the girl's
absorption in her
self through shal
low depth of field
limited to the sub-
ject, with every
thing else out of
focus From a pic
ture story on an as
pect of youth for
The Ladies Home
Journal.

70

DEPTH-OF-FIELD TABLE FOR 58MM BIOTAR F/2

F/	Depth	1'8"	1'10"	2'	2'2"	2'4"	2'8"	3'	3'4"	3'8"	4'4"	5'	5'8"	6'8"	8'	10'	13'	16'	26'	50'	∞	Set on Hyper Dist (Last Col) For Sharp Field To Inf From
2	Near	1'7½"	1'9½"	1'11½"	2'1"	2'3½"	2'7"	2'11"	3'3"	3'7"	4'2"	4'10"	5'5"	6'4"	7'9"	9'2"	11'11"	14'6"	21'8"	34'8"	113'	56½'
	Far	1'8½"	1'10½"	2'0½"	2'2"	2'4"	2'9"	3'1"	3'5"	3'10"	4'6"	5'3"	5'11"	7'1"	9'	10'11"	13'1"	19'6"	34'8"	90'	∞	∞
2.8	Near	1'7½"	1'9½"	1'11½"	2'1"	2'3"	2'7"	2'11"	3'3"	3'6"	4'1"	4'9"	5'3"	6'2"	7'7"	8'11"	11'5"	13'10"	20'	31'	80'	40'
	Far	1'8½"	1'10½"	2'0½"	2'2"	2'4"	2'9"	3'1"	3'5"	3'10"	4'7"	5'4"	6'	7'3"	9'3"	11'4"	16'	21'	39'8"	133'	∞	∞
4	Near	1'7½"	1'9"	1'11½"	2'1"	2'3"	2'7"	2'11"	3'2"	3'5"	4'	4'7"	5'2"	5'11"	7'3"	8'6"	10'9"	12'10"	18'	26'4"	56'8"	28'4"
	Far	1'8½"	1'10½"	2'1"	2'2"	2'5"	2'10"	3'2"	3'6"	3'11"	4'8"	5'6"	6'3"	7'6"	9'9"	11'	17'8"	23'8"	30'	∞	∞	∞
5.6	Near	1'7"	1'9"	1'10½"	2'1"	2'2"	2'6"	2'10"	2'11"	3'4"	3'11"	4'5"	5'	5'9"	6'11"	8'4"	10'	11'10"	16'	22'4"	40'	20'
	Far	1'8½"	1'10½"	2'1"	2'3"	2'5"	2'10"	3'3"	3'7"	4'	4'10"	5'8"	6'7"	8'	10'5"	13'3"	20'	29'4"	78'8"	∞	∞	∞
8	Near	1'7"	1'8½"	1'10½"	2'0½"	2'1½"	2'5"	2'9"	3'	3'3"	3'10"	4'3"	4'9"	5'6"	6'5"	7'5"	9'	10'6"	13'9"	18'	26'	13'
	Far	1'9"	1'11½"	2'1"	2'4"	2'6½"	2'11"	3'4"	3'10"	4'2"	5'1"	6'	7'1"	8'8"	11'9"	15'5"	25'4"	40'4"	∞	∞	∞	∞
11	Near	1'6½"	1'8½"	1'10"	1'11½"	2'1"	2'4"	2'7"	2'11"	3'1"	3'7"	4'	4'5"	5'1"	5'11"	6'9"	8'4"	9'2"	11'6"	14'6"	20'	10'
	Far	1'9½"	2'	2'2"	2'4"	2'7"	3'	3'5"	3'11"	4'5"	5'5"	6'6"	7'9"	9'8"	14'	19'3"	38'1"	86'8"	∞	∞	∞	∞
16	Near	1'6"	1'7½"	1'9"	1'10½"	2'0½"	2'3"	2'6"	2'9"	2'11"	3'4"	3'10"	4'	4'7"	5'3"	5'10"	6'8"	7'8"	9'2"	10'11"	13'	6½'
	Far	1'10½"	2'1"	2'3"	2'6"	2'9"	3'3"	3'10"	4'3"	4'10"	6'1"	7'7"	9'4"	12'4"	20'	33'4"	273'	∞	∞	∞	∞	∞
22	Near	1'5½"	1'6½"	1'8½"	1'9½"	1'11½"	2'1"	2'4"	2'7"	2'9"	3'1"	3'4"	3'8"	4'	4'8"	5'	5'8"	6'4"	7'5"	8'6"	10'	5'
	Far	1'11½"	2'1½"	2'5"	2'8"	2'11"	3'6"	4'1"	4'10"	5'7"	7'3"	9'5"	12'4"	18'4"	40'	266'	∞	∞	∞	∞	∞	∞

This chart is based on a circle of confusion of 1/500th inch

How to use the depth of field tables:

Select the point of focus, say 8 feet. Locate the figure in the top row opposite Distance Focused On. Then pick the lens opening, say f/11, in the extreme left vertical column, and glance horizontally across the table to the figures under the selected distance. The reading is 5 feet, 2½ inches for the nearest point of acceptable sharpness, 17 feet, 2 inches for the far limit. The depth of field is practically 12 feet for these distance and lens settings.

At the same distance, the depth increases with smaller lens apertures, becomes shallower as the lens is opened wider. Thus, at f/16, the depth is more than 30 feet, but at f/8 it is reduced to about 7. At the same aperture, a change in distance will affect depth. For example, at 12 feet the depth will be increased to about 55 feet, but at the closer distance of 5 feet, the depth will be cut to less than 4 feet.

The next to last column, under the infinity symbol, lists the hyperfocal distance of the lens at the various apertures. This term refers to the depth of field for a given lens opening when the lens has been focused on infinity. It varies with the lens opening, the smaller the lens opening, the closer is the hyperfocal distance. When the lens is focused on the hyperfocal distance, everything is reasonably sharp from half the distance to infinity (see last vertical column).

The tables on this and the following page are calculated on the basis of a circle of confusion of 1/500th inch (see text).

DEPTH-OF-FIELD TABLE FOR 50MM (2-INCH) LENSES

Distance Focused on		4	5	6	7	8	9	10	12	15	20	30	50	100	∞	Set on Hyper Dist (Last Col) For Sharp Field To ∞ From ▼
F/ 2	Depth Near	3'9¾"	4'8½"	5'7¼"	6'5½"	7'3½"	8'1¼"	8'11"	10'6"	12'8"	16'1"	21'11"	30'11"	44'9"	80'9"	40'4½"
	Far	4'2½"	5'3¾"	6'5½"	7'7¾"	8'10¼"	10'1"	11'5"	14'1"	18'5"	26'6"	47'7"	130'8"	∞	∞	∞
2 8	Near	3'9"	4'7¼"	5'5½"	6'3"	7'1½"	7'9¾"	8'6½"	9'11½"	11'11"	14'11"	19'9"	26'10"	36'7"	57'8"	28'10"
	Far	4'3½"	5'5½"	6'8"	7'11¼"	9'3"	10'8"	12'1"	15'1"	20'2"	30'6"	62'2"	∞	∞	∞	∞
3 5	Near	3'8¼"	4'6¼"	5'4"	6'1¼"	6'10"	7'6¾"	8'3"	9'6½"	11'4"	14'	18'3"	24'	31'7"	46'2"	23'1"
	Far	4'4¼"	5'7"	6'10½"	8'2¾"	9'7½"	11'2"	12'9"	16'2"	22'1"	35'1"	84'11"	∞	∞	∞	∞
4	Near	3'7¾"	4'5½"	5'3"	5'11¾"	6'8½"	7'4½"	8'1½"	9'3¼"	11'	13'5"	17'3"	22'4"	28'9"	40'4"	20'2"
	Far	4'5"	5'8¼"	7'1¼"	8'5¼"	9'11"	11'6"	13'3"	17'	23'9"	39'4"	115'	∞	∞	∞	∞
5 6	Near	3'6¼"	4'3½"	5'	5'8"	6'3½"	6'10¾"	7'5½"	8'6"	9'10¾"	11'10"	14'9"	18'4"	22'5"	28'10"	14'5"
	Far	4'7¼"	6'	7'6¼"	9'2¼"	11'	13'	15'2"	20'4"	30'11"	64'1"	∞	∞	∞	∞	∞
8	Near	3'4¼"	4'1½"	4'7¾"	5'2¾"	5'9¼"	6'3"	6'8¾"	7'6¾"	8'7¾"	10'1"	12'1"	14'5"	16'10"	20'2"	10'1"
	Far	4'11¼"	6'7"	8'5¼"	10'7"	13'1"	16'	19'6"	29'	56'7"	∞	∞	∞	∞	∞	∞
11	Near	3'2"	3'9¼"	4'3½"	4'9¼"	5'2½"	5'7½"	5'11¾"	6'7¾"	7'5½"	8'6"	9'11"	11'5"	12'10"	14'8"	7'4"
	Far	5'5"	7'5½"	9'11½"	13'1"	17'2"	22'7"	30'4"	62'	∞	∞	∞	∞	∞	∞	∞
16	Near	2'10¾"	3'4½"	3'9½"	4'2"	4'6"	4'9½"	5'3¾"	5'6¼"	6'3¾"	6'9"	7'7"	8'3"	9'2¼"	10'1"	5'2"
	Far	6'5½"	9'7¼"	14'3"	21'8"	35'10"	72'4"	∞	∞	∞	∞	∞	∞	∞	∞	∞
22	Near	2'7½"	3'1¼"	3'4"	3'7½"	3'10½"	4'1"	4'3¼"	4'7"	4'11½"	5'4¾"	5'11"	6'5"	6'10¼"	7'4"	3'8"
	Far	8'4½"	14'3"	29'4"	102'1"	∞	∞	∞	∞	∞	∞	∞	∞	∞	∞	∞

117 *Sam Falk, The New York Times Magazine. Depth of field can be achieved with fairly large lens stops if a wide-angle lens is used and the focusing point is carefully selected. In this shot of a French railway station, the photographer recorded a remarkably deep field at f/4 by focusing on the nearest porter taking suitcase from window*

1 The focal length of the lens. From the same viewpoint, a 35mm lens will yield a deeper field than say a 58mm lens, therefore the shorter the focal length the greater the depth; the longer the focal length the shallower the depth.

2. The lens aperture A relatively large opening will give a shallower field than a smaller aperture

3 The distance focused upon. The closer the lens to the subject the less deep will be the field Moving back or using a smaller lens stop will improve the depth (see notes on page 71 under depth-of-field table).

The Point of Focus

In this connection, photographers often overlook the fact that if they are careful in picking the point of focus, they can use fairly large stops (which may be essential in certain cases) and still get away with an acceptable field. Sam Falk illustrates the point in Fig. 117.

Since depth of field becomes more critical the closer the lens is to the subject, it is clear that the focus should be somewhere near the lens. A rough-and-ready-rule suggests about a third of the way into the desired field But here is a more exact method It's an old one, but still works. When photographing fairly close to the near plane of a subject which has considerable depth and which must appear sharp from front to back, here is the formula that will solve the problem ·

Measure the distance from the front plane, then measure the far distance, which comes to say 20 inches and 30 inches, respectively. Now multiply one by the other to get the total of 600; multiply this sum by 2 to get 1,200. Now add 20 and 30 to get 50. Divide 1,200 by 50 to get 24 Therefore, to show everything sharp from nearest to farthest plane of the 10-inch field, at the largest possible aperture, you must focus on a point 24 inches from the lens.

Depth-of-Field Tables

The limits of sharp focus from nearest to farthest planes at varying lens openings and varying distances from the camera are conveniently listed in the so-called depth-of-field tables for lenses of various focal lengths The fields for 50mm and 58mm lenses, which are the basic or normal lenses in Exakta-Exa photography, are given on pages 71 and 72 The figures are in feet and inches, the top line in each aperture bracket being the near distance, the one below it the far measurement The notes on page 71 give instructions on how to use the tables.

Reference is made in the notes to *hyperfocal distance,* or the nearest point in sharp focus when the lens is focused on infinity. This point varies with the lens aperture, the smaller the opening, the closer the near plane will be The principle has more practical usefulness when the lens is focused on the hyperfocal distance itself, in which case everything is sharp from half the hyperfocal distance to infinity. An extra column has been added in the tables to list these figures.

Hyperfocal distance is related to a criterion of adequate sharpness which is known as the *circle of confusion.* A photographic image is composed of a large number of pin-points or minute circles of light. Depth-of-field tables are calculated on the basis of a selected diameter of light. The smaller the point of light on which the calculations are based, the sharper the image will be recorded. A circle of 1/500th of an inch was used in preparing these tables.

The Depth-of-Field Scales

For general purposes, the depth-of-field scale on the lens barrel is fully

74

adequate. Figures 114, 115 show the scales for the 58mm Zeiss Biotar near the base of the lens.

The scales are all set at 10 feet, the focused point, and the aperture at f/8 and f/16. The depth-of-field scale, which shows duplicate sets of apertures on either side of the focus index, is brought into use after selecting the desired aperture The near and far limits of the field are then read opposite the selected opening on either side of the index. Thus, on the Biotar, at f/8, the field is 7 feet to 14; at f 16, 6 to 26 feet.

An alternative method is to pick the desired near and far limits of the subject and to focus on each separately to find the distance in each case For example, the nearest point focuses at about 7 feet, the farthest point at 16 feet. You can cover this range by using stop f/11 on the Biotar. Turn the focusing knob until these near and far limits are under the figure 11 on each side of the depth-of-field index The ground glass image will no longer be sharp, of course, but the depth of field will be there. Where the distance marks fall between the lens stops on the scale use one-half stops. For a deeper field, use a smaller stop. For a shallower depth-of-field, as when it is desired to emphasize a single object or person (Fig. 116) by rendering the other planes relatively out of focus, a larger lens stop is used and the corresponding faster shutter speed

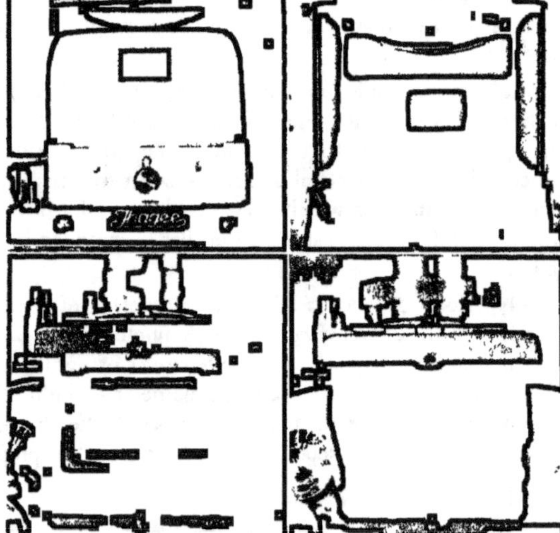

118, 119

The eye-level viewing position of the hooded reflex. The front flap is raised and the eye is held close to the rear peep sight (left), the open front aperture (right) frames the limits of the picture

120, 121

At right, the open hood is in the normal viewing and focusing position. At left, the magnifier flap has been lifted into place over the ground glass for increased focusing conven

Viewing and focusing positions with the Light-Meter IIa (left row) and Pentaprism Finder (right row)

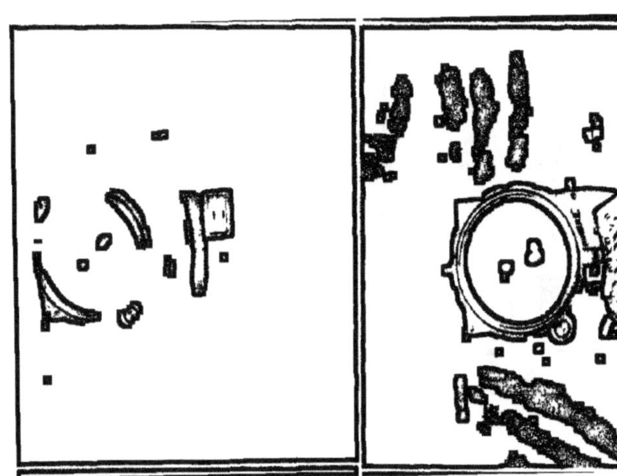

128-134

Shooting with Hooded Reflex: Waist level, overhead, eye level (horizontal and vertical). Bottom row: with cable release for time exposures, and horizontal and vertical shooting with open, or sports finder.

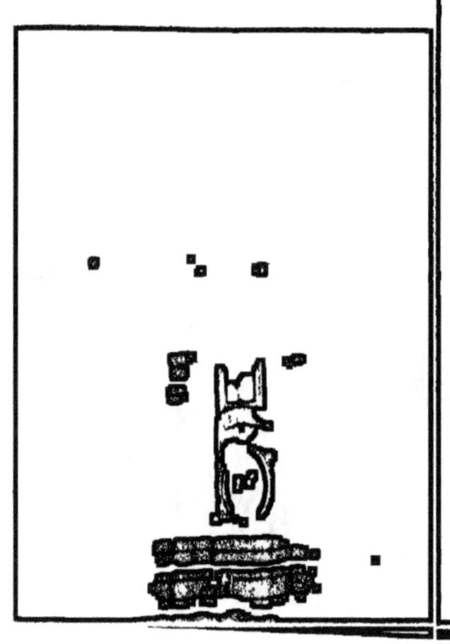

135 *Sam Falk, The New York Times Magazine. The cam-era was held high, as in Fig. 129, to show the crowd*

Zone Focusing, Prefocusing

For taking pictures of unpredictable action in a mobile shooting situation, as in the case of children at play, candid subjects, sports, and other action subjects, the zone focusing idea is a valuable solution. Consult the depth-of-field table, pick the depth at a given camera distance that you need and maintain this working distance throughout the shooting. Whatever happens within the preset zone will be in focus.

Prefocusing is another useful aid for stopping expected action, when the plane of action can be anticipated. Focus on the spot or the object the subject is due to pass. When he reaches this point, snap the shutter and the picture will be sharp. This technique is especially convenient when, because large lens apertures must be used for the needed shutter speed, the field is necessarily shallow. Such instances include poor light or heavily clouded days

The Camera Positions

The several ways of focusing and viewing with the Exakta (similai

78

STEADY DOES IT!

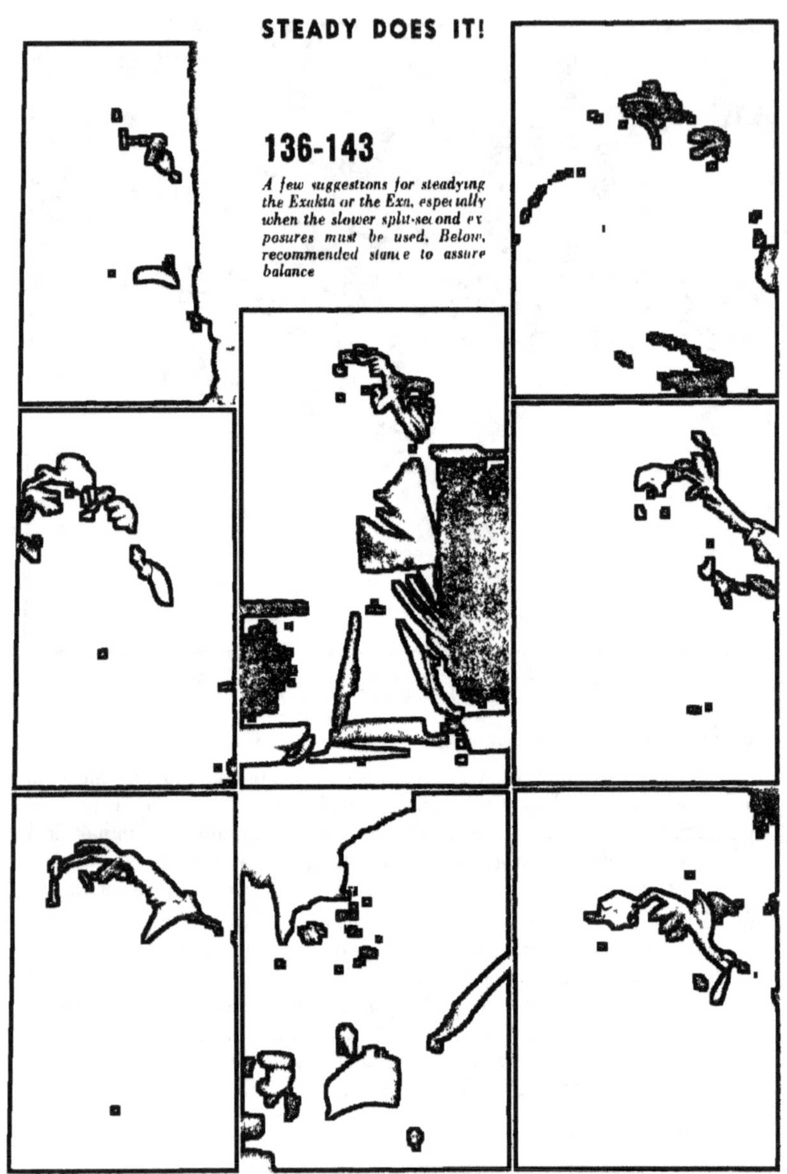

136-143

A few suggestions for steadying the Exakta or the Exa, especially when the slower split-second exposures must be used. Below, recommended stance to assure balance

methods apply also to the Exa) are illustrated in Figures 122-134, which are self-explanatory. When holding the hooded reflex at eye level (Figs. 118, 119) the eye should be close enough to the peepsight at the back to give the photographer a full view of the subject limits enclosed by the front frame.

Candid photography enthusiasts will think of other ways of holding the camera to get pictures without being observed, and in this connection will probably find the hooded reflex more adaptable to the purpose than the prism finders.

Steadying the Camera

Every photographer who shoots from the hand eventually adopts the one method of holding his camera that assures for him a firm grip and prevents camera shake. If the photographer is holding the camera in the most comfortable position to assure camera steadiness without strain, then he is doing it the "right way."

Individual preferences aside, however, there are certain principles upon which everybody seems to be agreed. Camera steadiness requires the use of more than the hands and fingers. The entire body is involved. Just as you must be sure that a tripod is free from shake or vibration when the exposure is made, so must the body be made rigid just before and during the brief instant of exposure.

Camera steadiness is promoted by several factors. First, grip the camera firmly (but not tensely) with both hands, leaving the finger or fingers, in the case of a cable release, of one hand free to operate the release.

Secondly, effect the release smoothly, avoiding the least jerkiness. The speed of the shutter is predetermined by the setting of the dial, not achieved by the rapidity of pressure on the release. Press the plunger gently and the shutter mechanism will do your bidding just as effectively as it will (and minus the hazards) if you exert a quick, jerky pressure. The latter will only shake the camera, even at high shutter speeds. Incidentally, the cautious photographer will use the shortest speed on the dial consistent with the stop required for control of field depth. This is particularly important in the case of miniature negatives where big enlargements are later to be made.

Thirdly, when using the camera at eye level, forehead, nose and cheek all become essential props. For waist or chest level use, the camera should be held against the body. If the camera is held freely in space, camera shake is almost inevitable. Propping the arms against one's sides keeps the camera fairly well anchored, and a momentary "stoppage" of breathing will help steadiness. A few ideas that have helped steadiness are offered in Figures 136-143.

Exposure Variables

Now that the mechanics of exposure as they relate to the Exakta VX, IIa and the Exa have been described and discussed in detail, the logical question is, how do we use these data to take pictures? What aperture is paired with what shutter speed to record an image on the film in the camera?

We know that, everything else being equal, a large lens aperture is paired with a short (fast) shutter speed setting, and yields a small depth of field; a small lens aperture calls for a longer shutter speed, and gives more depth. But we are not always free to make this simple choice, nor are we limited by it. Factors are involved which may dictate a choice or present alternatives. These are based mostly on lighting variables, often on the effect desired.

Exposure is governed by a variety of factors, including.

1. *The speed of the film* (see page 53). The actual speed should be established by the photographer as the rated exposure index is only a guide to the film's average sensitivity. Preliminary trials of shooting at the rated speed, and over and under, will soon give the photographer a personal figure that will be the "right one" for him. The speed he finally decides on will be related to his (or his photofinisher's) processing method and the developer used to process it. The film's speed is curbed to the extent of the factor when a filter is used. Thus, a fast film may be reduced to medium-speed or slower depending on the factor for the filter.

Indirectly, but none the less practically, film speed is also affected by lens extension, through the use of tubes or bellows, from its normal position on the camera (Chap. 9).

Light Volume

2. *The amount of light illuminating the subject.* Also, the type of light and its color. As we have seen (Chap. 5) film is more sensitive to blue light than to yellow or red. For this reason, a bluish light, however weak it may appear, is actually stronger than an exposure meter might indicate. The higher the color temperature of the light source, that is, the more it tends toward the blue, the shorter is the required exposure. For this reason, though fluor-

escent illumination is an artificial type, the daylight film speed rating should be used rather than the lower tungsten index.

The season of the year, the time of day and the weather condition will affect the light volume. Winter light is weaker than that prevailing during the summer months, and so is daylight early or late in the day whatever the season. That the amount of light varies with the appearance of the sky is a familiar fact to every photographer who reads his film instruction sheet Bright sun, hazy sun, cloudy-bright and cloudy-dull mean progressively larger lens openings (see also point 7, below) Pictures in the shade take more exposure than in the open, and in deep forest, where relatively little light comes through, more exposure still.

The candid photographer takes "no-light" for his province, often shooting in such weak light indoors or at night outdoors that pictures would not seem to be possible. But they are, as their results show (see Figs. 146, 147). Although a good deal of such shooting has been done successfully with 50 and 100 ASA film (frequently helped by an extra push in the development), the new faster films (with and without the push) are extending their exploits even further. As a result, smaller apertures and faster shutter speeds (with sharper pictures in consequence) may now be used safely in this type of work

Night-lighting outdoors provides another challenge in the matter of meagre light Limited views fairly well illuminated, like public buildings, store windows, etc., are much more easily handled, of course, than street scenes and similar subjects, particularly those away from the main thoroughfares The tripod can often be dispensed with now that we have fast filters and lens speeds of f/1 5 and f/1.9. However, where small stops are needed the tripod still comes in handy. A lens hood is inexpensive

In this connection, the slow-speed knob on the Exakta VX and IIa obviates guesswork in timing by providing accurately measured exposures of 1 /5th to 12 seconds, a range that will take care of practically any night exposure situation, especially when the fast films are used If the area being photographed is crossed by pedestrians during the required exposure, the T setting on the fast knob will be more useful. The shutter is opened on time (use a cable release); when someone passes, cover the lens with the hand. Keep track of the exposed periods until the allotted exposure total has been reached, then close the shutter.

Light Reflection and Distance

3 *The amount of light reflected from the subject.* Dark surfaces and colors reflect less light, light-toned surfaces and colors relatively more light to the camera. Here again one is reminded of the film instruction sheet:

82

144 Fritz Goro, LIFE. *Action at right angles to the camera plus a telephoto lens and a fast moving subject call for a top shutter speed. Data. 150mm lens, 1/500th at f/11.*

light, average and dark subjects call for progressively larger openings under any given light condition. By reason of exposure latitude the film takes in stride a considerable range of these reflected light values, the faster the film the greater the latitude. However, where the range of values exceeds the film's latitude the photographer favors either the lighter or the darker values or gives a compromise exposure somewhere between the two.

4. *The distance of the light source from the subject.* Except when using flash bulbs or electronic flash for a fill-in outdoors (see Chap. 11) this factor of course does not apply to outdoor daylight photography where the light source is the distant sun. With artificial light, the closer the lamp to the subject, the less the exposure needed, the farther away it is the longer the exposure. At twice the distance of a given setup, the exposure must be increased four times (the square of the distance). Thus, if the exposure is f/8 at 1/50th with the light 3 feet from the subject, at 6 feet the aperture must be opened to f/4, or the shutter speed cut to 1/10th. Incidentally, this is the basis for calculating exposure for closeups (Chap 9) except that the rule is applied to lens-from-film-plane extension rather than light-from-subject distance.

Proximity of the light is often the reason why "available-light" pictures succeed under apparently adverse lighting conditions. For example, Morris Gordon took his picture of the toolmaker at his lathe, Fig 146, by the light of a small fluorescent lamp just above the subject.

Light Direction and Contrast

5 *Viewpoint of the camera relative to the direction of the light.* A front light, from the camera position, will call for the shortest exposure; side lighting, or lighting at a 45° angle, double the exposure; backlighting (behind the subject), four times the front-light exposure. Example, if the front light takes 1/100th second, the side light exposure will be 1/50th, the back light 1/25th. The increasing exposures are based on the desirability of getting detail into the shadow areas. However, if a silhouette is wanted (Fig. 148), then the exposure will be as for front lighting.

Indoors, where a fill-in light must be used to illuminate the shadow areas, the exposure will of course depend on the distance as well as the direction of the light plus the ratio of main to fill-in light. In candid situations, the photographer either will accept the exposure limitations of the lighting angle as he finds it (deep shadows and all) or wait until the subject has moved into a better lighted position.

6. *Light contrast and quality* A shadowless, flatly lighted subject such as a distant scene will give better results if the normal exposure is halved Exposure is increased as the shadows become greater relative to the lighted

areas (see point 5, above) The terms "soft" and "hard" are used in photography to describe diffused, even light, and contrasty or sharply differentiated light values Daylight is softer and more pleasing in the morning and late afternoon than it is during the middle hours of the day, and exposure is less of a problem Because of soft lighting, pictures in open shade have more exposure latitude than in direct sunlight, with a minimized tendency to block up highlights through overexposure.

Overcast sky supplies more light than it may seem to because it looks dark Actually, the light may be stronger than it appears, as a meter reading will show, because the illumination is greatly diffused there are no strong shadows to contend with, as on sunny days, and contrast between sky and ground subjects is reduced One must be careful, therefore, not to overexpose as the atmospheric quality of the light on such days can be preserved only by fairly accurate exposures.

Snow, on the other hand, needs good sunlight at a cross-lit angle, as well as accurate exposure, in order to show its texture well In dull light, snow looks woolly In fact, adequate light contrast is generally desirable for the average run of material, and usually gives the most satisfying results with such subjects as landscapes, architectural details, street scenes, etc Shadow detail is not always wanted A bold light-and-dark effect is often preferable where pattern and design are the goal.

145 *Lou Bernstein Soft daylight at cross-lighting angle shows texture shadow detail.*

146 *Morris Gordon. A small fluorescent bulb above the subject's head furnished all the light for this hand-held candid shot*

7 Reflections from surrounding objects or surfaces Indoors, in addition to the illumination from a light source or sources, exposure under any lighting setup will be affected by the size of the room, the height of the ceiling, the lightness or darkness of the walls; the lightness or darkness of the subject's clothes, the presence of incidental light-reflecting surfaces, such as a white tablecloth, newspapers or open books, and the proximity of the subject to these surfaces and the walls.

Outdoors, extra light will be kicked into the subject area by an adjacent light wall or bank of light flowers or groups of people in light clothes. A large well-illuminated open area such as a beach scene will supply a good deal of extra light. For closeup subjects in such areas, however, the problem of light contrast can be severe. To help illuminate shadow areas, a reflector of news-

86

paper or a large white card or similar aid, may be positioned at the shadow side to reflect light for more detail.

Aubrey Bodine, who has done a good deal of night photography during his long career, prefers "bad-weather" nights when he takes pictures, because of the lighting help he gets from rain, snow, fog and mist, which spread the illumination of street, home and building lights Rain reflects the light on buildings, brightens the sidewalks, thus filling out the scene. Snow acts as a light-toned reflector Mist and fog spread the light around, often making it possible also to shoot directly into the light sources themselves.

Action Techniques

8. *Movement of subject* Five factors are involved. (1) the speed at which

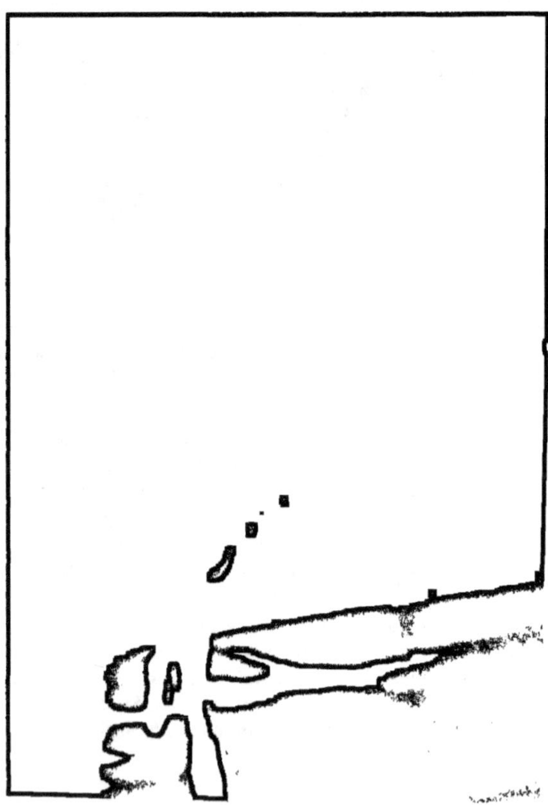

147

87

the subject is moving; (2) the distance of the subject from the camera; (3) the direction or angle of the subject movement in relation to the camera position; (4) the focal length of the lens and (5) the degree of "stopping" considered desirable or satisfactory.

The faster the subject movement the faster the required shutter speed, and the greater the distance between camera and subject, the longer the exposure may be. If, for example, 1/100th second is enough to stop a moving subject 50 feet away from the camera, twice this speed, 1/200th, will be needed for the same subject at a distance of 25 feet The longest (slowest) shutter speed is permissible when the subject is moving in a direction straight toward or away from the camera, the shortest (fastest) when the subject is moving at right angles to the camera, and an intermediate speed when the subject is moving in a diagonal direction. The diagonal is, therefore, the happy medium not only where shutter speed is concerned but also because a subject moving in this direction usually offers the most interesting picture angle

Focal length is involved in the scheme because it affects the size of the image moving across the film The larger the image (long focal length) the faster it moves, therefore requires a quicker shutter speed than a shorter lens, used at the same distance. In order to convey a feeling of motion, photographers sometimes deliberately use a longer exposure than the speed needed to stop motion "dead." The result ranges from movement of an arm or leg, which is normal and often unavoidable, to the extreme efforts of the "blur-it" devotees.

Panning and the Focal-Plane Shutter

Panning is the accepted method of shooting moving subjects, such as racing horses and cars, runners, etc. The photographer sights the subject in the finder and keeps it there while smoothly following the subject's movement, then snaps the shutter without stopping the camera The result is a blurred background, but the moving subject is sharp.

To avoid "stretching" the image on the film, owing to the nature of the focal-plane shutter, which exposes the film section by section (Chap. 4), the *subject* in the finder should move in the same direction as the shutter curtain will when it is released, but the *image* of the subject should move in the reverse direction to that of the curtain The Exakta curtains move from left to right, but the direction of subject movement as seen in the reflex ground glass is reversed. It is most convenient, therefore, to use the eye-level sight for such pictures. In this connection, the pentaprism finder makes an ideal companion for the Exakta's shutter, since the movement in the finder is in the same order of left to right as the shutter, but the actual image reaches the film from right

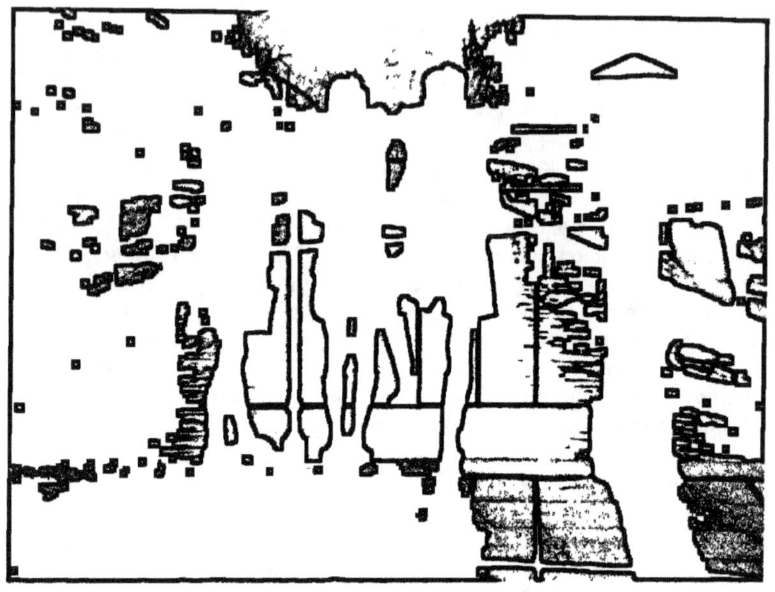

148 *Lies Wiegman. Backlighting, with no exposure allowance for the front part of the subject, results in a silhouette, which can tell a story of its own, as here*

to left, as it should

A useful technique in action photography is to watch for the peak in the movement of such subjects as a vaulter, a diver, a dancer, etc—the moment when the action pauses momentarily before changing its direction. Even very fast moving subjects can be caught with moderate shutter speeds this way, giving the Exa with its smaller range of speeds an almost equal advantage with the Exakta's higher top speeds.

9 *The processing technique* also has an important effect on exposure, since the developer used and the procedure followed affect both exposure and image quality (see Chap. 12)

Measuring Exposure

Exposure need not be guess work or based entirely on experience. Devices are available which if properly used will give accurate readings of subjects in practically all situations where sufficient light is reflected to make a reading possible. Today, the most generally used type of meter is the photoelectric, which is marketed in a very wide variety of designs and in a range of prices within almost any photographer's reach.

The heart of the photoelectric exposure meter is a light-sensitive cell; when the meter is pointed toward the subject being photographed, the light that strikes the meter is converted into electricity. The power thus generated moves a needle in the meter across a table of foot-candle values. By moving a dial on the face of the instrument, this figure is then lined up with scales which furnish at a glance a choice of lens aperture and shutter speed pairings, any one of which for the light indicated will give a satisfactory exposure. The readings are taken after the meter has been set for a specific film rating (all meters are now calibrated in the ASA rating system or include this with other systems).

Photoelectric meters are marketed in three types: (1) for reading reflected light (it is pointed toward the subject); (2) the incident-light meter, which reads the light source itself (the meter is pointed at the light from the position of the subject); (3) reflected-light meters that are convertible when desired to the incident type, usually with the aid of an accessory.

Using the Meter

The meter has a wider angle of view than most lenses in general use. The chief precaution to take in using the meter, therefore, is to hold the instrument close enough to the subject to cover only the areas to be photographed otherwise, values will be included that are outside the field covered by the lens angle. A practical rule is to take the readings from a distance about equal to the width of the subject. In the case of a portrait, for example, the distance would be a few inches. Outdoors in daylight, point the meter slightly downward to avoid the direct influence of sky light. When taking a reading close up make sure the meter does not cast a shadow on the subject, distorting the reading.

The same techniques apply in using the Exakta IIa light meter in the finder unit. If desired, the meter may be used off the camera.

Another type of meter, though less generally used these days, is the visual extinction meter. This one is held up to the eye, the user picks the dimmest figure in a line or circle of numbers that can be read clearly and without strain. The figure is then used in calculating the exposure with the aid of a table on the outside of the device. This meter is most useful indoors.

The exposure table in the instruction sheet that comes with every roll of film makes a reliable start for the beginner. It gives average exposures and is intended for average results. It is also a good general guide even for the photographer who uses an exposure meter, for it provides him with basic data on what he can expect from the film in terms of exposure speed. In addition, a number of calculators are on the market which are in effect an elaboration of the instruction-sheet table in that they may be used for films of different speeds and for an extended range of exposure settings.

Astronomical Sky Spectacles

These notes were supplied by Peter Austin Leavens, specialist in photographing sky phenomena. He has photographed many eclipses of the sun and moon for the American Museum-Hayden Planetarium in New York City.

Interesting pictures of stars as they move across the sky from east to west can be made by setting a camera on a sturdy tripod at time exposure and letting stellar paths record on the film while the earth rotates

Winter nights provide the best opportunity for long star trail photographs, but shots can be made over six-hour periods even in the summer season. It is of course necessary to work under a dark, clear sky, away from the glare of city or town lights. Exposures should not be started until the last glow of twilight has disappeared. Of course, the shutter must be closed before dawn begins. Tables of moonrise and moonset should be consulted to make sure that no lunar illumination will interfere.

A combination of fast film and lenses at full diaphragm will capture hundreds of star paths If a camera is directed toward the north pole star, Polaris, the trails will be circular, since the earth's axis of rotation also points to it. Often a meteor will flash in the field of view, enhancing the scene being taken with a brilliant, oblique track.

Exposure Data for the Moon and Sun

With very fast film like Kodak Tri-X and a shutter speed of 1/100th of a second, the lens aperture for representative phases of the moon will be:

f/8 for waxing crescent (best 94 hours after actual time of new moon).

f/11 for first quarter (actually one-half—best 4 or 5 hours after actual time of new moon)

f/16 for waning gibbous (more than half full moon but less than full; best 82 hours after actual full moon).

f/22 for full moon (not all full moons over western hemisphere; check time for particular month)

To photograph the sun, using the same speed film, the exposure is f/22 at 1/500th of a second with the Kodak Wratten Neutral Density Filter 4.0 (No. 96 series).

The Exakta may also be used to photograph the moon in conjunction with a telescope, either the refractor (Fig. 149) or the reflector type. Examples of the remarkable results are shown in Figs. 150 and 151.

The photographer has a choice of three methods·

1. With its lens removed, the Exakta can be mounted so as to seat the film plane at prime focus of the telescope's lens. Although this method results in the smallest image size, it will be the sharpest, and give the highest light transmission. The diaphragm ratings become simply those fixed by dividing the objective lens diameter into telescope focal length.

2 Another method is the use of the camera body without its lens, together with a telescope and eyepiece, the latter being adjusted to project and focus the image on the film plane In this case, ground glass focusing is essential. Diaphragm figuring is commensurate with the f/ number of the telescope objective, multiplied by the square of the magnification between telescope focal plane and film plane This will vary with eyepiece settings and can be best determined as the ratio of diameters of the image of the moon in the telescope focal plane, and the solar image on the film plane. The latter can be measured directly, and the former will be the focal length of the telescope objective divided by number 111.

3 Using an Exakta camera with 50mm lens set at infinity (Fig. 155), diaphragm wide open, and in parallel axis contact with the smaller exit pupil of a 4-inch Unitron telescope eyepiece This method produces maximum image magnification, but yields the least transmitted light. The actual aperture speed is computed as follow:

$$\frac{\text{Focal Length of Camera Lens}}{\text{Exit Pupil of Telescope}}$$

The telescope exit pupil is the objective lens or mirror diameter, divided by the magnification. The magnification is:

$$\frac{\text{Focal Length of Objective}}{\text{Focal Length of Eyepiece}}$$

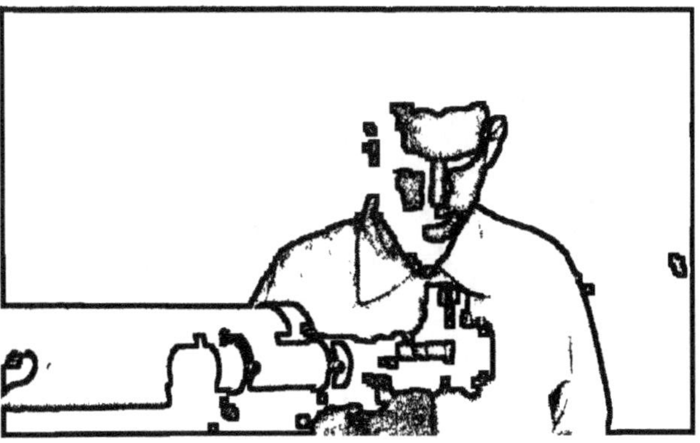

149

Frank Henrich with Exakta on refractor telescope with the setup he used to take the pictures reproduced in Figs 156 and 157 Photograph by **Peter A. Leavens.**

92

150

The full moon at perigee (closest to earth in elliptical orbit). This was taken with an Exakta, lens removed, at prime focus of 4-inch objective lens diameter, 60-inch focal length, Unitron telescope. Lunar image size on negative 9/16 inch Exposure on Kodak Super XX film was 1/100th second

151

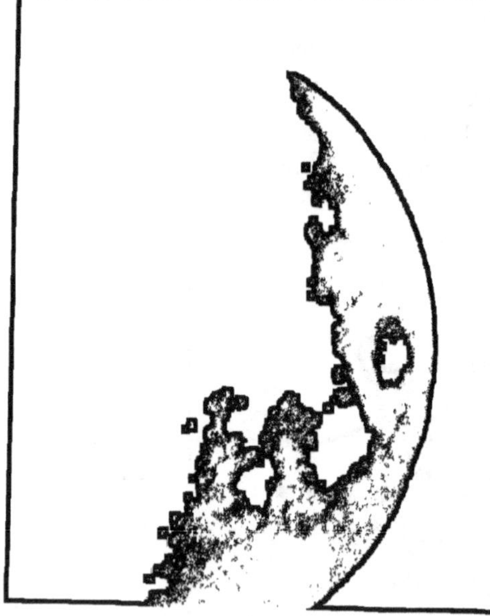

The half, or so-called first quarter phase, of the moon Craters and mountains become visible along the shadow line of sunrise or sunset Taken under identical circumstances as Fig 156, except that shutter speed was reduced to 1/25 second with fixed working telescope aperture of f/16 (approximately) Both photographs by **Frank Henrich.**

93

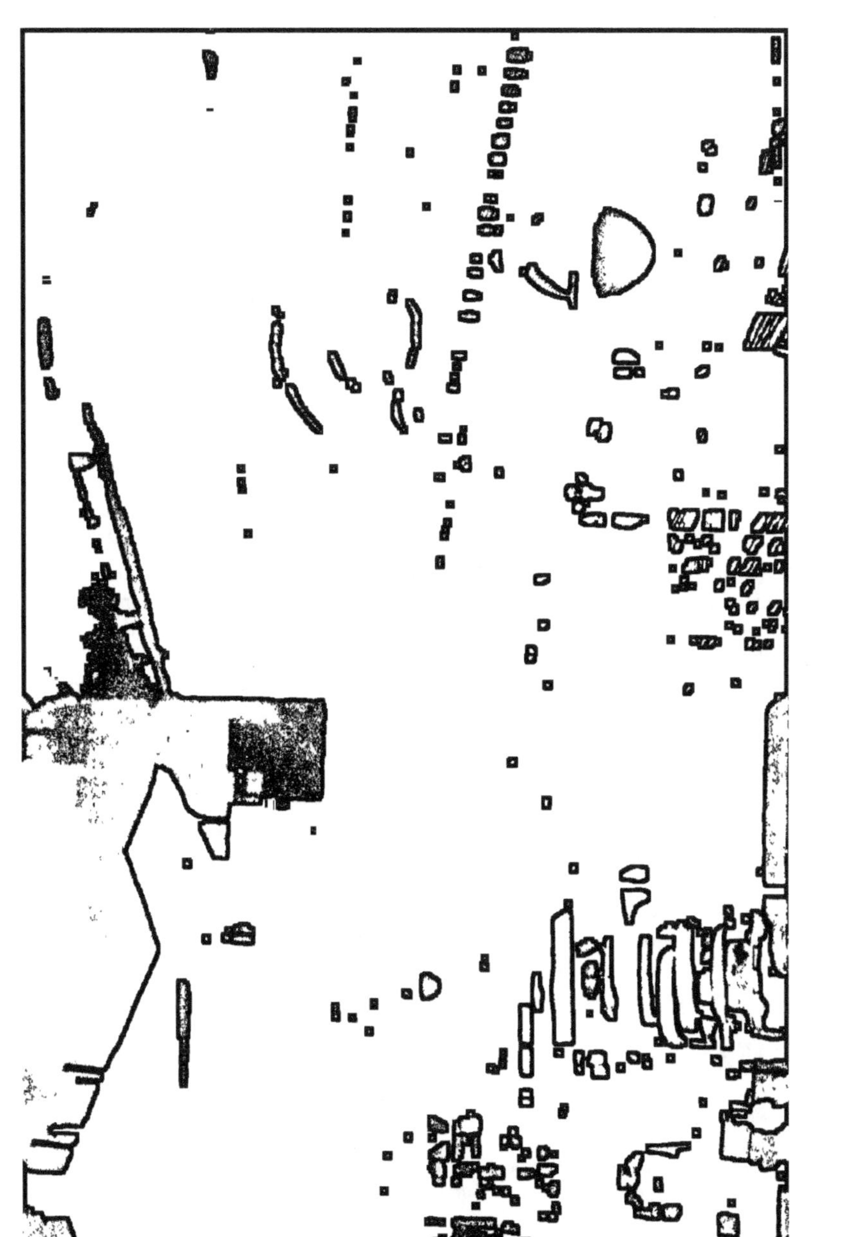

Lenses for the Exakta

From inches to miles, the range of coverage of lenses available for the Exakta-Exa cameras fulfills every practical photographic need. Nearly every lens manufacturer has made his contribution to the list, and incidentally to the photographer's problem of how to make a satisfying choice from a show-case of such abundance and diversity.

From the viewpoint of practical picture-taking, lenses are distinguished from each other basically, first by their focal length (see p. 29). Exakta lenses vary from 24mm to 1,000mm, Exa lenses up to 135mm and as fast as f/2 and f/2.8 (See p 97 for differences in area covered by lenses of varying focal length). The second consideration is the widest aperture, or speed of the lens.

When purchased, the camera is equipped with what is known as the "normal" lens, one with a focal length of 50mm or 58mm. The owner's first extra lens is usually a telephoto, next a wide-angle, although the order may be reversed, depending on the photographer's immediate needs In either case, the owner of a single-lens reflex camera has this advantage over others: whatever the focal length, the difference is seen directly on the ground glass without the aid of accessory viewfinders

Factors Affecting Choice

The speed of the lens is the first major factor in selecting a lens of a par ticular focal length. The decision will be affected by price (a slower lens usually costs less), although this may be offset by such other factors as the visibility of the image on the ground glass (the smaller stop of the slower lens will of course show a relatively darker image), and the kind of photography for which the lens is intended. With the introduction of the preset and

152   *Sam Falk, The New York Times Magazine*

The characteristic qualities of the long telephoto lens are dramatically illustrated in this shot of the now defunct New York City Third Avenue "El" Note how five cars have been squeezed so that they look like one and everything seems larger and closer together than it would be seen normally. Falk took the picture with the 400mm Tele-Megor at f/16 and 1/150th of a second from a station platform three blocks away

automatic diaphragm lens types for 35mm single-lens reflex cameras, these have added another important point in the choice of a lens (see p. 32)

The lens prospect will also examine such features as the range of apertures, the closest focusing distance and whether the scales are in meters or in feet. The nearest focusing distance may have influence with those who like to work close to the subject but not so close as to require the use of accessories. Although the scales on foreign lenses imported into this country are usually in feet and meters or sometimes only in feet, a few have only the meter scale. One can quickly become accustomed to the meter scale (see conversion table, p 114), but most American photographers prefer the foot scale or, in the light of other desirable points the lens may possess, are willing to settle for the double distance scale.

One may also be swayed by a variety of refinements, such as click lens stops, whether the lens mount extends beyond the lens surface to form a built-in lens hood, the placement and legibility of the scales, the finish of the mount, etc In this connection, one should bear in mind that because of the great activity in lens research by the various competing companies, perhaps more than in any other phase of photographic manufacture except that of film, lenses are constantly being changed in one detail or another. Therefore, several lenses, all apparently alike, may have slight variations in the mount, markings, coating symbols, engravings, mount dimensions, and differences in finish

Angle of Field Coverage

From a given camera position, the wide-angle lens, as its name indicates, includes more area in the picture, than does the normal lens, and the telephoto includes less This is the principal reason for interchanging lenses on the camera. Others are discussed in succeeding pages Typical results are illustrated on the opposite page. By comparison, the wide angle shows more in the picture, but everything is small; the telephoto selects a part of the photographed scene, and by "bringing" it closer and filling the negative with it, makes it look bigger.

The lens angle of view does it. All three pictures were taken from a window sill across the street. Note how progressively less area is included with each increase in focal length and, in consequence, reduction in the angle of view The most impressive illustration is the 400mm shot, which fills the full 1x1½-inch frame with a fraction of the subject area covered by the 58mm lens. The angle of view for the 58mm, 135mm and 400mm lens, respectively, is 40°, 18° and 5.6°. A list of view angles for representative focal lengths appears on page 114.

96

153

With 400mm Hugo Meyer Tele-Megor

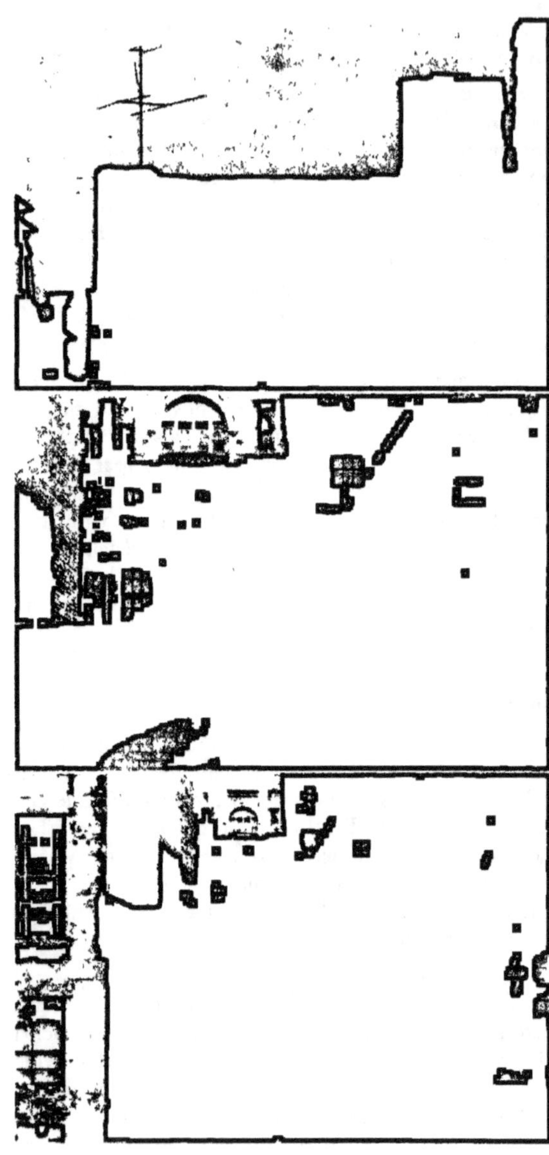

154

With 135mm Carl Zeiss Triotar

155

With 58mm Carl Zeiss Biotar

Preset and Automatic Diaphragms

The automatic diaphragm, which permits viewing the subject with the lens wide open and automatically stops down to a pre-selected aperture when the shutter is released, was described for the Biotar and the Primotar lenses in Chap. 3. Other lenses are available which follow the same principle but vary somewhat in operation

A semi-automatic type, the preset diaphragm, is available for a wide range of focal lengths. The desired opening is preset on a scale, and the lens is opened wide for maximum viewing and focusing convenience. Just before releasing the shutter, a short turn of the diaphragm ring stops down the lens to the preset opening. This is the basic principle; there are variations.

Because the advent of these devices and the prism finder eliminates the principal drawback of the single-lens reflex camera's darkened screen when stopped down, the idea has been incorporated in an increasingly growing assortment of lenses with automatic diaphragms

Range of Apertures

The range of apertures on lenses for the Exakta-Exa cameras extends down to f/11 or f/16 or f/22 and, particularly on the longest focal lengths, even to f/32 Although generally speaking lenses will give the best definition at two or three stops below the maximum opening, the smaller apertures will perform adequately when the depth-of-field is a critical requirement. But the smaller stops, like the widest aperture on the fastest lenses, should be used as a valuable reserve rather than promiscuously. In general photography, the inherent depth of the miniature lens will cover enough field at the medium stops and average distances to record the essential picture elements If this means resorting to high shutter speeds to compensate, then so much the better since steadier exposures will be the happy result.

The lens hood is an essential accessory for every lens. The combination or so-called "Series" type, which accommodates filters, etc. as well as the lens hood, is a convenient system that is deservedly popular Each lens should also be provided with lens caps for front and rear for protection when the lens is not in use.

The photographer who owns several lenses should provide himself with a combination compartmented case for storing the capped lenses when not in use and for carrying them into the field. Insurance against damage or loss for camera and lenses is obviously desirable but too often overlooked.

The "Normal" Lens

The 50mm or 58mm focal lengths are the standard for Exakta-Exa cameras, respectively covering a subject area 45° and 40° from the base of the camera They exceed slightly the diagonal of the film (44mm) which is considered normal, and the view angle is somewhat smaller than that of human vision, which is about 45°, but are generally accepted as the most useful for the average run of subjects, providing the most satisfactory limits for most purposes The speeds vary from the very high apertures of f/1 5 to the moderate one of f/3.5. Most normal lenses for these cameras are equipped with either the automatic or the preset type diaphragm.

The high-speed lenses are useful to the magazine and other photographers who do much shooting under unfavorable lighting conditions, but the need for lens speed is becoming less urgent even in these situations as film speeds spurt along. On the other hand, the large lens apertures do have the advantage that, coupled with the new fast films, they can record images under conditions where photography was not possible before and thus open up new opportunities for the medium.

Two lenses in this class are the 50mm f/1.9 Schneider Xenon fully automatic (see below) and the 55mm f/1.9 Steinheil Auto-Quinon fully automatic lens They are designed to give satisfactory overall definition even at full aperture, which is improved when the lens is closed down moderately Both stop down to f 22, and have distance scales in feet.

Although the normal lens can handle most subjects, an auxiliary wide-angle or telephoto lens, preferably both, will appreciably extend the photographer's range of picture opportunities The ease with which lenses can be interchanged on the Exakta-Exa mount (Chap. 3) and the fact that the image

156

The 50mm Schneider Xenon fully automatic lens.

change is seen immediately on the ground glass, make the transition as convenient and rapid as it is practical and effective

More Area With the Wide Angle

The wide angle is a short-focus lens compared with the normal. Because
it lies closer to the film, it covers a broader field than the normal at the same
camera-to-subject distance. However, individual subjects in the field are
smaller. The wide angle is therefore useful when the over-all scene is more
important than the individual details and when it is desirable to include a
large area, as in landscape photography, or in photographing a group It is
particularly useful when working in restricted areas, such as interiors, in
taking pictures of homes and buildings and wherever space does not permit
the photographer to back up far enough to include what he wants.

Among its other advantages over the normal lens are the greater depth-
of-field it covers even at wide apertures, and the fact that it renders valuable
service in controlling perspective (see p 108). Because focusing is less critical
with wide-angle lenses, particularly at ordinary distances, it is the ideal lens

157 *Harold Feinstein. The wide-angle lens is the happy solution when covering a group such as this at intimate range*

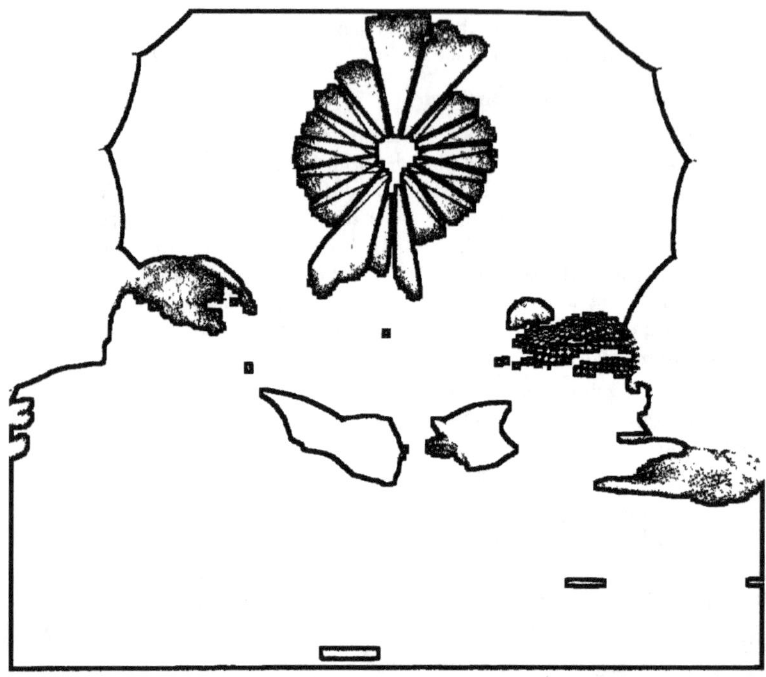

166 *Harold Feinstein. The deep perspective afforded by the close viewpoint with a wide-angle lens gives the observer a sense of participation in the experience*

for zone focusing (see p. 75) and similar situations where one is constantly faced with the possibility of unexpected action over a fairly broad area. Moreover, the relatively smaller size of the image permits the use of slower shutter speeds to stop moving objects (see p. 88).

The wide angle is a handy lens in candid photography and photojournalism generally. Indeed, it is the wide angle's unique characteristics that has made it so popular in recent years, to the point, in fact, that some photographers have made it their "standard" lens.

The presence of the mirror has long posed a problem in designing a wide-angle lens for the single-lens reflex camera since the lens must be so constructed that the rear elements do not interfere with the swinging mirror during exposure. The problem has been solved, however, in the extraordinary eight-element 24mm f/4 Isco Westrogon Super Wide Angle Lens, and the seven-element 35mm f/2.8 Steinheil Wide Angle Quinaron, both equipped with automatic diaphragm action. The respective angles of view are 82° and 62° for the 24mm and the 35mm Those who follow the contemporary trend to use the 35mm focal length as a "normal" lens may decide on the Quinaron as a general-purpose lens, with the added advantage that, as it can be focused from infinity down to 4 inches from the subject, it can also be used for close-up photography, and without the use of bellows or other accessories. The potentials of the 82°-angle Westrogon will be obvious to any photographer who has ever been faced with the need for taking in more area than his normal or moderate wide-angle lens would allow, and for working in extremely close quarters

The Telephoto Is More Selective

Working in the opposite direction to that of the wide angle, the telephoto narrows the camera's angle of view to a limited area, the longer the focal length the more narrow the area. The result is a relatively big image compared with that of the normal or wide-angle view from the same distance The telephoto in effect "pulls in" the distant object for closer attention.

Its usefulness is obvious for such subjects as sports from the sidelines or a grandstand, photography of birds in their nests or in flight, animal photography, mountain scenery, and in general for subjects that cannot be approached closely enough to isolate and emphasize the main subject in a desired composition. The telephoto is especially valuable in portraiture where pleasing perspective (see p 110) and in consequence natural results are obtained because of the distance from the subject imposed by the lens' focal length.

159 *The 24mm f/4 Isco Westrogon Super Wide Angle lens*   **160** *The 35mm f/2 8 Steinheil Wide Angle Quinaron lens*

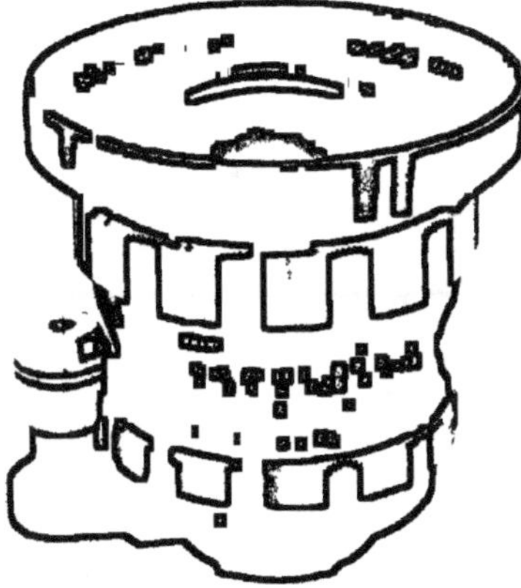 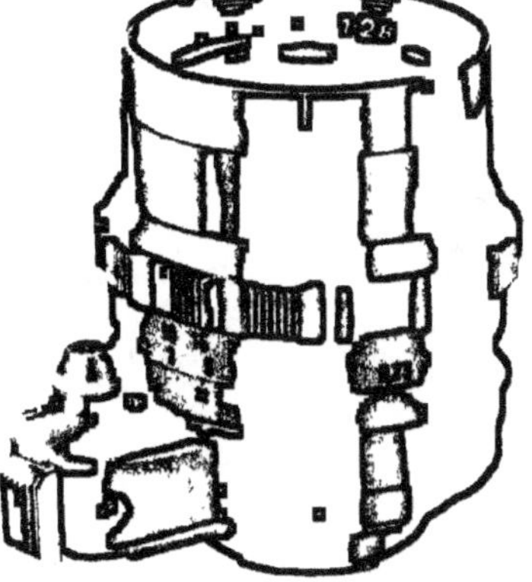

161 Harold Feinstein. *The medium telephoto lens, 75mm in this case, is generally favored for portraits*

Shallow Depth

A characteristic of the telephoto that may be considered a gain or a loss depending on the desired results, or one's acceptance of the result in the light of other advantages, is the fact that the telephoto image shows a flattening effect, the lens having a tendency to compress the field. This is illustrated with particular emphasis in Fig. 152, where a normal-sized train appears to have been compressed so that five cars look like only one.

Since all objects and planes in the field are seen from a distance (three city blocks in this instance), there is less apparent size differentiation between them than can be seen at the normal closer viewing distances. The height of objects tends to be equalized and the separation between them is markedly reduced (Fig. 169). Moreover, the background looms unnaturally larger in relation to the objects than we know from ordinary experience.

Actually, all these effects are normal; what makes them seem different is the fact that the greatly reduced lens angle of view gives us only the distant

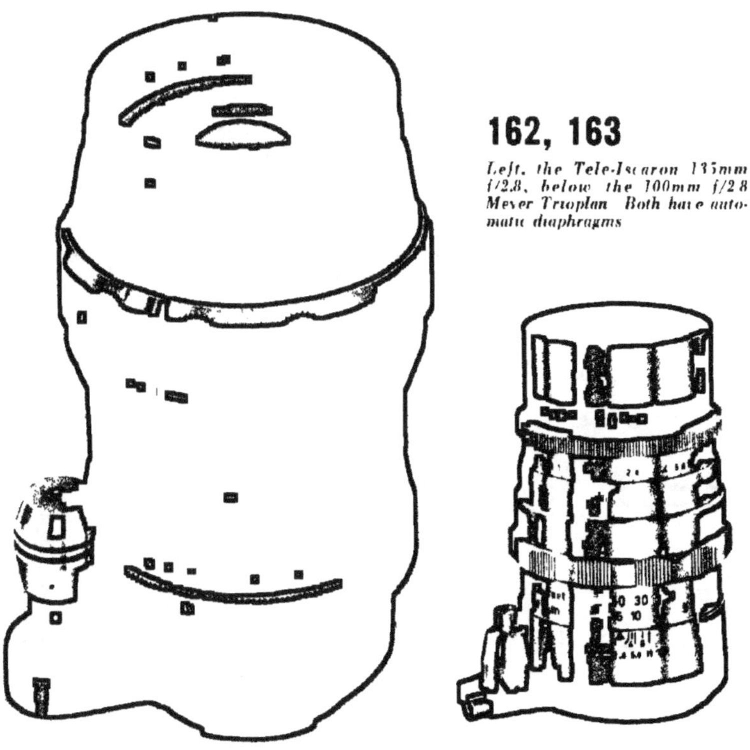

162, 163

Left, the Tele-Iscaron 135mm f/2.8, below the 100mm f/2.8 Meyer Trioplan. Both have automatic diaphragms

portion of the total scene encompassed by direct vision and cuts out all the rest. In so doing, our vision is deprived of normally seen relationships between near and far objects and thus we are able to see only the distant planes.

Telephoto Steadiness

Usually it is best to set the camera on a tripod when using a telephoto lens, particularly one of the longer ones Telephoto lenses magnify movement of camera and subject along with the size of the latter. Shooting with these lenses from the hand is therefore hazardous business and although it is done, the results are usually not as satisfactory as tripod exposures.

Some telephoto lenses have such long barrels that it is found more convenient to mount the lens on the tripod rather than the camera Some lenses are therefore equipped with a tripod socket on a rotating circular mount around the lens barrel The photographer is thus able to turn the lens and with it the camera, to any desired position Even tripod exposures are not secure from camera shake unless the precaution is taken to pick high shutter speeds, use a cable release and to wait until the slight vibration caused by handling in focusing and viewing has stopped If there is time, use the delayed-action release on the Exakta (see p 41).

When it is inconvenient to use a tripod and the camera must be hand-held, shutter speeds should be as short as possible. Because of the length of the long-focus barrel, a recommended technique is to grasp the camera in one hand and to support the lens with the other, somewhat in the manner of holding a rifle.

Because of the characteristically limited depth of telephoto lenses, focusing must be done very carefully, using the hinged magnifier if the field is too dark, as in the case of the slower lenses or in relatively weak light. How far to

164 *The Hugo Meyer Telemegor 400mm f/5.5, mounted on the Exakta, for long-distance photography*

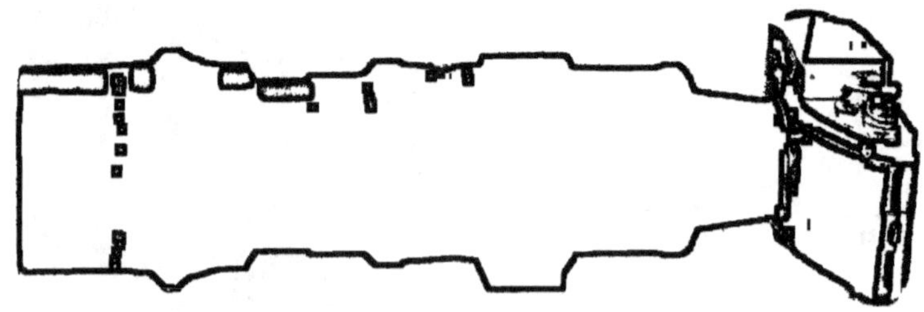

stop down the lens is a question that must be weighed against the problem of the high shutter speeds required in telephoto shots. Fast films may be the answer in many cases.

To facilitate the quick change from one lens to another, when using lenses of different focal length, professionals as well as some of the more affluent advanced amateurs, usually work with two cameras, one with a normal or wide-angle lens, the other with a telephoto. For the non-professional worker, the most convenient approach, if the situation will permit, is to decide on a series of shots with one lens, then to switch to a second lens for another series.

Choice of Lenses

The Exakta user has a choice of telephoto lenses ranging from 75mm to 1,000mm. For portraiture and average use, those of 75mm to 100mm should be adequate In this bracket is included the 80mm f/2.8 Carl Zeiss Tessar, the 75mm f/1.9 Hugo Meyer Primoplan, both with preset diaphragms, the 90mm f/1.8 Angenieux Pi, and the 100mm f/2.8 Meyer Trioplan with fully automatic diaphragm. A popular focal length for medium distance shots is the 135mm, which is available in the fully automatic f 2.8 Tele-Iscaron (Fig. 162) Another is the 180mm f 2.8 Tele-Iscaron.

For sports, animal and nature photography generally, the choice of focal length includes the 250mm and 400mm Hugo Meyer Tele-Megors and, for wild life and other long-range requirements there are available still longer lenses

Among the special lenses on the market are two interesting units. One is the Zoomar Reflectar (Fig. 165), a 20-inch f 5.6 lens which incorporates the new mirror-optics principle, which makes possible the use of a relatively short barrel (7¾ inches long) in spite of its long focal length The other is a Kilfitt Macro-Kilar, a unique lens that focuses from infinity to 2 inches (Model D) or to 4 inches (Model E) See also Chapter 9

Picking the First Extra Lenses

The choice of extra lenses, whether wide angle or telephoto, should be based on one's usual needs rather than the occasional one For the general photographer who likes to shoot "everything," a telephoto of 75mm to 90mm focal length and a 35mm wide angle (if the standard lens is 50mm or 58mm) will make a good start The specialist who works at close range may find he cannot use a telephoto at all, whereas the bird photographer, for example, may consider only the long telephoto Other lenses, of which there is increasing variety as the lens makers keep bringing out new products of advanced design, may be added later as one's interests change or expand into new directions.

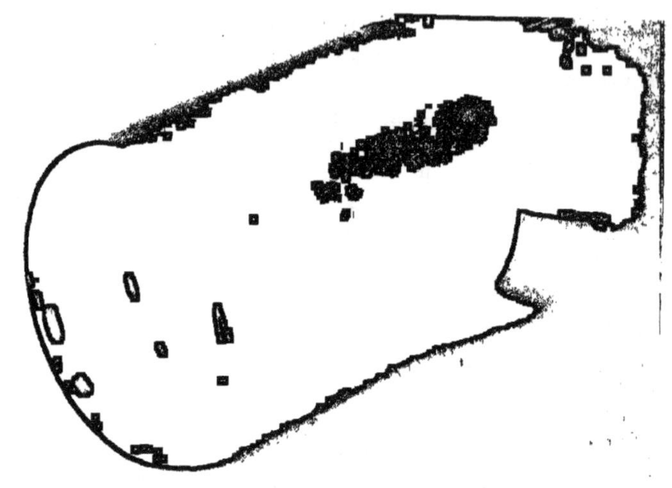

165 *The 500mm f/5.6 Zoomar Reflectar, a telephoto lens that employs the mirror optics principle It is 7¾ inches long, 5 inches in diameter, and weighs 3½ pounds off the camera*

166 *Candid 180mm telephoto shot from a window*

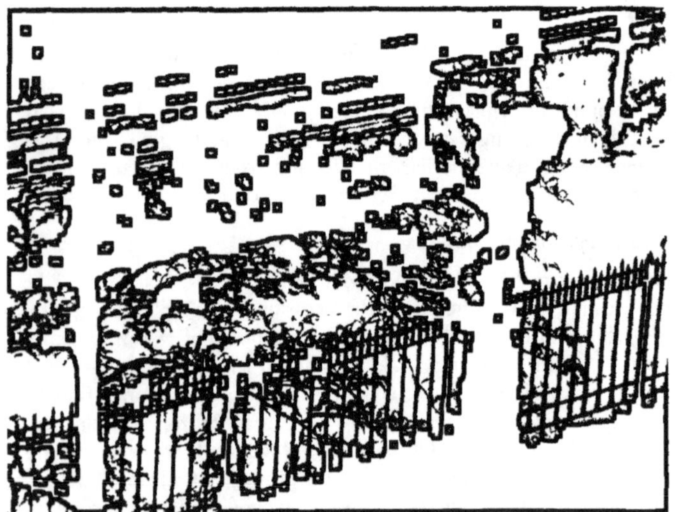

Camera Distance Key to Perspective

Perspective in photography is the technique of reproducing in a photograph the distance and size relationships between objects as they are normally seen We gain perspective by moving closer to near objects, thus making them appear to be larger than those farther away. We minimize perspective as we move away. The more we move back from the subject, the less pronounced become the size differences and separation between objects.

The representation of perspective therefore is achieved by the distance of the lens from the subject, regardless of the lens focal length At the same distance, the individual elements in the picture will be smaller when using a wide angle (because it includes more area) than in a long-focus shot (because the lens includes less) but the relationships between the objects will be the same. To alter perspective, therefore, move the camera back or forward from the subject and change lenses to cover the desired area. If the new lens covers more than is wanted, and a lens of longer focal length is not available, crop out the wanted portion and make a smaller enlargement than you had intended, since cropping of the small negative requires much caution to avoid graininess and poor print quality.

Control Through Perspective

Perspective offers an important control for the photographer when he understands and exploits its possibilities By an appropriate choice of lens and viewpoint, he can emphasize an object in a scene by making it larger than other objects (Fig 158), and he can vary at will the relative proportions of one object or figure and another (compare Figs 169 and 170). Therefore, if he wants only a moderate reduction in the size of distant figures or objects relative to those in the foreground, he will move back to get this effect (Fig 170). To produce a pronounced, or exaggerated effect of depth the photographer will use a wide-angle lens and come close (Fig. 167).

Distorted perspective occurs when, in order to get a larger image on the negative, the camera is brought unusually close This impulse is particularly tempting when using miniature cameras. Move back a reasonable distance (unless you want the exaggerated effect), and distortion disappears. Confusion about perspective also is caused by the kind of images one sees produced by the wide-angle and long-focus lenses With foreground objects near the camera a picture taken with a wide-angle gives a dramatic impression of great space due to the abrupt way in which parallel lines recede into the distance.

A small room can be made to look tremendous by this technique. Replace the wide-angle with a normal lens and the effect is different. The perspective is the same in both cases, but there is less area. The camera is too close for

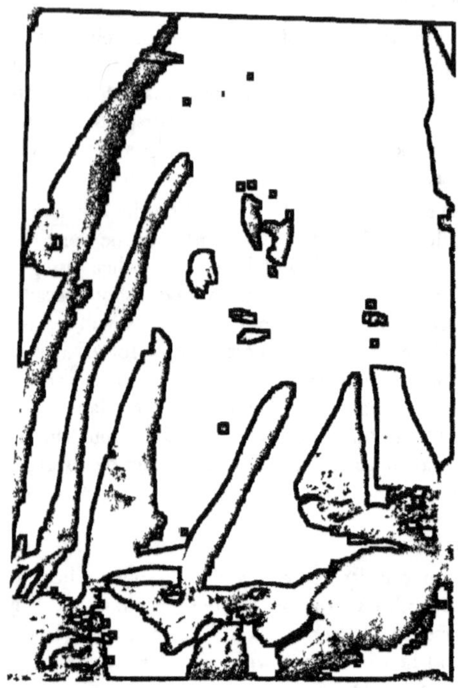

167

Harold Feinstein. *Space rela
tionships are well indicated in
this wide-angle shot at close
range with a 35mm lens*

168

Arthur Leipzig. *The shallow depth of the 300mm telephoto compressed space un
realistically (the player seems to be part of the score board) exaggerating the
size of the background relative to the player*

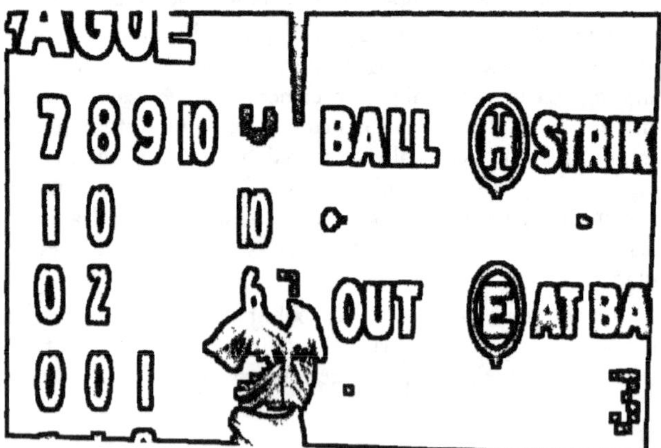

the normal lens to achieve the same result. By stepping back with the normal lens, one could include the same area as the wide-angle, but the perspective will have changed because of the new camera position and with it the effect. Similarly, although flattening of the field is characteristic of the telephoto lens, this result occurs only when the camera is at a considerable distance from the subject. Bring the camera as close as the lens will permit and the perspective (within the comparatively limited area), though not the effect, will be the same as that obtained with a lens of shorter focal length.

Characteristically, the wide-angle expands relationships, thus emphasizing the idea of space; the telephoto narrows relationships, thereby promoting the idea of compression and flatness. Granted that perspective is a matter of distance from the subject, nevertheless, because of practical usage among photographers, the wide-angle lens is associated with steep perspective (when this is wanted), the telephoto with the opposite effect The wide-angle achieves its effect because it can move in closer to more area, front to back, than the telephoto. The latter, on the other hand, because it obliges the photographer to move back from the subject in order to include the wanted area, has the advantage of showing the subject proportions more naturally. This is a particularly valuable consideration in portraiture and in nature photography.

The control of background and foreground relationships is one of the most important functions of perspective control through interchange of lenses.

169 *(Left)* **Sam Falk, The New York Times Magazine** *This shot was made at about 300 feet from the foreground group with the 400mm Tele-Megor. Note how the telephoto effect closed up the distances (about 150 feet from the surf's edge) between the other groups in the picture. Compare with Fig 168.*

170 *(Above)* **Sam Falk, The New York Times Magazine.** *The wide-angle lens at the appropriate distance shows the school children in natural size and distance relationships*

If the background is minimized too much relative to the subject when using the normal lens, switch to a telephoto and move back. This will be the result: the subject will be the same size as with the normal lens at the closer distance, but the background will be larger, the size differences between subject and background will be reduced.

If the foreground is too large, use a telephoto and move back to make the foreground objects smaller relative to the background. Conversely, if the background is too large, move in closer with the normal or use a wide angle lens to show the same field as before

Perspective also is achieved through other means than lens interchange and variation in camera-to-subject distance. The illusion of space can be created by using a large aperture to focus the subject but to keep the other objects out of focus (Fig 173). Aerial perspective, the atmospheric effect produced by a gradual lightening of distant planes because of haze, mist or light fog, is a favorite with pictorialists Lighting the subject from the side or the back, or cross-lighting for texture, gives a dimensional effect by rounding out forms and emphasizing planes.

The perspective achieved in taking the picture can be minimized in viewing the resulting print if one fails to observe the rule that in order to see the print in the same perspective as did the camera lens, the distance of the eyes from the print should be equal to the focal length of the camera lens for a contact print, or the diameter of enlargement multiplied by the focal length. Thus, a picture taken with the standard 50mm lens and enlarged say seven times should be seen at a distance of 14 inches.

171, 172 *Bob Henriques. After taking the 50mm shot (opposite page), the photographer switched to a 300mm lens and took the picture below from across the street, both at 1/500th Note differences in perspective*

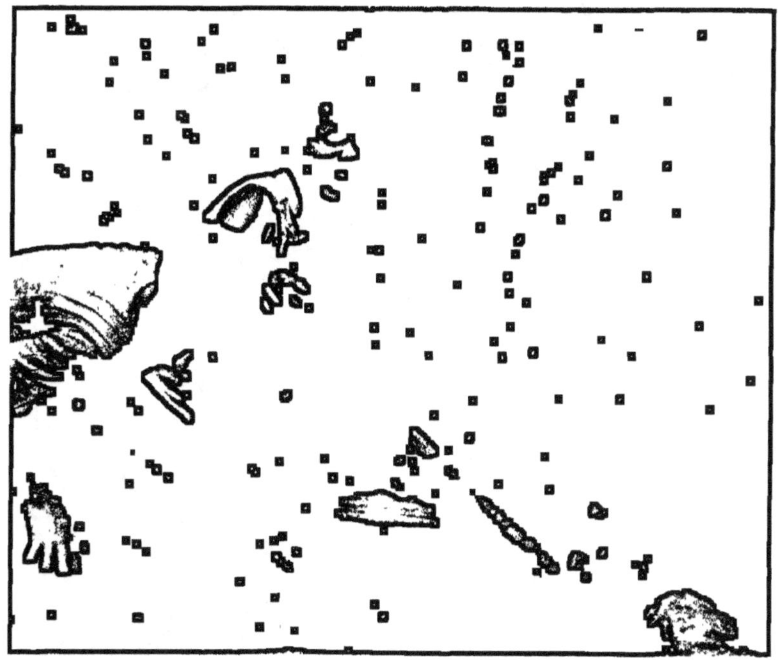

METRIC CONVERSION TABLES FOR AMERICAN USE

Focal Length Equivalents

Millimeters	Inches[1]
28	1 1
35	1.37
38	1 5
40	1 58
50	1 96
58	2 27
75	2 94
85	3 33
90	3 53
100	3 92
150	5.88
200	7 84
250	9 80
300	11 76
400	15 68
500	19 60
600	23 52
800	31 36

Distance Scale Conversions

Meters to Feet/Inches	(approximate)		Feet to Meters	
1	3	3	3	91
1 25	4	1	3½	1 07
1 5	4	11	5	1 52
1 75	5	9	6	1 83
2	6	7	7	2 13
2 5	8	2	8	2 44
3	9	10	9	2 74
4	13	1	10	3 05
5	16	5	12	3 66
6	19	8	15	4 57
7	23	0	20	6 10
8	26	3	25	7 62
9	29	6	30	9 14
10	32	10	40	12 19
15	49	3	50	15 24
20	65	7	75	22 86
30	98	5	100	30 48
50	164	0	150	45 72

[1] Usually rounded off to the nearest ¼ inch of ½ inch, as 50mm = 2 inches, 100mm = 4 inches, 300mm = 12 inches

For other measurements
1 millimeter (mm) = 0 03937 inch
1 centimeter (cm) = 0 3937 inch
1 meter (m) = 39 3701 inches

For other measurements
1 inch = 25 399mm = 2 5399cm = 0 0254m
1 meter = 3 2808 feet
1 foot = 0 3048 meter

TABLE OF LENS ANGLES

Lens	Angle
28mm	74°
35	64
38	61
40	57
50	45
58	40
75	33
85	28
90	27
100	22 5
105	22
135	18
150	16
180	13 5
200	11
250	10
300	8
400	5 6
500	5
600	4
800	2 5

173 Harold Feinstein. The 75mm telephoto at a distance of about 12
feet and medium aperture gave satisfactory perspective. The out-of-
focus figure in the background helped create an illusion of space.

The Camera Moves Closer

Close-up photography is divided into two general classes, pictures in the area near the limit of the fully extended lens, and pictures at the much closer lens-to-subject distances made possible by the use of accessories that permit greater than normal lens extensions. The goal in both cases is to get a larger image of the subject and/or to isolate a part for more detailed scrutiny.

An interesting example of the first type is Fritz Goro's (Fig 174) in which a technical detail is dramatized by the use of the close-up with a 50mm lens. Close-ups with the unaided lens are also taken with the wide-angle lens, which can be placed closer to the subject, and the telephoto, which must be placed farther away (see Chap. 8)

But the concern of this chapter is with the still closer working distances, the problems they introduce and the solutions that are available. In order to move the camera closer to the subject and thereby magnify the image on the film, two general facilities are at hand. One can either shorten the focal length of the lens by attaching a supplementary lens (a thin optical glass) like a filter, or extend the lens itself by means of tubes or bellows between camera and lens.

The supplementary (or "portrait" lens, as it is sometimes called) is available in many powers known as diopters and named $+1$, $+2$ and $+3$, etc, the higher the number the closer the permissible working distance, therefore the smaller the subject field and the greater the magnification on the film. The supplementary has the advantage that it can be used without altering the normal exposure (see below) But the flexibility and range of tubes and bellows, in spite of the exposure increase they impose, have made these the mediums generally preferred by Exakta photographers.

Extension Tubes

When a lens is removed from a camera and placed at some distance in front of it, it is possible to come closer than usual to the subject and, in consequence, to obtain a larger image The extension tube makes this possible by closing the gap between camera and lens, and in the Exakta permits viewing the change directly, without the use of auxiliary viewing-focusing devices.

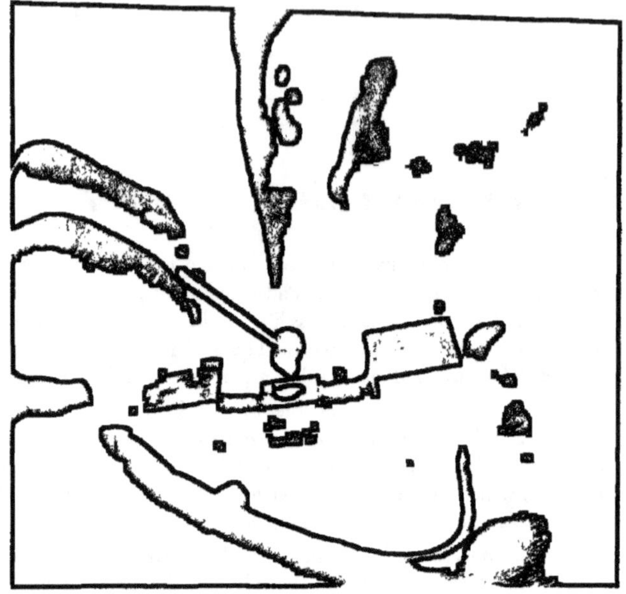

174

*Fritz Goro,
LIFE. The nor-
mal closeup
without accesso
ries is achieved
in the single-
lens reflex cam
era directly
Because the eye
sees what the
lens does, there
is no parallax
problem, even at
the closest dis
tances This shot
was made with
a 50mm lens,
1/50th at f/5 6*

The key to the method is the adapter ring, a bayonet ring at the back to fit the camera lens flange, and an adapter at the front to hold the lens Each is threaded to take the required length and number of extension tubes.

The Ihagee extension tube set for the Exakta consists of three tubes threaded at both ends, to be used singly or in combination, depending on the desired film-lens separation, and a pair of adapter rings The tubes, which are blackened on the inside against light reflections, are in three lengths, the 5mm size, the 15mm and the 30mm ring. The adapter rings add another 10mm to the tube length used, and in fact may be used alone if desired, one screwed into the other.

Where a shorter extension is needed than even that afforded by the 10mm adapter combination, the Two-in-One Adapter accessory does the trick. This is a one-piece unit with the camera mount on one side and the lens mount on the other, the distance between the two, when mounted on the camera, being 5mm This takes care of the "blind space" not covered by the regular extension tubes when using a 50mm lens or the 58mm Biotar with the preset or the automatic diaphragm, but not the earlier Biotar lens, which cannot be focused close enough. The Two-in-One may be added to any tube combination to gain an extra 5mm (see table, p. 121) Supplementary lenses are sometimes used together with tubes to increase magnification (see Chap. 9).

What is in effect a variable extension tube is incorporated in the unique 40mm f/3.5 Kilfitt Macro-Kilar lens, which can be focused on any point from infinity down to as close as 2 inches, simply by turning the focusing collar. Scales engraved on the collar carry the working data—lens-to-subject distance, image-to-subject ratio, and the exposure factor.

Bellows Extension

Use of the bellows extension is similar in effect to the extension tube system but offers the advantage that the lens-to-film distance can be altered quickly simply by racking backward or forward, and the disadvantage that the bunching of the folds when the bellows is fully retracted rules out small extensions. The bellows unit for the Exakta has a bayonet mount on the back to fit the camera lens flange and an adapter ring at the front to take the lens, the distance from the camera body to the front of the bellows when fully extended being about 5 inches. The bellows rides on a carriage consisting of two rods etched at one-half-inch and one-inch intervals for a 50mm and a 105mm lens, respectively, with numbers indicating the exposure increases required at various lens-to-film distances. The rod at the left gives the 50mm factors of 3 to 12 times, the rod at the right the 105mm factors of 2 and 3 times. Focusing is done with a knob on either side of the unit, the one at the left being also used to lock the focus by turning the knob counter-clockwise.

There are two versions One is the single-carriage model which attaches directly to a tripod The other is the considerably more flexible double-carriage unit which has an extra pair of rods and its own focusing rack (Fig 180), which is attached to the tripod Thus, the lower carriage offers supplementary focusing by permitting the entire camera-bellows-lens assembly to be moved. It is also equipped with left and right-hand knobs, the left one being turned counter-clockwise to lock focus. In addition, the double-carriage unit allows the camera to be swiveled a quarter-turn from horizontal to vertical or the other way around.

If more extension is required than the limits of the bellows will allow, extension tubes may be added or a lens of longer focal length. Special 105mm and 135mm Steinheil Culminars and Schneider Xenar lenses have been built into short mounts to work as a unit with the bellows. Thus the latter provides the extension that is normally part of the lens barrel. The effect is to achieve continuous focusing from infinity to 9 inches with the 105mm lens, to 16½ inches with the 135mm lens.

The Close-Up Factors

The extension between lens and film is related to the distance of the lens

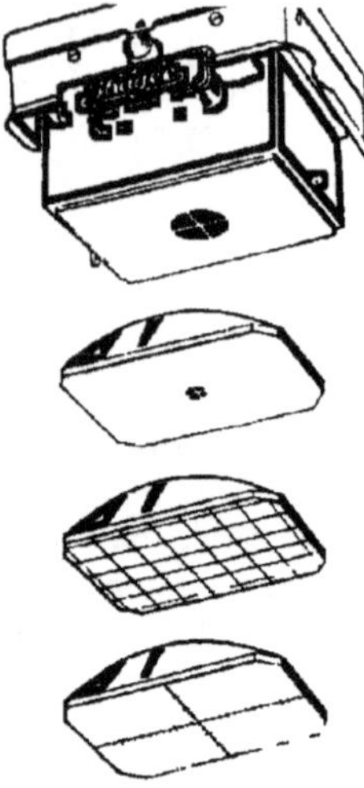

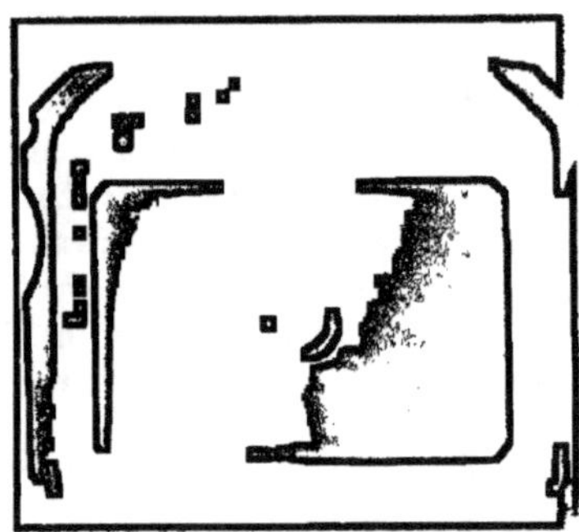

175, 176

Left, variety of special focusing glasses inter-changeable on the Exakta-Exa finders. Below, the rangefinder glass on the Pentaprism.

from the object. The greater the separation between lens and film, the closer the distance between lens and object, therefore the greater the magnification of the object image As the lens-to-film distance is narrowed, the lens-to-subject distance is widened, the object image is progressively reduced. The amount of reduction or magnification and in consequence the ratio of subject-to-image size determines the exposure required. The exposure factors for combinations of these data are covered in the table on page 121, the notes to which give the formulas involved. The field dimensions covered at the various distances from the object are shown directly on the ground glass.

Exposure for Close-Ups

When a lens is worked at a distance from the film plane greater than its focal length (which happens when an extension tube or bellows is used), the f/ values on the lens scale no longer apply (The problem does not arise with supplementary lenses as the camera lens is not extended). The exposure formula is based on the fact that the light image entering the lens becomes weaker with increasing separation of lens from film surface (lengthening of extension), for every additional extension of the lens means that the light must travel a proportionately greater distance before it reaches the film. The exposure time must therefore be increased since the f/ value is cut down in proportion to the lens extension. To reproduce a subject in its natural size (1-to-1 ratio), for example, the camera lens is extended to twice its focal length. To compensate for the weaker image resulting from this extension, the exposure is increased four times (the square of the distance) because the amount of light reaching the film is cut down to one-fourth of the normal strength.

Data tables giving the exposure changes in terms of factors (as in the case of filters) are listed on page 121.

Close-Up Meter Readings

To assure an accurate estimate of the light reflected from the small subjects in close-up photography, meter readings should be made by holding the meter closer to the subject (short of casting its own shadow on the measured field) than in average photography in order to avoid the influence of the background area lighting. Hold incident-light meters as close as possible to the subject and pointing toward the camera. The 8x10-inch Kodak Neutral Test Card, which is gray on one side, white on the other, is often used as a substitute exposure-reading surface when photographing very small objects. The card is held in front of the subject and a reading is taken at a distance of a few inches. Ordinarily, readings are taken from the gray side. But when the light level is rather low, use the white side instead. This reflects five times the quantity of light reflected by the gray side, therefore the indicated exposure must be multiplied by five to find the correct exposure. Because of the small stops and, in consequence, relatively long exposures used in most close-up

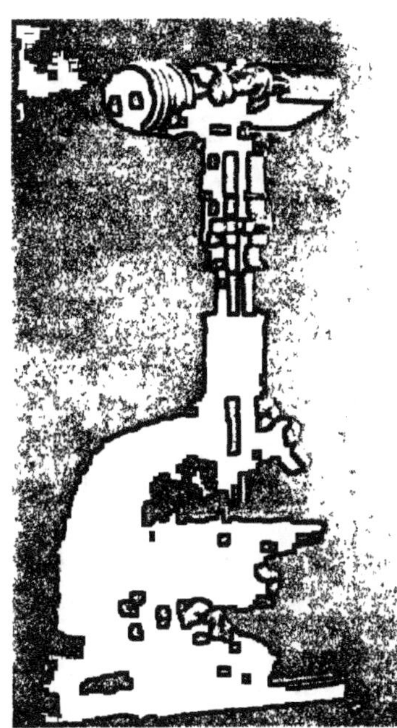

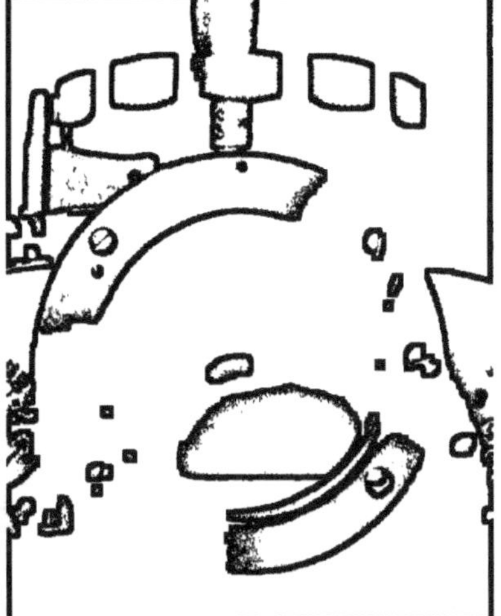

177, 178

Left, Magnear finder with lens attached, mounted on microscope attachment for photomicrography. Below, Magnear finder (open to show focusing glass inside), which interchanges with prism and hood finders on camera.

CLOSE-UP DATA FOR 50MM LENSES

For extension tube units (see text) [1]	Length of extension in mm	Distance from subject to lens in mm [2]	Distance from lens to film in mm [3]	Total distance from film to subject in mm [4]	Scale of subject image to life size [5]	Required exposure increase [6]
	0	infinity	50	infinity	variable	1.00
2-in-1	5	550	55	605	0.1	1.21
Adapter rings	10	300	60	360	0.2	1.44
[1]5mm	15	217	65	282	0.3	1.69
5mm 2-in-1	20	175	70	245	0.4	1.96
15mm	25	150	75	225	0.5	2.25
5mm 15mm	30	133	80	213	0.6	2.56
5mm, 15mm 2-in-1	35	121	85	206	0.7	2.89
30mm	40	113	90	203	0.8	3.24
	45	106	95	201	0.9	3.61
5mm, 30mm 2-in-1	50	100	100	200	1.0	4.00
5mm 15mm, 30mm	60	92	110	202	1.2	4.84
	70	86	120	206	1.4	5.76
	80	81	130	211	1.6	6.76
	90	78	140	218	1.8	7.84
	100	75	150	225	2.0	9.00
	110	73	160	233	2.2	10.20
	120	71	170	241	2.4	11.60
	130	69	180	249	2.6	13.00
	140	68	190	258	2.8	14.40
	150	67	200	267	3.0	16.00

CLOSE-UP DATA FOR 58MM LENSES

For extension tube units (see text) [1]	Length of extension in mm	Distance from subject to lens in mm [2]	Distance from lens to film in mm [3]	Total distance from film to subject in mm [4]	Scale of subject image to life size [5]	Required exposure increase [6]
	0	infinity	58	infinity	variable	1.00
2-in-1	5	731	63	794	0.09	1.18
Adapter rings	10	394	68	462	0.17	1.37
[1]5mm	15	282	73	355	0.26	1.59
5mm, 2-in-1	20	226	78	304	0.35	1.81
15mm	25	192	83	275	0.43	2.05
5mm 15mm	30	170	88	258	0.52	2.30
5mm, 15mm 2-in-1	35	154	93	247	0.60	2.60
30mm	40	142	98	240	0.69	2.85
	45	133	103	236	0.78	3.17
5mm, 30mm 2-in-1	50	125	108	233	0.86	3.46
5mm 15mm 30mm	60	114	118	232	1.03	4.14
	70	106	128	234	1.21	1.87
	80	100	138	238	1.38	5.66
	90	95	148	243	1.55	6.51
	100	93	158	250	1.72	7.42
	110	89	168	257	1.90	8.39
	120	86	178	264	2.07	9.42
	130	84	188	272	2.24	10.50
	140	82	198	280	2.41	11.70
	150	80	208	288	2.58	12.90

The figures are for 50mm and 58mm lenses set at infinity. For intermediate distances use the lens focusing ring as usual.

If inch measurements are desired rather than the millimeter lengths shown multiply by 0.03937. Since lenses differ even those of the same focal length these data should be considered only as guides. For more precise information, use the formulas on page 128.

[1] From third line down, add adapter rings to the tube lengths indicated

[2] Measured from the center of the lens to the plane of the iris diaphragm

[3] The extension plus the focal length of the lens measured from the diaphragm plane of the lens to the film plane

[4] The sum of the two preceding columns

[5] The ratio of the subject to the size of the image on the film

[6] This is the factor by which the normal exposure (without extension) must be multiplied to allow for the extension

Films For Special Uses

① Kodak Infrared	—	20	20 cart., 100-ft. bulk
Kodak High Speed Infrared	—	—	20 cart., 100-ft. bulk
② Kodak Direct Positive Panchromatic	64	50	100-ft bulk
Du Pont Microcopy (line copy)	—	30	100-ft. bulk
Du Pont Microcopy (continuous tone)			100-ft bulk
Eastman Microfile (line copy)	—	16	36 cart., 100
③ Du Pont Fine Grain Safety Positive (line)	—	5	100-ft bulk
③ Eastman Fine Grain Safety Positive (line)	12	3	100-ft bulk
③ Eastman Fine Grain Safety Positive (continuous tone)	1	25	100-ft bulk

All above films except infrared Take meter readings by incident light when using these films Read reflected light from a gray card of 18% reflectance such as the gray side of a Kodak Neutral Test Card placed in the position of the original to be photographed Alternatively read from a white card giving five times the indicated exposure ①Use with Kodak Wratten Filter No 25 (A red) Eastman Kodak Company says No settings are given for daylight since the ratio of infrared to visible radiation in daylight varies considerably and meters respond principally to visible light but this ratio for tungsten light is sufficiently constant to warrant use of a meter ②This film is for black and-white transparencies exposed directly in the camera and processed by reversal to a positive for projection like color slides The Kodak Direct Positive Developer Outfit is indicated for developing this film ③These are color blind films sensitive only to blue light

work, especially with the slower films, as well as the shallowness of the field, a tripod or other steady support for the camera, such as a clamp that may be attached to any handy support, is strongly advised

Films for Close-Ups

The films generally associated with close-up photography include the popular Kodak Direct Positive Panchromatic Film, a medium-speed reversal film which is processed to a positive for use as transparencies for lecture and other purposes, and Kodak Fine Grain Positive for processing to a negative. For making line copies, available films are Kodak's High Contrast Positive and Micro-File, Ansco's Minipan and Du Pont's Microcopy. Color film is being used a great deal, especially in the technical, scientific, medical and nature fields (Chap. 12 and 13) Moderate and medium-speed films also have many uses in this connection. Occasionally, one of the fast films is needed. For data on all films see above and the table on page 53

Focusing

Since image definition is of paramount importance in close-up work, focusing must be done very carefully. This phase of the work is facilitated by the bright image shown on the Exakta and the Exa condenser ground glass, which can be supplemented by swinging up the hinged magnifier when required, or the pentaprism finder. For greater precision, as in scientific work, special focusing glasses are available (see below).

Depth of field (see pp. 70-74) is very shallow at close distances, becoming
increasingly so the narrower the lens-to-subject distance becomes. To assure
overall sharpness, it is necessary to establish the correct point of focus. The
formula is: measure the near limit of the subject, say 4 inches, then measure
the far limit, say 6 inches Multiply the one by the other, then multiply the
product by two. Divide the result by the total of the near and the far distance.
Thus, $4 \times 6 = 24 \times 2 = 48$ · $10 (4 + 6) = 48$, the point on which the
lens should be focused. Then stop down the lens to take in the field.

Special Focusing Glasses

Reference is made on page 170 to interchangeable focusing glasses for
specialized purposes An assortment of these glasses is available with a ground
or a clear base variously modified to provide suitable aids to accurate focusing
in photomicrography and similarly exacting work. The glass is held in the
pentaprism finder by springs and is easily removed and inserted. To facilitate
viewing on the camera ground glass in photomicrography but to focus by
the more brilliant microscope image, the glasses are designed with clear or
cross-hairline center spots through which the microscope image is seen When
this image and the hairline cross are both seen sharply, the picture is in focus.

The variety of such glasses includes ground or clear glasses with a center
cross, ground glass with a clear center spot, ground glass with a hairline cross
in clear center spot; clear glass with a checkerboard pattern, or with crossed
vertical and horizontal lines divided into eighths and sixteenths of an inch

179 *Schematic drawing by* **Edward S. Ross** *from his book, "Insects Close Up" showing how the Exakta is adapted for close-up work with extension tubes or bellows*

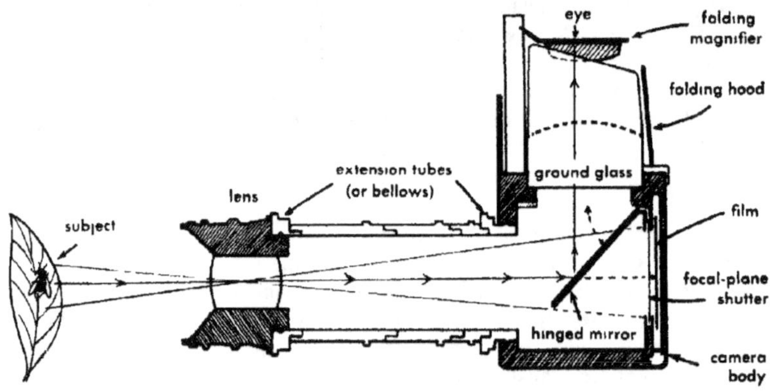

(see Fig. 175). Similar special focusing glasses are available for the reflex finder hood, but the finder must be interchanged as a whole.

The Magnear Lens-Viewfinder

A unique focusing and viewing device, which is interchangeable with the hooded reflex and the pentaprism finders on the Exakta VX and IIa, the Magnear (Fig. 178) utilizes an actual camera lens for critical focusing. A bayonet lens flange like the one on the camera is mounted on the top part of the finder and accepts any lens with an Exakta mount On the bottom is a ground glass with a clear center spot and cross, which is held by the same kind of spring catch as on the pentaprism finder and therefore can be easily exchanged for one of the special focusing glasses available for that finder (see descriptions on page 123).

An advantage of the Magnear is the magnified image (five times with a 50mm lens, for example) it affords, a particularly valuable feature in specialized technical photography and wherever very fine detail is to be reproduced, as in various phases of scientific photography. Any lens may be used on the front of the camera, of course. The device is best employed in conjunction with the extension tubes or bellows or with the microscope attachment.

180 *Edward S. Ross. (From "Insects Close Up") The Exakta with double-carriage bellows focused on specimen in laboratory setup An old enlarger head furnishes back lighting to give translucency to mosquito larvae in a micro-aquarium Electronic flash was used in front to stop movement of the specimen and to permit the use of a small lens stop*

181

Edward S. Ross. This closeup shot of a fence lizard on a rock is a hand-held shot at 1/50th f/8, using extension tubes and sunlight illumination Note how limited depth of field emphasizes main features

The Microscope Adapters

Photomicrographs can be taken with the Exakta by using an adapter to connect the camera to the drawtube of standard microscopes. The subject is viewed and focused as normally, directly on the ground glass of the camera. Since the microscope's objective and eyepiece are used to take the pictures, the camera lens is removed and the microscope adapter unit attached to the camera in its place by means of the standard adapter ring, as when installing regular extension tubes. The microscope attachment is then slipped over the drawtube and locked securely in place by a slight turn of the clamping screw.

The attachment consists of the camera adapter ring, two extension tubes and the drawtube connecting piece. It is available in two types, one hinged (Type I) so that the camera may be swung aside for critical focusing by means of the microscope eyepiece directly. The other (Type II, shown in Fig. 177) is a two-part unit held together by a bayonet fitting and set screw, and permitting quick removal of the camera, leaving the bottom or connecting piece

firmly attached to the microscope drawtube. The bottom part of the attachment is fastened to the drawtube by turning the outside lugs which tighten a
three-part metal sleeve around the tube.

Copying Techniques

The variety of resources described for the photography of small objects
of course apply as well to copying documents, stamps, pages from books and
other printed, drawn or painted originals. With at least one problem eliminated, depth of field (since the subject is in a single plane), although the lens
is usually closed down two or three stops to assure overall sharpness and
definition.

For the occasional copying requirement the makeshift setup of the camera
on a tripod and the original pinned up on some support, will do reasonably well
if great pains are taken to make sure that the plane of the copy material is
exactly parallel to the plane of the film in the camera. If the photographer
intends to do a considerable amount of copying, he would be wise to acquire a
device specifically designed for the purpose. The CopyMat shown in Fig
182 is typical of the more advanced units available. A more versatile unit is the
Vielzweck which, with its accessories, will handle a wide range of needs (see
pages 129-130)

182

*The Copy Mat, a copying
unit based on the prin-
ciple of the optical bench.
The reflectors each house
two lamps for even illum-
ination A swinging holder
takes filters or supplemen
tary lenses.*

126

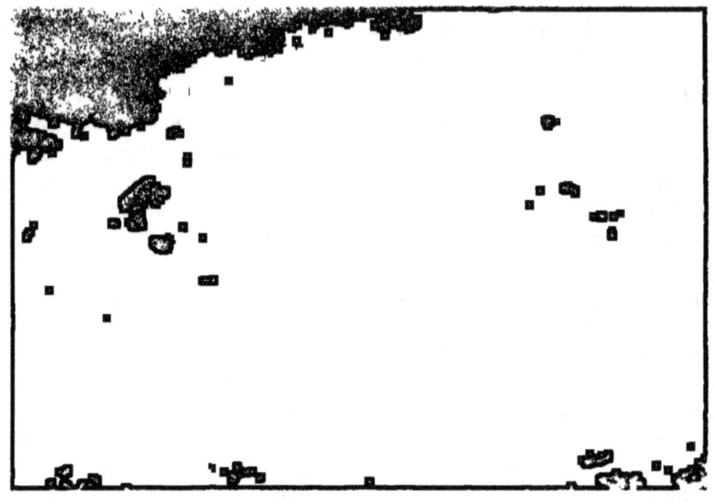

183

The original of this copy is a print made in 1908 which had become yellowed and flat in tone over the years. A yellow filter and slow film were used to achieve satisfactory contrast

In addition to parallelism between film and copy original, successful copying technique makes three demands: 1, the material to be copied should be placed as near as possible to the lens in order to fill the film frame; 2, it must be evenly illuminated to avoid reflections and paper texture, and 3, the film used should be one of the slow, fine-grain variety, such as those listed previously, in order to permit development to good contrast. Use the panchromatic type film for colored originals, such as paintings

Lighting, Filtering

Even illumination of the original is achieved by placing a light on each side of the subject (two on each side, one above the other, for large originals, like paintings), at an angle of about 45 degrees to the plane of the copy easel. In addition to equality of angle and distance of the two lamps, the lights must also be identical. The result is the desired perfectly flat illumination. When spotty reflections appear, a polarizing screen over the lens will be found useful. Fairly satisfactory results may also be obtained by using daylight as the light source; an overcast sky or shade will provide the most even lighting. Be sure to use a lens hood.

To minimize or eliminate slight or rough textures in copy originals, soak the print in water, squeegee it face down on a sheet of clean glass and copy it through the glass, or place the original in a tray of water, or rub down the print with a good coating of white vaseline.

Filters are used in copying to eliminate defects and/or to add contrast in the copy. To eliminate colored markings, such as ink stains, from photographs, documents, etc., use a filter the color of the stain. For example, a red filter over the lens will cause a red stain to disappear from the original. To add contrast to a fading and yellowed photograph, copy it through a deep yellow or a blue filter.

Size Ratio Formulas

To find the *scale of reproduction* or the *ratio of subject to image size*, the formula is $\dfrac{Object\ size}{Image\ size}$

Thus, with a subject 5 inches long and the image on the film 1 inch $\dfrac{1}{1}$ would yield 0 2, a ratio of 1 0 2, or an image size one-fifth that of the subject

To find the *ratio of reduction* or the amount by which the subject is made smaller in the image, the formula is

$$\frac{\text{subject to-lens distance (say 150mm) minus lens focal length (say 50mm)}}{\text{lens focal length}}$$

Thus, 150 minus 50 comes to 100, which, divided by 50, yields the figure of 2, or a ratio of 1 0 5, the image is one-half life size

To find the *ratio of magnification*, or the amount by which the subject size is made to look larger on the film, the formula is

$$\frac{\text{lens focal length (say 50mm)}}{\text{lens-to-film distance (say 160mm) minus lens focal length}}$$

Thus, 50mm into 160-minus-50 (110), yields the magnification 2 2, a ratio of 1 2 2, the film image is 2-1/5ths the size of the subject

Extension Exposure Factors

Three methods of increasing exposure to compensate for tube or bellows extension

1 Add 1 to the ratio of magnification and multiply the total by itself. Thus for a magnification of 1, the total will be 2 and the final answer 4. The normal exposure time without extension therefore must be increased four times

2 The same answer is found by the second method. Multiply the lens-to-film distance by itself (in this case a 50mm lens extended to 100mm) and divide the result by the square of the lens focal length. Thus, 100x100 comes to 10,000 50x50, 2,500. The second into the first gives a factor of 4

3 Since the marked lens aperture no longer applies when the lens is extended by tubes or bellows, one may increase exposure simply by finding the new aperture and basing the exposure on that. The formula is

$$\frac{\text{normal lens stop x lens-to film distance}}{\text{lens focal length}}$$

For the 100mm extension (50mm lens focal length plus 50mm extension) used in the second method and a lens stop of say f/11, the new or real aperture will be the product of $\dfrac{11\text{x}100}{50}$ or f/22

Vielzweck Copying Stand

Versatile over an extremely wide range of application, the Vielzweck consists of a group of basic and accessory parts that are used in a variety of combinations for close-ups and copying with the Exakta or Exa camera.

The 12½x15¾-inch wood baseboard, which offers a 12½-inch-square subject area when using the Vielzweck in vertical position, has two adjusting screws for leveling the board on the support. The stand may also be used without the baseboard, resting on a table or mounted on a sturdy tripod.

There is a choice of three units to vary the camera height on the Vielzweck (1) the short basic or foot column, which is attached to the baseboard and has provision for installing lighting equipment, and two longer posts which may be used singly or, for increased height, together. The lower column also has a stop ring for use in photomicrographic work. Two lever arms are supplied that help to tighten the columns in place.

The Exakta is mounted by means of a headpiece, which is attached to the column in use, and a focusing slide assembly screwed to the headpiece. The headpiece may be positioned for either vertical or horizontal movement of the camera. The focusing slide rides on a block-shaped track which is heavy enough to serve as a support when the Vielzweck is placed on a table; its base is threaded for attachment to the headpiece or for tripod mounting. Focusing is by rack and pinion knobs.

Bellows and Other Attachments

The bellows, swing angle, and transparency copy units, all interchange-

184, 185

(Left) Assembly of Vielzweck stand components including lower column, connecting pieces focusing slide and bellows attachment. (Right) With bellows extended on focusing scale, using foot base as support.

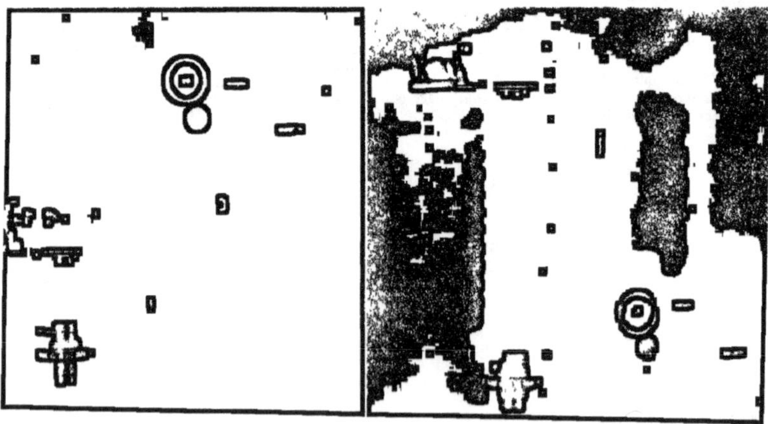

able on the focusing slide, expand the Vielzweck's versatility in many directions. To use the bellows attachment, the camera lens is removed and mounted on the front of the bellows, the camera on the back, thus permitting variable extension of the lens from the film plane according to the desired reproduction scale.

The extension may be varied from 35mm to approximately 210mm A 50mm f/2.8 special lens with sunk mount is available for bellows focusing at distances up to infinity, and for reduction of large originals The red figures on the focusing slide are used with the special lens; the black figures with all other lenses.

The swing angle, which is used for close-up work in conjunction with extension rings and tubes, may be worked in either vertical or horizontal position merely by swinging the camera around. The focusing slide scale is inoperative when using the swing angle The swing angle also is useful in stereophotography of non-moving objects.

When using the Exakta with a long-focus or a heavy lens on a tripod, satisfactory balance is aided by mounting the camera on the swing angle The latter is attached to the tripod by the intermediate tripod plate on which a gliding rail is used either to balance the lens or as an aid in focusing

The transparency copy assembly, used in conjunction with the bellows and focusing slide, is designed to make 1.1 (same size) transparencies from 35mm color or black-and-white negatives, and 35mm duplicate negatives from transparencies. The film gate, which includes a pressure plate to keep the original flat, takes single negatives or positives, or filmstrips. An opal glass plate distributes the illumination evenly

186, 187

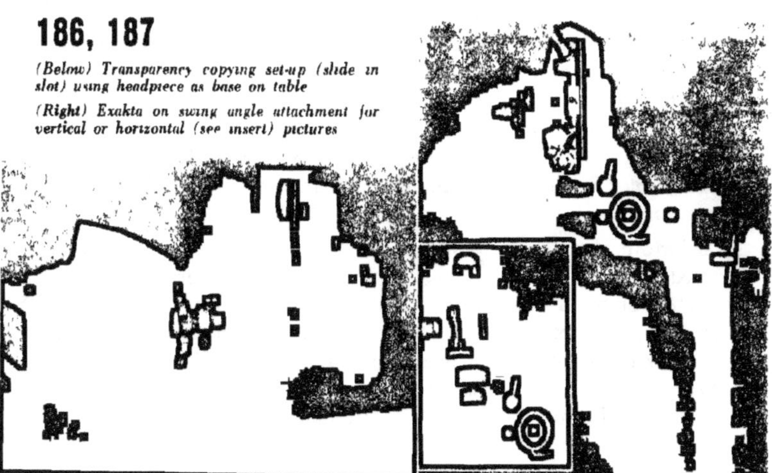

(Below) Transparency copying set-up (slide in slot) using headpiece as base on table

(Right) Exakta on swing angle attachment for vertical or horizontal (see insert) pictures

Exakta Photography in Color

The potentials of color photography both as recording and creative medium have been greatly expanded in recent years. The Exakta photographer now has a choice of speeds from the traditional Kodachrome Daylight index of 10 to the phenomenal sensitivity of High Speed Ektachrome's index of 160 In between are Super Anscochrome's 100 and Anscochrome's and Ektachrome's 32 The table on page 137 shows the complete list for 35mm photography, indicating the films' basic exposure indexes and the variations in speed when used under different types of illumination.

Miniature color film is balanced during manufacture for use in specified illumination—daylight, tungsten, flash, 3200K (studio lamps). If one type is used in lighting intended for another, distorted color will result, unless a special filter is used to bring the light into balance with the film.

The exception is Kodacolor, a color negative material now available in 35mm, which may be exposed either by daylight or flash, compensation being made through the use of filters in printing the color print or enlargement. Miniature color film is packaged and loaded the same way as black-and-white.

All of these films are processed to a positive transparency except Kodacolor, which results in a negative form from which any number of color or black-and-white prints or enlargements can be made All may be processed by the user or sent to a color photofinisher; Kodachrome cannot be processed by the user but must be sent through a dealer either to Eastman Kodak or to one of the many color finishers in the country. Kodak also makes slides from Koda-color negatives.

Color film should be processed as soon as possible after exposure. It should be stored in a cool, dry place, never in the glove compartment or trunk of an automobile, or warm closet or drawer at home. Color balance can be markedly affected by undue exposure to high temperatures and humidity. File the finished slides in light-tight containers, such as the slide files available on the market in wide variety. Expose to light, as in a viewer or projector, for only moderate periods, thus avoiding premature fading.

Lighting and Exposure

Color film has a shorter range than black-and-white, hence requires a closer ratio of highlight-to-shadow illumination in order to show color and detail in both. This varies from 2 to 1 for Kodachrome to 4 to 1 or a bit longer for the faster color films. Since less light is reflected from the darker hues, or areas, more from the lighter ones, the amount of light actually reflected, called the brightness range, depends on the light intensity and the ability of different parts of the subject to reflect the light impinging on them.

To lower the ratio when the contrast is too high, supplementary illumination is used for the darker areas, such as light-toned natural surroundings, neutral-colored wall, a white cardboard or newspaper, aluminum foil crumpled and then smoothed out over a board. Professionals make use of such a device as a white umbrella or one covered on the inside with aluminum. A favorite technique is that of fill-in flash (see page 144).

Light reflected from colored walls when working indoors will alter the subject colors. In such cases, either pick an interior with neutral-colored or white walls and ceiling, or place the subject far enough away from the walls so that the reflected light does not reach it

Although, generally speaking, exposure has to be fairly correct, today's fast color films allow for some latitude in this respect "Correct" exposure is in fact a relative matter even in color, as slight overexposure will yield a softer, pastel effect that may be more pleasing in some cases, slight underexposure a deeper, more saturated color.

In estimating exposure, it is usually best to favor the highlights, unless these are negligible The exposure table that comes with the film you buy is satisfactory for a start and as a general guide, but for exacting requirements a photoelectric exposure meter will be indispensable

The photographer should make tests to establish the most satisfactory index for his equipment and purposes, one for shutter speed (at the rated lens stop, and at a half stop larger and a half stop smaller), the other for lens stop, at the rated shutter speed, and half and double the speed. When the results are returned check them, against your test records, in a viewer or by projection on a screen. When shooting particularly important subject matter, or when in doubt as to the proper exposure, use the professional's bracketing method— three shots of the same subject, at the "correct" setting, and below and above this figure, as assurance that at least one of the three will be right.

Balancing Light Quality

Correction filters are available mainly in two classes: light-balancing filters and color-compensating filters. The first are used when color film

must be exposed to light for which it is not balanced; for example, Ektachrome Type F will give satisfactory results when exposed to the light of
clear flash lamps, but will need a Wratten No. 82A filter when the same film
is exposed by photoflood lighting. Color compensating or CC filters are used
to correct color deficiency, rather than color balance, in the existing illumination, and to effect changes for desired effects. They are used most often for
deliberate departures from normal color balance in order to introduce a mood
or to satisfy personal tastes

To convert one film type to another, so-called conversion filters must be
used. The Type A No 85 filter permits the use of tungsten type Kodachrome
and Anscochrome in daylight, the No. 85C conversion filter does the same for
the Type F Kodachrome and Ektachrome. To use daylight type color film by
photoflood illumination, convert all 35mm color films with the No. 80B filter.
Follow the maker's instruction as to filter factor

UV filters are designed to absorb ultraviolet and some blue light, thereby
reducing the bluishness of haze-screened subjects. The UV15 gives slight
haze correction, the UV16 medium correction, the UV17 more. To minimize
or eliminate the pronounced bluishness in slides exposed under certain outdoor lighting conditions, color photographers use a slightly pink filter called
the Skylight No. 1A, which "warms up" the blue without affecting the other
color values (see notes under table, page 136). The skylight filter reduces
the ultraviolet, cuts out some blue and a little green, (no exposure increase).

The polarizing screen (see p 63), the unique anti-reflection filter reduces the slight bluish haze in distant scenes that are lighted by a clear sun
from the side or overhead. It clarifies detail and strengthens the color values
In addition, the screen is used to darken blue skies, the depth of the tone may
be varied by rotating the filter The exposure increase generally recommended
by manufacturers is two and one-half times

Viewing Color Slides

The minimum facility needed for looking at color slides is a white surface
with light shining on it, and the slide held at an angle over the illuminated
surface. The light is thus diffused and comes through the slide evenly Slide
viewing devices on the market use basically the same scheme of diffused transmitted illumination, but show a larger, more brilliant image

The slide is inserted in the viewer and observed through a magnifying
lens while holding the device up to a light Better viewers have a built-in light
source powered by batteries or operated on AC, when a cord is plugged into
a convenient outlet. There are many variations, some permitting table viewing
as well as in the hand. The light is switched on by slight pressure on the slide,

by on-off switch, or by pressing a button. Several have automatic or semi-automatic slide changers. Table viewers have a built-in optical system that projects the slide on a built-in screen. Light boxes, mainly for professional use, have a light source which trans-illuminates a large viewing surface on which the slides are placed for direct viewing.

To show slides at their best, however, nothing compares with actual projection on a screen. Much progress has been made in projector designs, aided largely by innovations in lamp design, principally the small low-wattage lamps with built-in reflectors, which have made possible attractive low-silhouette models and small, compact, efficient units.

Other advances include automatic operation at pre-selected intervals, or by remote push-button control, choice of lenses to cover various working distances, a "previewing" box for use before projecting individual slides, slide pointers for use by lecturers, pre-heating of slides to avoid popping With the aid of an accessory some also permit filmstrip projection.

The most favored projection screen is glass-beaded for image brilliance. The lenticular screen, which offers a wider viewing angle, was coming into prominence as this was being written. The screen, operating like a window shade enclosed in a tubular case, is mounted on legs to provide its own stand, or designed for setting on a table or hanging from a wall.

Processing Color Film at Home

Complete kits of chemicals with step-by-step processing instructions enable the user to develop Ektachrome or Anscochrome 35mm rolls in a little under an hour after exposing the film in the camera The Kodak Ektachrome Processing Kit (specify Process E-2 Improved Type) and the Anscochrome Developing Outfit contain all the materials required except a No 2 photoflood for the reversal exposure and black-and-white darkroom accessories.

The procedures have been so thoroughly routinized that all one has to do to assure satisfactory results is to follow the carefully spelled-out instructions to the letter. The film is developed in two stages, the first in a light-tight tank, the second by normal room lighting. In the interim period, the film is exposed to the light of a No. 2 photoflood lamp to achieve the reversed (positive) image which in due course is developed as a color transparency. The user may also process Kodacolor with kits supplied by the film maker The result is a color negative (see below).

The temperature, which is particularly critical for the first developer, can be controlled by placing the tank and bottles of solution into a tray and running hot or cold water into it. The water-jacket tank of the BFI Processor (Figs. 188, 189) simplifies the procedure.

To permit the light to reach all surfaces of the film, a tank reel is specified in which at least half the end surfaces are open. The Nikor reel is recommended for this purpose. A transparent reel such as the one supplied with
the BFI Processor is equally suitable. Ektachrome film is exposed to the light
for 15 seconds on each side of the reel one foot from the lamp. The Anscochrome process stipulates a three-foot distance for a total of six minutes.

Both sets of instructions lay stress on the importance of agitating solutions
and the proper technique to use to assure uniform development. If using a
closed tank such as the small Nikor rollfilm units, agitate by turning the tank
end for end for the period and at the intervals indicated. In the case of an
open tank, such as the BFI Processor, agitate the film by lifting the reel out
of the tank and reimmersing it continuously.

The BFI Processor is well suited to home processing of color film. Made of
polystyrene, it consists of a 15-inch-diameter tank with a revolving light-proof
lid, which holds seven pint-capacity removable cups, a film reel of clear plastic
(ideal for flashing during the reversal step), which is attached to a handling
stick to raise and lower the reel for transferring it to successive baths and for
efficient agitation Four floating lids are supplied to protect solutions against
oxidation during storage. The tank is equipped with a hose inlet and outlet,
making a reliable circulating water jacket for wash and rinse as well as for
regulating temperature.

Color Prints from Slides

Processing kits for making color prints at home are also available. Anscochrome Printon and Kodak Ektachrome Paper (Type R) are designed to
make color prints by contact or enlargement from positive color slides by a
single exposure. More satisfying results but requiring somewhat more skill,
are achieved in printing from color negatives, such as Kodacolor, on Kodak
Ektacolor Paper (Type C).

These materials can be manipulated to a degree approximating in many
respects the flexibility of black-and-white, including dodging, "burning in,"
etc., using the appropriate filters. Careful adherence to the detailed instructions, especially with regard to developer temperature, the timing of the baths,
and agitation of the solutions, will assure success. Total processing time is
under an hour. Color prints using these materials are also made by color
finishers.

Those concerned with the preparation of visual aids material for distribution to teachers and others, or who would like to send the same slide to several
persons, may order duplicates through dealers.

FILTERS FOR USE WITH COLOR FILM BY DAYLIGHT AND ARTIFICIAL ILLUMINATION

(Required filter in top rows, exposure index, with filter, in lower rows)

Color Film Name	(1)Daylight	(2)Clear Flash 3800K	(3)Photo flood 3400K	Studio Lamp 3200K	Electronic Flash
Anscochrome, Daylight	None	80C	80B	80B	81A
	32	*	12	12	32
Anscochrome Tungsten	85	81C	None	82A	NR
	25	*	32	25	
Super Anscochrome, Daylight	None	80C	80B	80B	81A
	100	*	40	40	100
Super Anscochrome Tungsten	85B	81D	81A	None	81A
	80	*	100	100	80
Ektachrome Daylight	None	80C	80B	80B + 82A	**
	32	*	12	8	
Ektachrome, Type B	85C	None	82A	82C	NR
	16	*	16	12	
High-Speed Ektachrome, Daylight	None	80C	80B	80B + 82A	**
	160	*	50	40	
High-Speed Ektachrome Type B	85B	81C	81A	None	85B
	100	*	100	125	100
Kodachrome, Daylight	None	80C	80B	80B + 82A	**
	10	*	5	3	
Kodachrome, Type A	85C	None	82A	82C	NR
	10	*	12	10	
Kodachrome Professional, Type A	85	81C	None	82A	NR
	10	*	16	12	
Kodacolor	None	None	82A	82C	85
	32	*	20	16	12

The filters listed in this table are the light balancing type designed to correct the film's response to a type of light source for which the film was not specifically intended. The correction is for the total illumination. No filter is available for correcting mixed light sources of different qualities such as daylight and non-tinted artificial light sources (except electronic flash). When the use of a filter changes the basic exposure index, the new index is shown just under the required filter. The letters NR indicate the film is not recommended for use with that particular light source.
*See guide numbers on flash bulb sleeve.
**See instructions with film

①Color pictures in bright sunlight on cloudless days from two hours after sunrise until two hours before sunset. Daylight has a bluish cast in open shade, under overcast skies, on rainy days, in distant scenes, views around large bodies of water, from or at high altitudes. Use Skylight Filter No. 1A to reduce the bluish effect. ②These are clear wire filled flash lamps (see Chap. 11). ③These data are for new white photoflood lamps. Blue photofloods are not recommended as the sole light source but may be used for supplementary illumination.

188, 189

The BFI Processor for simplified development of miniature color film. The seven cups hold a pint each of solution or rinse. Water is circulated in the tank to maintain proper temperature.

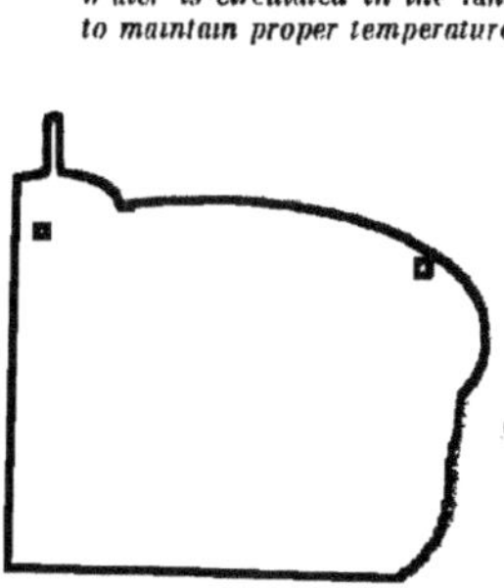

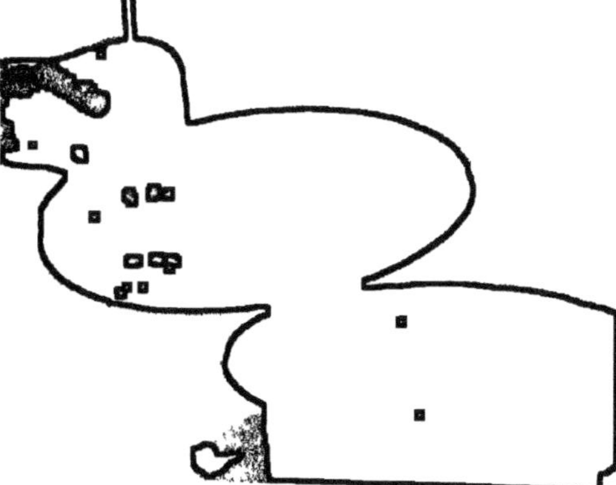

Black-and-White Prints From Color

The negative-positive concept familiar to black-and-white workers and now extended to color work in the combination of Kodacolor negatives and Ektacolor printing paper, opens the way to what is generally acknowledged as a new era in photography The color possibilities have been mentioned, but even black-and-white is benefited, as in the making of black-and-white prints from color originals.

The usual method has been to print a color negative or intermediate black-and-white negative from a color slide, on conventional papers. The result was inevitably only an approximation of the true tonal values of the original for the reason that the paper lacked red sensitivity. With the advent of Kodak Panalure Paper coated with a panchromatic emulsion more satisfying results are now possible. Using an original Kodacolor negative or Kodacolor intermediate from a color slide in an enlarger equipped with the usual tungsten light source, and without the aid of filters, Panalure yields a black-and-white print in which the tones are similar to those obtained from an ordinary black-and-white negative exposed in the camera.

Moreover, since the projected image is in the colors (complementary) of the original subject, improvements can be made in the print through the use of filters normally used in camera exposure to darken or lighten subject color areas. For example, a red filter on the enlarger lens will darken a blue sky, giving the same result as if the subject were being exposed all over again.

Although Panalure is available in only one grade (E surface, normal, grained, lustre, semi-white, matte) it is possible to vary contrast over a full grade, depending on the developer used and the time of development Because of the paper's red sensitivity, a special safelight filter is required, the Series 10, the same as for processing Ektacolor paper

Light Sources:
Flash, Electronic, Flood

Both the Exakta IIa and the Exa are internally equipped for flash-shutter synchronization of flash lamps and electronic flash As you face the camera, the Exakta has a socket at the left marked M (Fig. 16), for use with focal-plane lamp exposures at all the shutter speeds. On the right are two sockets (Fig. 15) marked with a red X on top, for use with electronic flash units, a green F below it, for SM, SF lamps with the shutter set at 1/25 or 1 50 The Exa has two sockets left of the lens (Fig. 29). The green F marking is for flash lamps, the red X for electronic flash.

CAUTION· Do not insert the plug in the camera or a flash lamp in the reflector socket until the shutter has been fully wound—each time Otherwise, the lamp will flash prematurely in the hand. Reason· When the shutter is not wound, the flash contacts are ready to fire, when the shutter is wound the contacts are in the "off" position.

Focal-Plane Flash Lamps

Because of the nature of the focal-plane shutter (see p. 36), the Class FP (flat peak No. 6, No. FP26, etc.) lamp must be used with the Exakta at most of its shutter speeds in order to provide uniform illumination of the film during the total period of exposure. With the Class M lamps (No. 5, No. 25, etc) used with iris-type shutters, the lamp builds up intensity toward a peak position and brightness point, then falls off again. Since a focal-plane shutter essentially exposes the film a segment at a time as the curtain slit moves across the film's surface, the use of a Class M lamp would result in some of the segments receiving less light than others.

However, if the speed is set at 1/25th or 1/50th the shutter will stay open long enough to receive the peak light of the Class M lamp uniformly. But these speeds are impractical for general flash exposures, with some exceptions The long level of even illumination is achieved in the focal-plane lamp at the cost of lighting intensity. It packs plenty of light but spreads it out, whereas the Class M lamp delivers a strong light with a single wallop. Therefore, when more light is needed and shutter speed is not a factor, use the Class M lamp but remember to set the speed at 1/25th or 1/50th (using the X sockets). Of course, one could resort to the larger No. 31 and No. 2A focal-plane flash lamps, but the powerful illumination supplied may prove to be too much of a good thing for the purpose in hand.

Another reason for being obliged to use the Class M type is the special lamp which is not available in the focal-plane class. Examples are most of the amber-tinted lamps for use with tungsten type color film and the black bulbs used with infrared film (see table, p. 140).

The Exakta flashgun is attached to the tripod screw at the bottom of the camera, with the reflector positioned right or left of the lens, the lamp on a level with the lens. The reflector has a satin finish, mounts on the gun by a single twist and may be turned in two directions. Other guns may also be fitted to the Exakta or Exa cameras. The gun is ready for pictures as soon as the shutter has been wound and the plug inserted in the camera flash sockets

Flash Exposure

The required exposure for a given situation is based on a system of guide numbers supplied by the maker of the lamp and listed on the carton, along with other useful information. The number varies with the speed of the film used and the shutter setting. For a given shutter speed, the guide number will be higher for the faster film. To find the exposure, which is determined by the distance of the flash lamp from the subject, divide the guide number by the lens stop. Thus, for a guide number of 100 and lens stop of f/8, the distance is approximately 12 feet. Where a specific working distance is needed, divide the guide number by the distance to get the lens stop.

Exposure varies also with the type of reflector A 4 or 5-inch satin-finished reflector requires a half-stop larger opening than that indicated for a polished reflector of the same size, but yields somewhat softer illumination. It's a fair exchange, since the latter will give more pleasing results.

In addition to the reflector, the flash source has a number of supplementary sources, the character of which determines the total amount of light made available for exposure. These include the reflections from surrounding objects, from walls, fences, etc., and from the clothes of the subject A small room with light-toned walls gives an appreciable boost to total light, especially when the subject is fairly close to the walls. The amount of reflected light will vary according to the lightness or darkness of the walls and the clothes worn by

FOCAL-PLANE AND SPECIAL FLASH LAMPS FOR USE WITH EXAKTA AND EXA CAMERAS

Lamp No and Maker	① Type of Base	② Output in Lumen Sec	③ Degrees Kelvin	Uses, etc
PH/6 (G E.)	Bayonet	16,000	3,800	For general flash work at all shutter speeds
FP26 (Sylvania)	Bayonet	15,000	3,800	
PH/31 (G E.)	Med Screw	81,000	3,800	Powerful sources for large-area coverage, all shutter speeds
2A (Sylvania)	Med Screw	77,000	3,800	
PH/6B (G E.)	Bayonet	7,500	6,000	For average use with daylight color film
1 P26B (Sylvania)	Bayonet	7,500	6,000	
PH/31B (G E.)	Med Screw	37,000	6,000	For use with daylight color film, large area
6A (Dura-Flash)	Bayonet	8,000	3 200	Amber-tinted, for use with indoor color film
5A (Amplex)	Bayonet	14,500	3,400	Same as above
25C (Sylvania)	Bayonet	14,000	3,400	Same as above
22A (Dura Flash)	Med Screw	60,000	3,200	Same as above, but more powerful
5R (Dura Flash)	Bayonet	———	Infrared	Used with infrared film, absorbs blue and red, lets through infrared radiation
22R (Dura-Flash)	Med Screw	———	Infrared	

Special Class M Lamps— see p 139

① The bayonet base is used on midget type flash lamps Most flash units have a bayonet socket which includes an ejector which forces out the flashed lamp mechanically when an external button is depressed The medium screw base is similar to that on ordinary household lamps and requires the use of a flash reflector with a corresponding socket The standard reflector size for use with bayonet base lamps is 4 to 5 inches, with medium screw base lamps 6 to 7 inches ② The *lumen* is a measure of the quantity of light produced by a light source and, issuing in all directions within a sphere falling on an area 1 foot square and 1 foot distant from the source at every point A single lumen therefore measures only a part of the total output of the source the output in the direction of a designated area, as just indicated To get the total light of the source it is necessary to measure the entire area surrounding it and upon which the light is received This is the way the total lumen output of light sources is measured in laboratories and given to us in total numbers The *lumen-second* is a measure of the light falling on a surface for one second and is the yardstick used for flash sources In arriving at the totals indicated both the intensity of the flash and its duration (longer with focal plane than with high peak Class M lamps see p 138) were considered thereby providing a useful means of comparison between the light output of different lamps The amount of light actually reaching the subject or area being photographed depends on the type and efficiency of the reflector being used and other factors (see p 86)

③ Differences in the color quality of light are stated in terms of color temperature or degrees Kelvin after Lord Kelvin the British scientist who established the principle The "hotter" (the higher the temperature) the whiter the light hence producing a greater volume of blue rays the colder the lower the temperature), the yellower the light For example the noon day sun is practically a perfect white, the comparatively dim light of the ordinary household bulb is yellowish In black and white photography these differences in color temperature are important chiefly in terms of exposure and are referred to generally as 'warm' or 'cool' colors In color photography (see Chap 10) Kelvin rating is vital, since it indicates color balance or capacity of the film to record faithfully under specific types of illumination

the subject, for example. Moreover, when shooting with color film, reflections from colored surroundings may affect the color of the subject. If the background is important it should be illuminated by a separate lamp unless it is close enough to the subject to be covered by the lamp or lamps (if a second light is used). Blue-tinted flash lamps generally are used with daylight color film outdoors or indoors, as supplementary illumination. Alternatives are a blue filter over the flash reflector or to tint clear lamps in a blue "dip".

Flash guide numbers are also supplied for use with electronic units (see below) and the principles relating to incidental reflections apply regardless of the type of light source employed.

Electronic flash is rapidly gaining adherents among professionals as well as attracting increasingly larger numbers of upper-bracket amateurs. Advantages of this light source over conventional flash include its repeatability; high inherent speed—1/500th, 1/1000th and much shorter—independent of the camera shutter; the convenience of not having to change bulbs between shots, as in ordinary flash (a new flash can be made at intervals of 3 to 30 seconds, depending on the unit); distinctive light quality favorable to highlight detail, coolness, and a daylight color balance, permitting its use with daylight type color film without a light-balancing or conversion filter.

The heart of an electronic flash unit is a power pack in which one or more capacitors at intervals supply current to the flashtube from the regular AC electric outlet, from a rechargeable wet-cell battery, from a dry-battery pack ordinary D-cell batteries, and other sources. The flashtube itself, a spiral or U-shaped gas filled lamp containing electrodes and mounted in a reflector, emits its light when electrical energy from the power source passes into the tube, causing it to glow brightly for a brief moment. Following the flash, the unit becomes recharged, and after several seconds, is ready for the next flash

Typical of the units powered by D-cell batteries is the Exakta Electronic Flash Unit, Model A (Fig. 190), which uses three of these inexpensive sources The unit may also be operated by plugging a cord into the home AC line A set of D cells will power 50 to 60 flashes, any number when using AC

The reflector covers the normal 50 angle of view, recycles for another shot every four seconds on the AC line, somewhat longer on D-cell power, has a flash duration of 1 1000th of a second, and the flash tube has a life

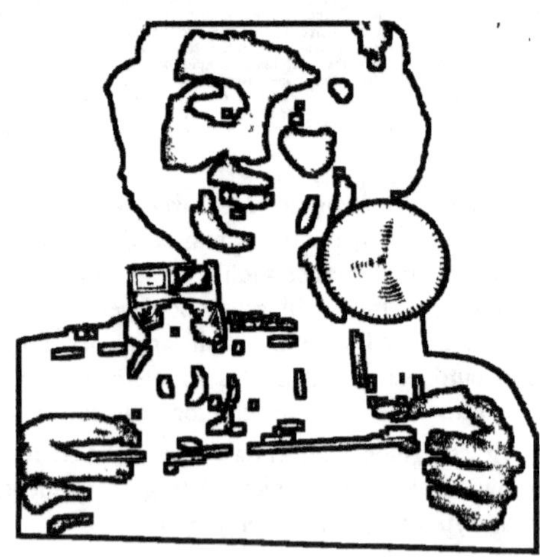

190

Exakta Electronic Flash unit operates on three D-cell batteries or directly on AC house current

191 **Sam Falk, The New York Times Magazine** *A fine example of electronic flash control that simulates ordinary flood-light illumination Two lamps were used, one at the side of the stage, the other at the camera but held high to kick a little light into the audience and at the same time provide a fill-in for the main subject*

capacity of about 50,000 flashes. The color of the light approximates daylight quality, about 5500° Kelvin, hence may be used when shooting daylight color film

To operate the unit, attach the bracket to the base of the Exakta or Exa, slide the gun into the shoe on the bracket, plug the three-prong plug into the side of the leather battery case, and insert the cord tip in the Exakta or Exa socket For AC operation, set the control button on the case in the *down* position, and plug the AC line into the socket on the case and into the AC wall outlet. When using the battery power, make sure the cells are fresh, and set the control button in the *up* position. A continuous, slight buzzing sound will indicate the unit is working. Return the control button to the *down* position when through shooting

An indicator on the back of the flash reflector will light up when the unit is ready for flashing. When camera shutter button is pressed, flash and film exposure are synchronized For time or bulb exposures, or for fill-in flash, use the red button on the back of the reflector

142

Accessories for the Exakta unit include the new nickel cadmium battery, more efficient than the D cells but more expensive; a battery recharger for the D cells, and a ring light attachment. The latter is a circular light tube that fits around the camera lens and is designed to provide even illumination in close-up photography.

Flash Techniques

The flash photographer can greatly extend his opportunities by removing the gun from the camera and directing it from any other desired position. Lamps on extension permit him to use two or more lights simultaneously to achieve effects similar to those obtainable with flood lamps (see below). Fig 191 is a splendid demonstration of one such technique. Mr. Falk used one electronic flash lamp on the stage for the main lighting and another one high above his camera as a fill-in. He held the lamp so that a small amount of the light would spill over onto the foreground. This sparing use of flash for realistic effects also has been employed successfully by Morris Gordon of Western Electric in his industrial photography by normal room lighting. In order to retain the authentic appearance of the subject yet perk up the lighting a bit, he uses an electronic flash lamp on extension about 30 feet away. The flash has little effect at that distance but that little is all he needs—just a wee kick into the shadows

Bounce Light Flash photographers have been bouncing flash off light-toned ceilings and walls in recent years to exceedingly good effect, and happy to pay the cost in exposure (two to three stops larger because of the light loss). For the resulting illumination is pleasingly soft and diffused, with little if any shadows, something like daylight under a hazy sky. It is a particularly useful light for shooting groups and for large-area illumination generally.

Electronic flash, flash lamps and floods all have been used in this technique. The lamp is held at arm's length or placed on a light stand and turned toward the ceiling or a wall. (For color photography the surfaces should be white to avoid unwanted color reflections). In addition to the speed of the film (the new fast color films make their use much more practical for this purpose than hitherto), exposure is based chiefly on the height and lightness of the ceiling and the distance of the lamp from the ceiling. The closer the source, the stronger will be the bounced illumination, and incidentally, the more contrasty the lighting. At greater distances from the ceiling, the lighting is softer, also weaker. Because the light is broadly distributed, there is considerable exposure latitude, especially with fast black-and-white film.

Sun-Flash Synchronization: Because of its convenience and effectiveness, flash has become quite popular as a means of filling in the deep shadows created

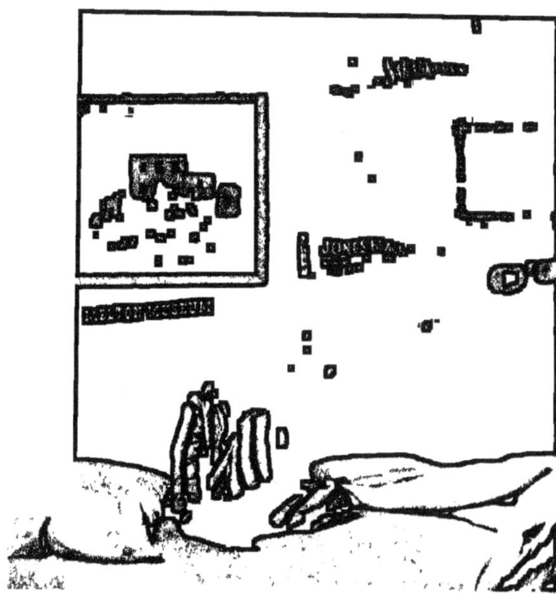

192

Harold Feinstein. The bounce-flash technique furnished the diffuse illumination needed for this subject Mr Feinstein estimated the exposure on the basis of the distance from the camera (on which the flash lamp was mounted) to ceiling to boy and back to camera.

by sidelighted subjects on sunny days outdoors. Although black-and-white film has the latitude to take a considerable contrast range in its stride, color film, even the new fast material, is not so fortunate in this respect The fill-in formula, using either blue flash or electronic flash, the color temperature (see notes, p 140) of either of which is close enough to that of daylight to give reasonable satisfaction, is similar to the standard method of determining flash exposure (see p 139) with certain exceptions If the flash is closer than about 8 feet the shadows may be unnaturally light In such cases, cover the reflector with a plastic diffuser or with one or two thicknesses of handkerchief, depending on the distance and one's notion, based on experience, of the most desirable depth of tone. For closeups, use an extension flash unit at the required distance, thus freeing the camera for the closer approach.

Flood and Spot Lights

The most popular, convenient and efficient of the other artificial light sources is the photoflood lamp, which comes in two types. One is shaped like the ordinary household bulb, and is frosted on the inside to diffuse the light evenly and so make it more effective photographically. It is available in three sizes. the No 1, which supplies 250 watts of light, the No 2, 500 watts, and the No. 4 (with the special large mogul base), 1,000 watts. These lamps are used in adjustable metal reflectors mounted on stands. The other lamp type is

the mushroom-shaped reflector flood, so called because it includes its own
reflector in the form of a silver coating on the outside of the neck Three lamps
of this type on the market are: the RFL2 and the RSP2, each 500 watts, and
the RFL1, 375 watts. Because they are independent sources, these lamps may
be used either in a light stand or any household light unit.

The RSP2 lamp is a handy version of the spotlight, the narrow-beam light
source, the basic purpose of which is to concentrate light on an isolated area
rather than the broad coverage for which the flood is used. Regular spotlight
units consist of a housing with a convex condenser or Fresnel-type (grooved)
lens at the front, and a reflector at the back. A projection lamp is centered
in front of the reflector. By means of an adjusting lever, the lamp is moved
toward the reflector to narrow the light beam, forward to broaden the beam
until it approaches flood characteristics. Large spotlights use projection lamps
of 500 watts or greater. A number of miniature spotlights are available which
perform in a similar way but produce a much narrower light beam and use
150 or 200-watt projection lamps.

Reflectors come in various shapes and diameters — the larger and more
shallow the reflector the greater the area covered The sizes range from about
fifteen and twenty inches in diameter down to the popular ten-inch reflectors
and smaller The deeper, cone-shaped reflectors are for limited area lighting,
as in illuminating the hair in portraiture or to isolate a feature of a setup.

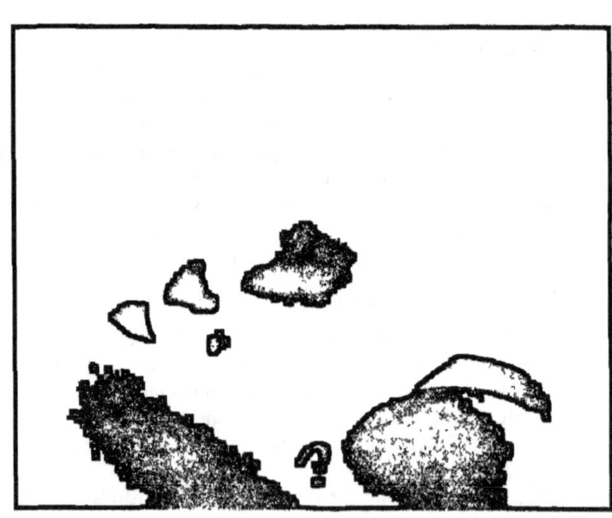

193

The reflector is mounted on a telescoping sectional light stand, which rests on folding legs, and is raised or lowered to any desired height, then locked with wing nuts or knurled screws. A photoflood bulb is screwed into the swiveling socket which holds the reflector, and a light cord which ranges in size from six to twenty feet is plugged into the electric outlet. The light is switched on and the reflector is adjusted at a suitable angle relative to the subject. If a reflector-type lamp is used, no other reflector is needed.

The market offers compact and inexpensive reflector-and-stand outfits which contain two or three reflectors and stands enclosed in a corrugated carrying-case or paper box for convenient storage. For overhead lighting, an adjustable boom light device is available for extending the light over the subject without including the light stand in the picture

Among the accessories available for use in conjunction with reflectors and spotlights are diffusion screens, barn doors to prevent light spill, masks with circular apertures for pin-pointing the light, low-high switches (weak light for focusing, bright for the picture), and cut-out holders for spotlight projection of background designs

Steinheil Flash Calculator

Just under the focusing ring on the Steinheil lenses are two scales, a green one marked Film ASA, and below it, Guide Number with red figures Also on the green ring is an aperture scale, which lies adjacent to the distance scale. To learn the flash apertures needed for a given exposure index (ASA) and guide number at various camera-to-subject distances, turn the green ring until the two are opposite each other. A glance at the aperture-distance scales will show the required lens stop for the required shooting distance Both the ASA and Guide Number scales may be set between the engraved figures when necessary.

For example, the film in use has an exposure index of 100. Turn the green ring until it is opposite the guide number of the flash lamp in use (for a given shutter speed), say 130. The green aperture scale shows that at 18 feet the aperture f/22 should be used. Since guide numbers are just that, guides, the photographer is advised to establish his own figures by test.

The easiest way to operate the calculator is to rack the lens all the way out (as if for extreme close-ups), then turn the green ring as far as it will go to the right Next, turn the lens to infinity position. This will provide the leverage needed to set the scale conveniently.

194 *Extreme closeup of the head of the cicada.*

Nature Photography—An Introduction

The "available-light" photographer has more in common with the nature photographer than he might suspect, for both are sold on the candid approach. Although the similarity is closest when the nature man stalks birds, animals and other lively creatures which will fly or run away even at the suspicion of a photographer's presence, the candid spirit is implicit in the whole realm of nature work. The photographer looks in on the most intimate aspects of private lives and photographs what he sees—the lives of ants, mosquitos, bugs, moths, caterpillars, turtles—often in amazement, always in wonder, sometimes amused, usually with a sense of exciting discovery. How he does it is the subject of this chapter.

Lynwood M. Chace, who lives in New Bedford, Mass., has been a leading professional nature photographer for many years. Some of his experiences, what he has learned from them, and practical information on valuable techniques in nature work with the Exakta are covered in the pages that follow. All of the illustrations are the work of Mr. Chace.

Nature Photography With the Exakta

LYNWOOD M. CHACE

Nature photography is a highly specialized and technical field which offers a vast variety of material, as your subject may vary from a mosquito sucking human blood (with its very specialized instrument, the labium) to a tall and rangy giraffe feasting on leaves from the treetops in far-off Africa. Just as the watchmaker must have his precision tools to perform his skilled work, so must the nature photographer have the right equipment to accomplish the type of work that is to be achieved.

In my years of experience in nature photography I have found, through trial and error, that the Kine Exakta is the ideal camera for successful results in this field. This is due mainly to the great advantage of the reflex system with which this type of camera is equipped, an essential feature when you go into the field to photograph such nature subjects, for example, as the life cycle story of the black swallow-tail butterfly and the black-eyed Susan.

In establishing the camera setup for such closeup shots one realizes the very important role played by the reflex feature. Ordinarily, when working

195

A field of black-eyed Susans. How they grew from buds is developed in the camera sequence on the facing page.

148

196, 197, 198

Right, first stages of the budding Susan With 3-inch extension tube, exposure 1/5th at f/16.

199, 200

Below, bud begins to open during final stage Camera was pulled back slightly to cover larger picture area. The full bloom is seen in Fig 195

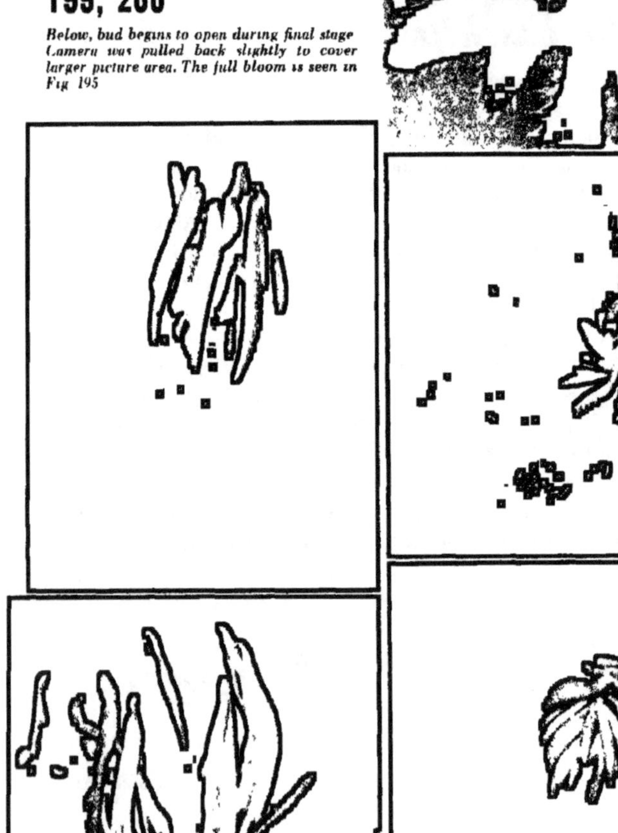

so closely as 3 inches from extremely small subjects, the parallax problem is a critical one. In the Exakta system, parallax does not exist, as the photographer views the subject directly through the shooting lens. In consequence, the camera is always perfectly lined up with the subject, regardless of the distance from the camera. Moreover, one can follow the slightest movement of the subject, quickly maneuvering the camera to keep the subject on plumb center, in the field of focus at all times.

The Burgeoning Susan

The camera's usefulness is well demonstrated in my experience in photographing the blossoming bud of the black-eyed Susan. To photograph successfully such a series, one needs first of all several yards of white mosquito netting to build a tent around the plant to be photographed, this as a protection against wind, minimizing or eliminating the problem of subject movement. This precaution is necessary because of the slow shutter speeds that will be required to compensate for the small lens stops needed to achieve the necessary depth of field A good tripod is another must, to keep the camera rock-steady. A 3-inch extension tube and at least one No 3 portrait attachment complete the equipment list.

Select a bud of a black-eyed Susan and set up the camera and accessories. Take the first picture of the closed bud, then check periodically to get successive stages of the gradual opening of the blossom. As the blossom opens and becomes larger, the camera will have to be moved back slightly to cover the greater subject area. In the more advanced stages, possibly the No. 3 portrait

201

The caterpillar of the black swallow-tail butterfly has just attached its tail to a twig and spun a strong line of silk about its body to support it while it begins the weaving of its chrysalis Other steps in life cycle on facing page

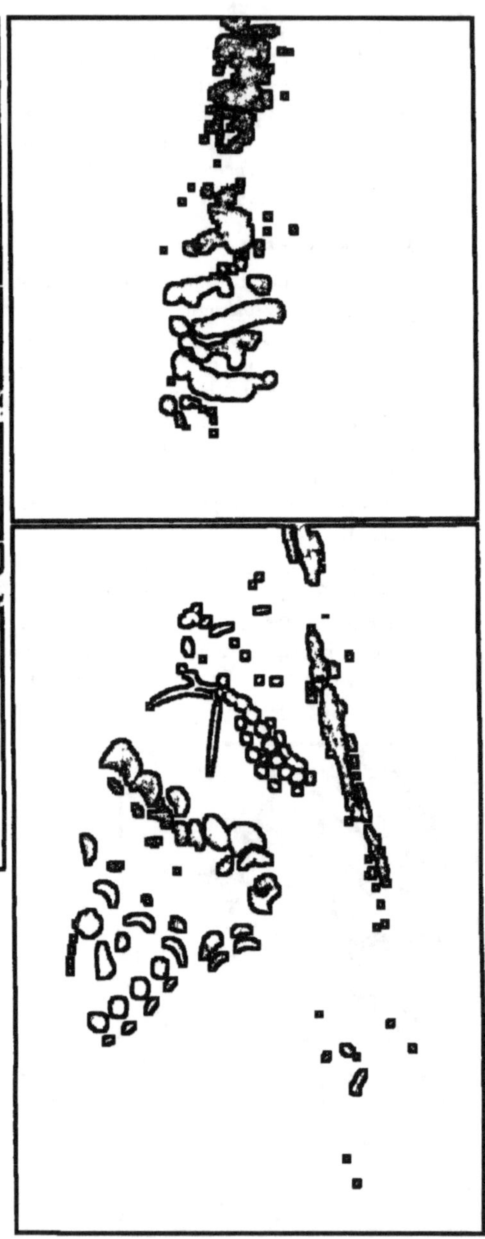

202-206

*The life cycle of the insect
with a yen for carrot leaves
Above, butterfly laying eggs,
and one it laid on carrot leaf
(shot with No 3 extension
tube and No. 3 portrait attachment to increase size
from a pin head)   At right,
emergence from chrysalis
(Fig. 207, above right, is in-
between stage)*

151

attachment may have to be eliminated in order to get the full blossom in the camera field. In taking the series reproduced in Figs 195-200 I stopped down the 50mm f/2.8 Carl Zeiss Tessar lens to f/16 for adequate depth of field and set the shutter at 1/5th.

I used similar techniques in photographing the life cycle story of the black swallow-tail butterfly (Figs. 201-206). The first shot to go after is a striking picture of the jewel-like egg which has been deposited on a carrot leaf by the female butterfly. This photograph is most important as it is the establishing shot of the story. You may have to use a magnifying glass to find the tiny egg as it is about the size of a pin-head. This shot therefore calls for an extreme closeup, so the camera has to be assembled with the proper equipment for extreme closeup work as the egg should stand out boldly in the finished picture.

A 3-inch extension tube and a No. 3 portrait attachment will do the job. When working at this close distance, the depth of field decreases rapidly, so it is necessary to stop down to f/16 to assure a fair degree of overall sharpness, and of course to use a tripod. When in some doubt as to proper exposure, it is a good idea to make three different shots at different speeds, especially in the case of subjects that are difficult to find, one taken slightly faster and one slower than the reading called for by the meter. Thus you will be sure of getting at least one good result.

The Caterpillar At Home

After photographing the egg, the next step is to find the caterpillar —or at least one belonging to the same family of butterfly. For convenience in photographing, the caterpillar may be brought home and put into a prepared container with a cover of wire screening. This is to insure that the caterpillar gets the necessary air as well as to prevent it from escaping. After the caterpillar has been fed for a time, with carrot foliage or tops, it finally attaches itself to some object (perhaps some twigs or branches, the container having been prearranged accordingly) by a silken thread which the caterpillar produces It fastens one end of the silk thread to the twig, then passes it around its back and affixes the other end to the twig (Fig 201), thus suspending itself for its next performance.

The photographer now watches patiently and intently in order not to miss the opportune moment to photograph the caterpillar in the act of shedding its skin and transforming into the chrysalis stage. To line up the camera and lights for this spectacular performance, and then obtain shots of the chrysalis, and finally the butterfly when it emerges from the cocoon sometime later, is a fascinating experience, and carries with it a great feeling of satisfaction of accomplishment.

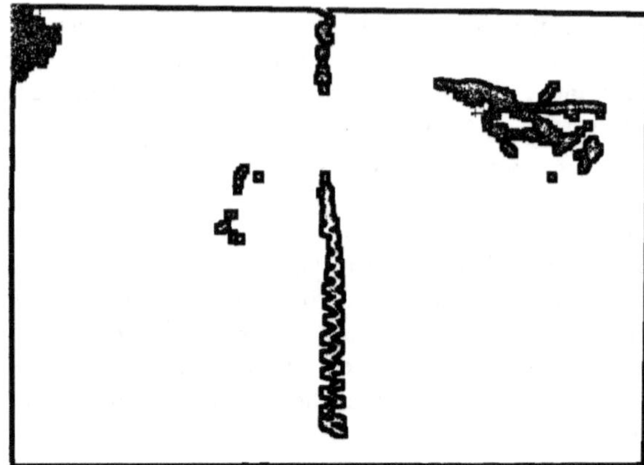

207

The Mirror Reflector

For crisp lighting, an excellent combination is clear sun falling on the subject at a 45° angle and a reflector filling in the shadows. I have found that covering a mirror with white mosquito netting works out most successfully in many cases. For stronger reflected light, I dispense with the netting. For example, when photographing such a subject as a spider wrapping up a victim with shrouds of pearly-white silk, I have found this the best lighting to use: the sun striking the web from the back, and a strong light reflected from the other side by a sizeable mirror with no covering. This arrangement will make the silk sparkle and the strands to stand out boldly

It is best to shoot from the side of the mirror, where the photographer may adjust the mirror as needed; I have obtained striking Kodachromes of spiders and of tent caterpillars applying silk to their homes, by working out the lighting with this mirror method. It makes the silk strands just dazzle, if ordinary light is used the silk structure is dull and uninteresting.

Techniques for Turtles

A mirror served another use when I photographed a group of snapping turtle pictures. It was quite a large project. First, I had a ton of sand trucked to my premises and a pond 15 x 20 feet constructed. An advertisement for snapping turtles and snapping turtle eggs in the local newspaper and over the radio brought fifteen turtles and 200 eggs within a week. I planted the turtle eggs in the sand, and placed a mirror upright in the sand in front of the eggs so I could see when the eggs began to hatch. I put the adult turtles in the pond so I could watch for an opportunity to get shots of the turtle laying eggs.

The reason for wanting such a large number of turtles was to make sure

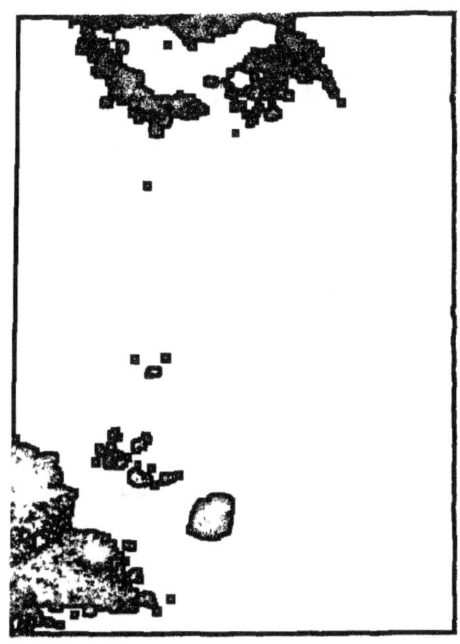

208, 209

The snapping turtle lays an egg first she digs a hole with her hind feet then deposits the eggs in it one a minute for a total of 20 to 30 Photographed by photoflood illumination (see below)

of getting some subjects, as many of the eggs might not hatch and there was no way of telling which of the turtles would lay eggs However, one turtle finally did perform (Fig 209), but just at sundown, which necessitated a more complicated setup for photographing than would have been the case in good light.

I ran extension cords from my studio and set up four No 2 photofloods, two were placed at a low angle and two set for top lighting. The exposure was 1/50th at f/3.2, using a 50mm lens I worked from a tripod to assure steadiness.

The Turtle Lays an Egg

Another experience with the snapping turtle had to do with one of the most interesting assignments I have ever had It was to photograph the life cycle of the creature, starting with the laying of its eggs. When the awaited moment arrived and my subject began to produce, I found myself maneuvering around the turtle to get closeups, high shots, low shots, etc. This was the critical, brief period when the shots had to be made, for once the turtle had

154

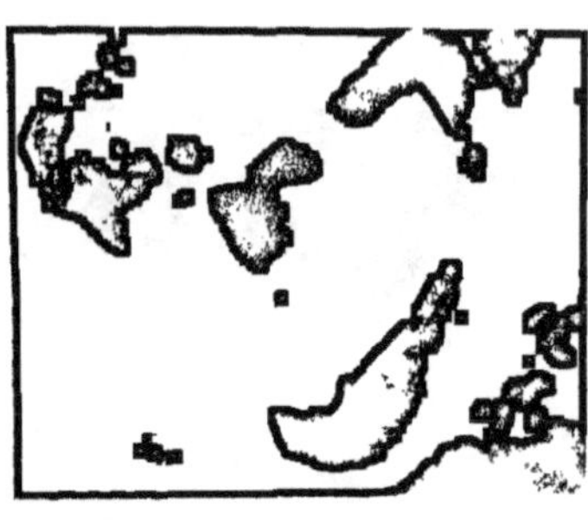

210, 211

*This snapping turtle did not get its
name for nothing Here it is in an ugly
mood. The extreme closeup, above,
shows the razor-like jaws*

finished her egg-laying, that would be it, at least for the time being. During
the rapid sequence of shooting I appreciated the flexibility and viewing control the reflex principle afforded me, making it possible to work rapidly without sacrificing exactness of timing and quality of results.

The project was fascinating I was intrigued by the idea of photographing the embryo in the turtle eggs at different stages of development. Indulging
in this adventure I opened up eggs at various stages of incubation, first at
one-month development, then a two-months' embryo, then at three months,
completing the period of incubation The sun's heat did the job of incubation,
its rays furnished the light for photography

Most unusual were the baby turtles as they broke out of the eggs. With

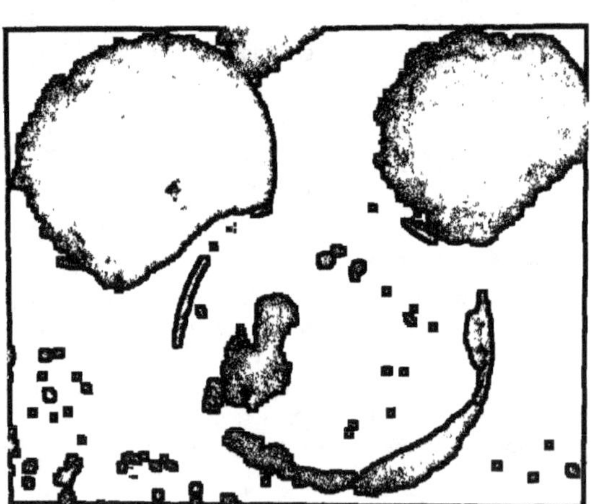

212

*His curiosity getting
the better of him, the
photographer cut away
half a turtle egg two
weeks before hatching
and photographed by
sunlight what you see*

155

the Exakta ready for closeups I waited for one to come through the shell
When its egg tooth had pierced the shell, the head came poking through,
giving me the shot I had anticipated and for which I had patiently waited,
for it was the picture I needed to complete the story.

Underwater at the Aquarium

You do not have to be a skindiver to take underwater shots in nature
photography. Most of the underwater pictures I have taken have been photographed in large aquariums holding 30 to 60 gallons of water and carefully
set up with natural underwater plants, gravel bottom and rock to simulate
exactly the natural appearance of underwater scenery. I shot a frog swimming
to the surface (Fig 213) by this method, and once took pictures of sun fish
in the act of spawning in a lake. To eliminate reflections from the glass I used
a polarizing screen (see page 63). A good lighting arrangement for shooting
in large aquariums can be obtained by using No. 2 photofloods (I prefer the
built-in reflector type). To avoid reflections from the glass walls of the aquarium, the lights have to be set up above and to the extreme side of the aquarium.

When photographing such small subjects as the head of the cicada (Fig.
194), the cecropia moth on a daffodil stalk (Fig. 214) and the greatly magnified head of the cecropia showing its fern-like antennae (Fig 216), I usually
work in a studio, using two No 2 photofloods. Thus I avoid the possibility of
even a slight breeze moving the subjects, an especially important precaution
in such a case, for example, as the delicate antennae of the moth Also, I have
better control of the lighting arrangement.

The photograph of the water bug with eggs on its back (Fig. 215)—the

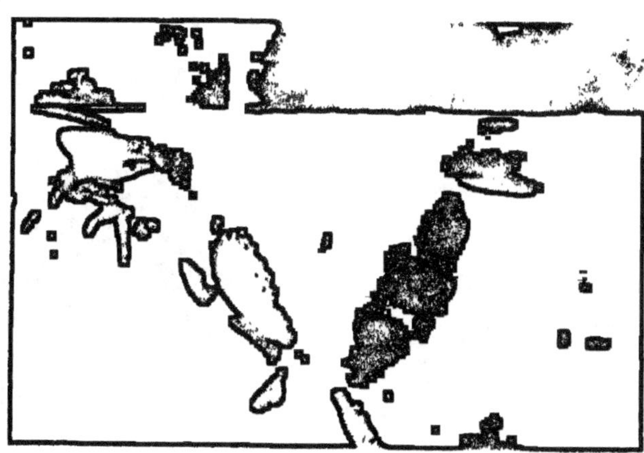

213

*For shooting in
an aquarium the
proper lighting
is above and to
the side to avoid
reflections. A
polarizing
screen also
helps.*

bug was removed from the water to facilitate photography—was taken indoors the same way, using a 3-inch extension tube. The exposure was 1/5th at f/8. When using the photofloods much care must be used to avoid getting the lights too close to the subject as the heat will destroy it. A light strength that will register up to 25 ASA is plenty strong enough for photography and will be safe for the creatures.

Tripods and a Blind

The tripod is one of the most useful accessories in the photographer's kit. True, it adds to the weight and bulk of the equipment and involves the routine of setting it up, but this trouble pays off in finer results For work in the field, the nature photographer's equipment should include two good tripods, one baby tripod for low-level work close to the ground, such as photographing ants at work; the other a normal-sized tripod for landscape and bird photography.

For the latter, a blind is also needed. A very practical blind can be made by sewing burlap bags (that have been opened up completely) to the top of a

214

The cecropia moth on daffodil stalks. This is an inside job The photographer brought the subjects into his studio, set up two No 2 photofloods. The original was a color slide. Mr. Chace prefers shooting color even when he wants black-and-whites as he likes the results.

157

beach umbrella. When the umbrella is closed it is a compact blind to carry and a simple one to set up, as it requires merely driving a stake into the ground and sliding the top of the umbrella into it. After stubbing down the edges of the burlap, the blind is ready.

I have also learned that it is a good idea to make a hood out of burlap to fit over the lens that protrudes from the blind, as in most cases the sight of the black lens hood alarms the birds. However, the burlap lens covering should be made fast to the camera with a string to make sure it does not slip over the front of the lens when focusing At least a half dozen retaining rings should be included in the equipment, and at least two No 3 portrait attachments along with a 3-inch extension tube for extreme closeup photography of small subjects. For a reflector for these subjects I use a small round shaving mirror that works on a swivel, covering the glass with white mosquito netting to reduce the hardness of bright sunlight

215 *The water bug of the male species takes a hand in child bearing Here is the rare proof When ready to lay her eggs, the female bug lays them on the back of the male, where they remain his responsibility until they hatch—at least Incidentally, what progeny!*

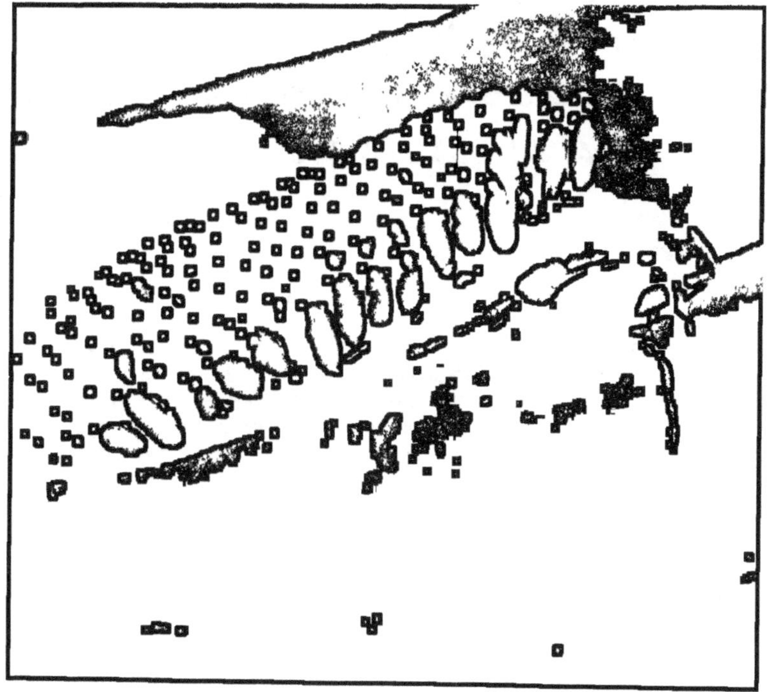

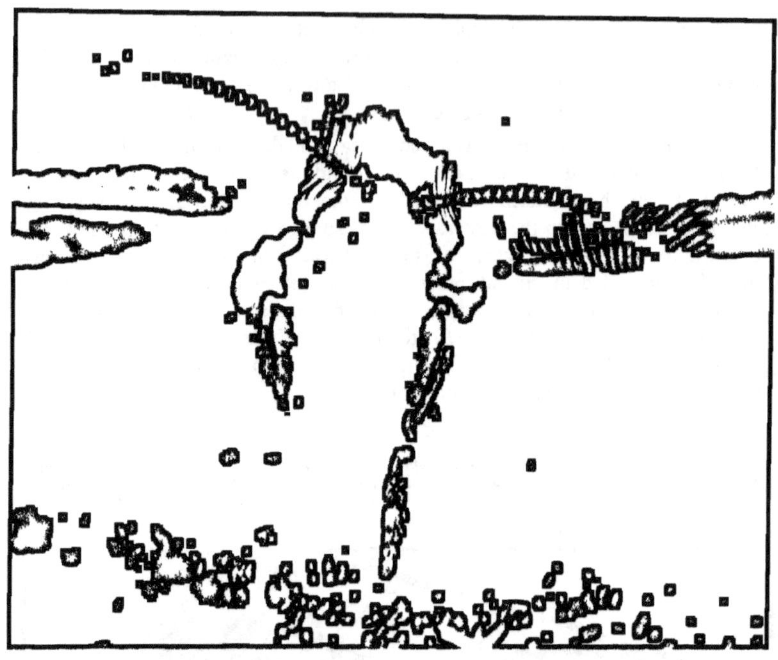

216 *Greatly magnified head of the cecropia moth showing its fern like antennae A 3-inch extension tube brought the camera close enough to show this amazing detail*

The Medium Telephoto Is Best

In photographing birds from a blind I prefer a 3-inch or 4-inch lens, as sometimes you have to work in tight places where a lens of longer focal length would be impractical When using a blind you can always get close enough to the subject so that a 3-inch lens will do the job well. The lens should never be slower than f/4.5, for if Kodachrome is being used the average exposure is 1/50th at f/5.6 under good light, and it is good policy to have at least one stop more in reserve in case the lighting is not up to standard. *(The situation with regard to the speed of color film has been greatly improved, of course, with the introduction of the new fast color films—see Chap. 10).*

A favorable feature of the 35mm Exakta is that it is light in weight and compact, which makes it ideal for field photography, especially when you are striking out on a long hike to hunt for the unusual in nature subjects. Often, when traveling in timber country you are quite likely to discover your prize nature subject is high up in a tree. As in the case of the hawk's nest (Fig. 217), for example, for in order to get the desired shot looking down into the hawks' nest, it is necessary to climb up.

The Photographer Up a Tree

The camera's compactness was ideal for this rather difficult operation. I hiked up the tree opposite the one that held the nest and, in order to get satisfactory lighting, tied back large branches that were casting shadows on the nest I was about 10 feet from the nest but a 100mm lens brought me "closer." The exposure was 1/50th at f/5.6. A 3-inch lens might also serve in such cases. In addition, you will need some sort of makeshift blind, which can be constructed by arranging the branches of the tree from which you do the shooting. Projects like this often entail much waiting, but frequently result in exciting shots of a bird's family life.

Sometimes one can climb a tree and bring the subjects down for a better photographic look. This was the case with the baby squirrels (Fig. 218). After the shooting, I fetched them back to their nest again. The lighting used was diffused daylight and a mirror reflector, with a 50mm lens, and a No. 1 portrait attachment. The exposure was 1/25th at f/8. I used the slow exposure as there was practically no movement and I needed the depth of field.

I use Kodachrome film mostly, even when I need black-and-white prints, as I prefer the quality of black-and-white prints made from the slides to those shot directly on black-and-white film. This is advantageous too. When covering a life-cycle set of photographs of a nature subject in Kodachrome you have the beauty of the color and in addition a set of crisp, sharp black-and-white negatives that can be enlarged up to 11x14 inches with no difficulty. Rather than change from one type to another, I have standardized on Type A for both indoors and outdoors, using a conversion filter for the latter. To assure good color values, I shoot between 9 A.M. and 4 P.M. during the late spring and summer

The Exakta's feature of permitting closeup photography the most direct way led me years ago (before the days of the bellows units now on the market— see Chap 9) to adapt the camera for use on the back of a Recomar bellows camera with double extension. This arrangement worked very successfully. It eliminated the need for extension tubes as the bellows of the Recomar could be extended to get just the desired size of enlarged image. With the bellows extended full length, for example, a life-size image of a mosquito could be obtained.

Exakta and Microscope

The Exakta may also be adapted to microscope photography by masking off the lens hood to fit the eyepiece of the microscope. As the camera is set

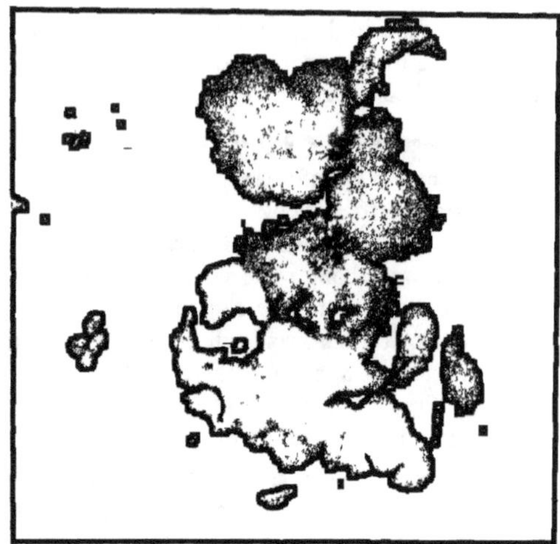

217

*Mr Chace climbed a tree adja-
cent to the one that held these
baby hawks in their nest and
photographed them with a
9-inch lens*

for shooting down, the focusing hood rests rigidly in the most convenient focusing position, enabling the operator to sit at the assembled microscope and camera and to view the image in comfort.

Fabulously striking effects can be obtained in color with such a setup; for example, the dazzling color and pattern of the scales on the wings of butterflies and moths, and countless other subjects that would go unseen by the human eye were it not for microscopic photography.

The reflex principle continues to be the Exakta's chief attraction for me as a nature photographer, offering both the facility of retaining full control of the image at any desired angle, from the worm's-eye level and up, and framing the subject to suit exactly the needs and tastes of the photographer.

218

*Baby squirrels apparently are
easier to handle, so the photographer brought them down
from their home in the tree
to photograph them at leisure
on the ground.*

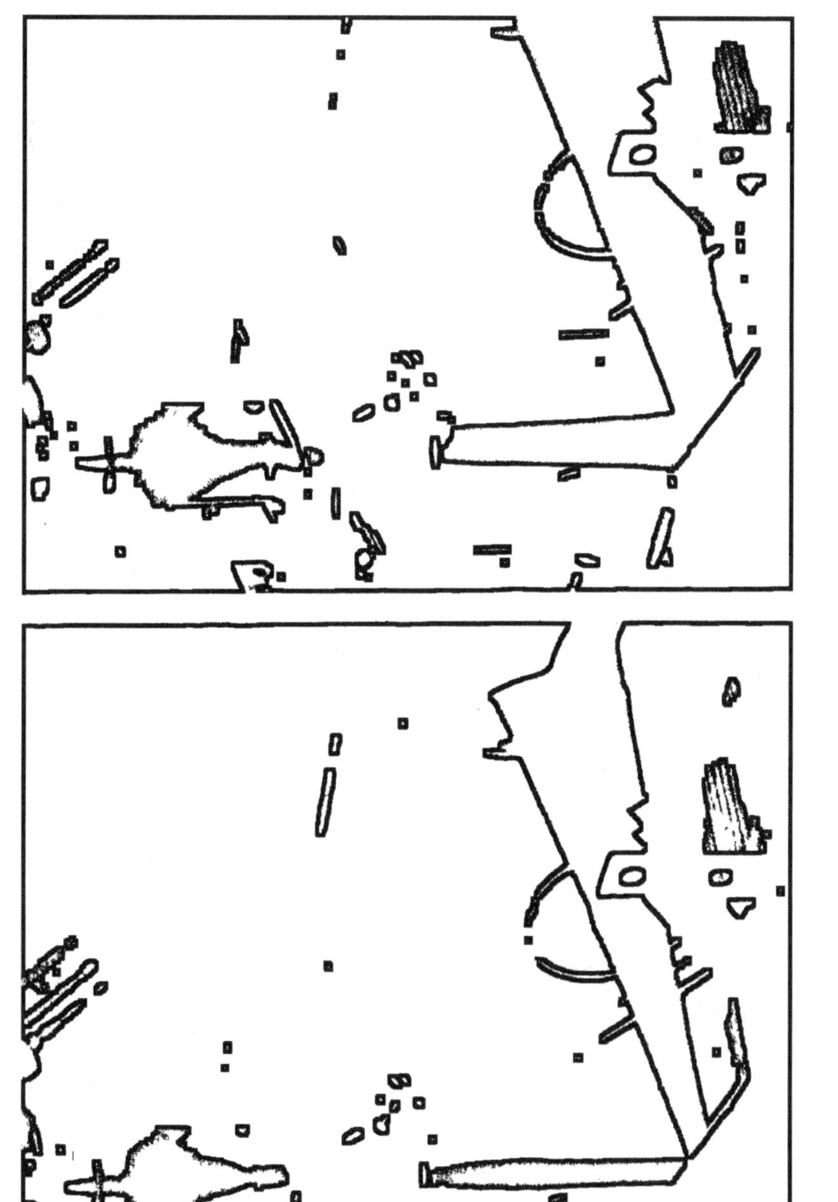

219 *Two electronic flash lamps were used to illuminate this chick fetus for lighting convenience and to stop subject movement The heat from photoflood lamps would have caused the subject to move about so much faster that photography would have been difficult*

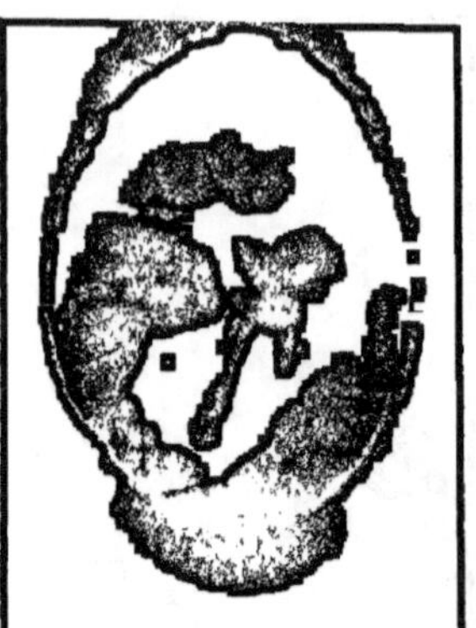

CHAPTER   THIRTEEN

Medical Photography with the Exakta

JULIUS WEBER

It is consistent with the progress of the last twenty five years in photography to find that during that time the functions of medical photography also have undergone significant change. Instead of merely requesting an infrequent record of an unusual lesion, modern medical men welcome the photographic technician as an aggressive participant in teaching and research   In fact, it is a rare hospital indeed which is now without some photographic facilities, no matter how small. This is an excellent indication of the special insistence of the younger physician to take advantage of the cornucopia of methods, tools and facts which is available from photography   Today's medical scientist recognizes that this medium offers not only the best means of teaching through visual aids, but is also unsurpassed for recording, by means of infrared and ultraviolet, so much of what would otherwise be completely invisible to us.

How Photography Helps the Doctor

The first and immediate problem which confronts the doctor is a rapid identification of the pathology presented by the patient. This is often made more difficult because the appearance of a disease may never be quite alike in any two individuals, therefore, the lesions themselves and the case histories often show subtle variations. One of the most important functions of pho-

220, 221 *The importance of centering the condenser in photomicrography The uranium cube resting on the surface of the glass slide illustrates the condenser has been properly centered at left, off-center at right. This unique demonstration was visualized by Julius Weber by blowing smoke into the path of the light rays continuously during the exposure. Note the improvised cradle for the filter and the filter's position away from the direct heat of the lamp. The device permits convenient interchange of filters and the use of smaller (therefore cheaper) ones than would be required ordinarily. Incidentally, the glass for the slide should be the thickness recommended by the manufacturer of the equipment; if too thick it will bend the light rays unduly, thereby interfering with the proper image formation by the microscope objective.*

tography is the permanent record it provides. This record becomes part of the physician's illustration library where, classified and indexed, it may be referred to at any time for study, lecture projection or publication.

The arrangement of all parts to be photographed should be planned so that the finished photograph will relate the fullest possible story. Such a record has greatest value when it is as instructive to the general physician as it is to the specialist. Therefore the field must be oriented at a glance. This is the paramount concept, and the photographer must take any and all views and introduce any technique to accomplish this. Sometimes the photograph can emphasize fully only a single aspect of a lesion. In such cases, other features present should be demonstrated by changing any or all of the photographic conditions This may mean changing the lighting, the lens focal length, the film, the filter or the processing. It should be added that as the diseased area borders on normal tissue, the relation of the pathological locale to its more normal surround should always be included. Indeed, it is wise to include such periphery somewhere in the photograph even when a comparatively high magnification closeup is being taken.

The photographic record is invaluable to the doctor in the following ways:
1. It establishes a permanent living library of his own experience. It keeps the case "alive" and insures that the information is kept up to date.
2. It provides a means of comparison with previous cases.
3. It enables him to describe his findings at medical conferences.
4. It is the basis for his illustrations in medical publications.
5. He retains the personal interest, a memory of the case which is impossible with notes alone.

It is important to remember that the essential object facing the photographer's camera is always the pathological site. This one place continues to be the crux of all activity throughout the entire course of clinical evaluation, surgical or pharmacological treatment, and laboratory diagnosis. It will be returned to the photographer again and again for more information, and each time he may move his camera closer and closer to it.

He will record perhaps a smaller portion of the scene, but this is because he seeks greater magnification and resolution. First he sees it clinically and records it *in situ;* his lenses and lamps may help film its surgical excision and the intricacies involved in its removal. He next trains his camera on the total gross specimen and photographs its external character and, when the involved laboratory procedures are completed, magnifies tiny internal portions of the tissue with powerful microscope optics in either visible or invisible light.

It is this constant concern with the single aspect of the patient—the aspect which remains the photographer's "model" throughout—that provides us with a logical plan for describing the various techniques which are so useful

164

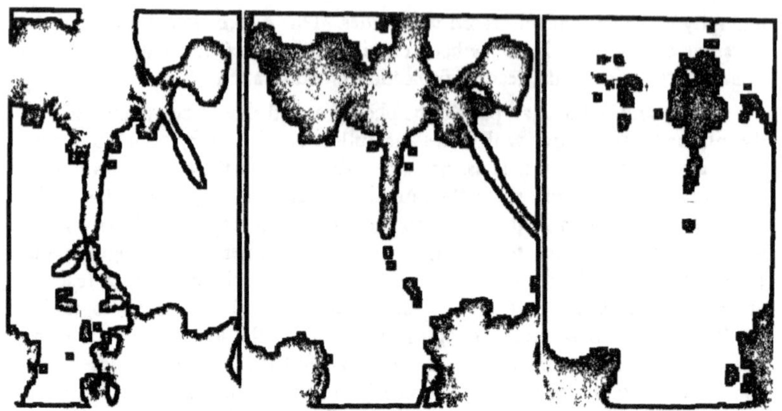

222, 223, 224

Choice of film and development to suit the photographer's needs Medical photographers who face a variety of assignments, from copying of documents, where line rendering is required, to subjects like this X-ray of the aortagram, tend to try to do all the jobs on the same film. The first picture, left, shows the unhappy result of this practice, particularly for a subject like this one, in which vital information about the heart and the large heart blood vessels is lost when the film used is unsuitable for the purpose This X-ray picture was copied on Microfile film, left, on Super XX, center; and at right on Super XX later processed in a very soft developer Since detail is important here, the Microfile negative is practically useless The center one is adequately rendered for reproduction in a publication The third, richly detailed, but soft, is ideal for projection

in medical photography We shall therefore discuss each problem in the order in which it may come to the physician, beginning with the patient's clinical appearance and continuing through all the various stages of the diagnosis and treatment When all the photographs are assembled afterward, the case is ready either for teaching presentation in the lecture room or for the editor for publication.

Let us begin with the patient in the doctor's office or hospital clinic.

Photography of Patients

In medical photography, we are faced with two paramount questions: 1, what means of illumination shall we use, and 2, how shall patient, camera and lights be arranged? We will obtain the best answers when in all decisions regarding the choice of equipment and its arrangement we are guided by one philosophy The apparatus must be capable not only of providing the best results photographically, but must also possess optimum versatility of camera movement and ease and speed of lighting operation. The importance of insisting upon these conditions becomes obvious when we remember that the patient may not be subjected to prolonged discomfort. Therefore the photographer must work as quietly and efficiently as possible.

These demands are readily met by the Exakta. Two features in the camera make it easily adaptable to the most precise medical photographic requirements. The first is its small size; the second, and more important, its reflex construction. The best way to safeguard the proper orientation of the photographic field is to keep it under constant scrutiny. The ability to observe the area until the instant of exposure is invaluable in assuring perfect medical photographs. When we add to this the further advantage that we may move as close as is necessary to even the smallest lesion without adding any expensive, auxiliary optical systems, we can see how greatly this enhances both the usefulness and efficiency of the camera.

The Exakta is light, small, easily positioned. It should be stationed on a sturdy, pan-tilting head. Some workers find the use of a gooseneck stand suitable; others prefer the elevator type tripod. However, maximum maneuverability will be gained when the camera and pan-tilt base are located on a stand with wheels. Such an arrangement consists of a hollow tube which rises from the center of a heavy T-shaped metal base. The base moves on three rubber-tired wheels and drags a small chain for grounding static electricity. To the tube should be added a number of off-set arms which are designed to slide up and down and may be fixed at any height by set screws. One offset arm can hold the camera directly. The others may accept lamps mounted on counterbalanced rods

Advantages of a Small Camera

The small size of the camera enables it to be used in close conjunction with a spot lamp, a feature which is especially attractive for photographing a small area within a narrow working space. When the camera is brought so close to and directly above the patient's body, it will enable us to take photographs when the patient's position may not be disturbed. Moreover, such views can be made with the camera angle distortion held to a minimum. The cables of the illuminating unit may be located in the hollow tube. Hidden in this manner, there is increased freedom of working with all parts and annoying wire tangles are avoided. If desired, the tube can also be filled with sand and capped, to provide a low-vibration, highly rigid unit.

This last feature is very important. Indeed, the necessity of holding vibration to a minimum when exposures must be longer than 1/50th of a second cannot be overemphasized. Unless flash lamps are used, the greatest care should be taken to insure the security of all parts of the apparatus. This problem, always pertinent, is more pressing when the lens is used with the extension tubes or when the area being photographed is in constant, albeit imperceptible, movement. We should be as meticulous in photographing with 35mm film as we would be with 5 x 7 or 8 x 10 sheet film. In choosing the best lamp for our

166

purpose, we must respect the size, shape
and surface coating of the reflector, for
these factors will govern the amount
and direction of the light

In many clinics, during the study of
a particular problem, it is often possible
to plan a fundamental arrangement
which is based upon a distinctive patient position and specific area view.
Under such circumstances an inflexible
setup is best Most laboratories need the
very opposite—many camera angles and
quick, elaborate lighting changes Permanent setups are recommended for
full-length body photographs, especially
where a grid or other comparison is
being simultaneously recorded. Other
specialized static arrangements are advantageous when photographing the
face, ears, nose for plastic surgery or
otolaryngology, in recording the feet or
lower limbs for orthopedics or derma-
tology and in taking closeup views of
the exterior of the eye for general features, or recording the conjunctival
blood vessels with infrared.

In all the above cases, the apparatus may be kept fairly immobile and,
in fact, may rarely need even minor adjustment. However, in a studio where

225, 226, 227

*The effect of using different condensers in the
optical setup of the microscope is illustrated in
these pictures of bread mold (rhizopus). By interchanging and adjusting condensers to give a
bright field (center), a dark field (top) or a
medium field (bottom), the photographer is able
to adapt the lighting to different specimens and
to make it yield the type of information he
wants to show This vital control provides the
photographer with an important means of describing detail, texture and form.*

many types of photographs are constantly being made, it is not feasible to tie up too many lamps and reflectors in such static arrangements Again, the logical plan is obviously to determine beforehand the scope of required photography and to plan the work accordingly. As we noted previously, the one situation which works best with a permanent lamp setup and wiring is the full-length photograph of the body. Here it is best to have the main lamps set back far enough to provide a basic, even illumination covering an area approximately 7 feet high by 7 feet wide. This will permit views of the patient with arms outstretched. Additional fill-in or spotlights may then be added where needed.

Use of Electronic Flash

If photoflood or filament lamps are used, a permanent bank of reflectors to cover such an area should be built and wired with a series-parallel circuit for dimming and brightening the lamps The control switch itself should be kept within reach of the camera. The patient is posed with the light dim and the bright circuit turned on just before the actual exposure is made. This will keep the patient more comfortable and extend the lamp life. There are a number of reasons which mitigate the use of conventional flash bulbs when

228, 229

Left, arrangement for copying negatives, using an Aristo grid lamp unit, and masks for negatives of varying sizes Right, a complete copying outfit. The insert board, which can be placed at several levels for originals of different sizes, is for copying documents and other opaque subjects. At bottom is a light box containing twelve 40-watt lamps, with switches for individual dodging control in photographing transparencies (see Figs 230-233, see opposite page). On shelf at left is a densitometer for accurately measuring image densities, on shelf at right is an automatic electronic timer.

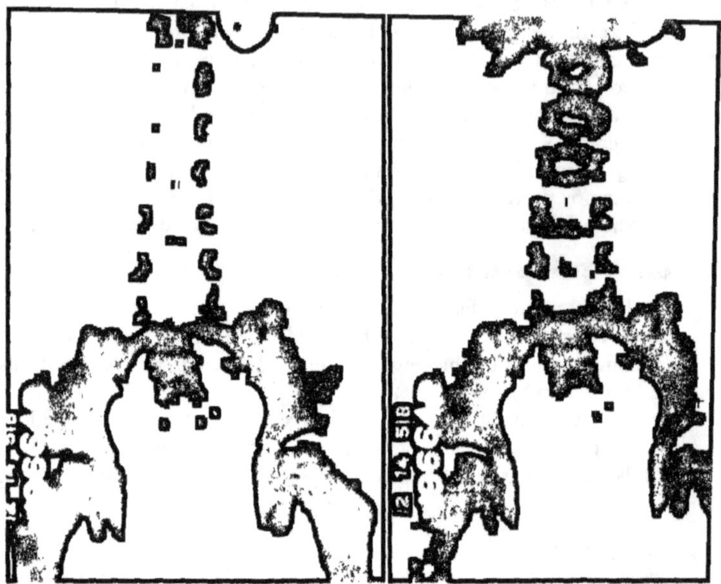

230-233

Correct tonal values and full detail were achieved in photographing the X-rays at top, left (showing a key swallowed by a child) and at bottom, left (calcification of the shoulder) by dodging with lamps in the light box (Fig 229) Individual lamps were switched off where too much light was coming through the thinner parts of the original As a result, the total illumination was evened out to give a much more satisfactory picture than that possible without dodging, as in the picture at top and bottom, right

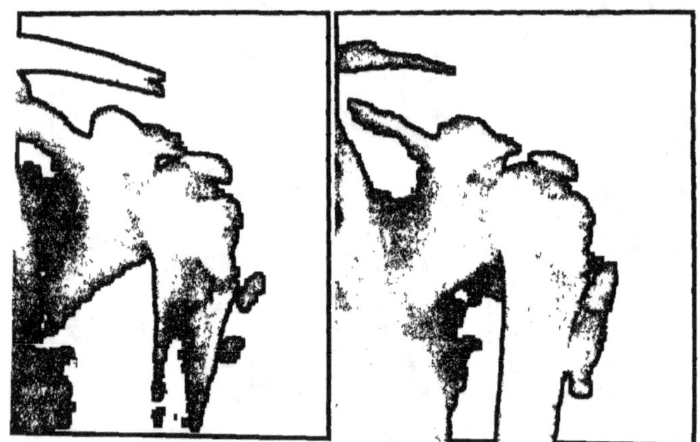

the photographic requisition calls for more than one exposure. Chief of these are the damaging effects to the patient of the blinding light, the delay and distraction occasioned by defective lamps, and the possibility that the lamps may explode.

It is interesting to note how eagerly medical photographers have turned to electronic flash since its inception. By June, 1954, reports from medical photographers here and abroad showed that from 75% to 98% of their clinical work is presently being accomplished with illumination from gaseous discharge tubes.

It is important to note that a problem which is often encountered with some electronic flash equipment is that the photographer is unable to check the lighting on a subject before actual exposure. There are at least two ways to solve this very serious defect. One is to incorporate modeling lamps into the electronic flash reflector; the second is to substitute conventional lamps of higher intensity on a swivel arrangement. In this method the electronic flash lamp and a photoflood lamp are mounted at opposite ends on a bar which is center-drilled to revolve When illuminating the subject, the lamps are positioned so that both their angle and direction of illumination are similar. The subject is then modeled with the photoflood and the electronic flash is swiveled into illuminating position just before exposure.

The Background for the Clinical Photograph

The consideration accorded the background is usually a reflection of the carefulness of the photographer's technique. Naturally there is always the rare instance when it is impossible to interpose anything between the patient and any annoying particulars which surround him. Even here, however, a combination of careful back lighting and judicious focusing will lessen the emphasis upon the undesirable detail. Such rare occasions aside, the choice and composition of the clinical background is too often given very little consideration or, at best, treated as a mere expedient for hiding some very obvious distraction. Besides its larger size, and therefore increased cost, the features of the background which present problems are its color, reflectivity and totality. Both the texture and the color of the material used for the background should be selected carefully. Only an even, unobtrusive texture should be chosen, while the color should be solid and the dyes resistant to fading.

A definite degree of background color change is always possible by controlling the intensity of the background illumination. The desirability of an even tone throughout requires that the material be mounted flat and taut to avoid folds and shadows. To reduce the possibility of glare, highly reflective substances should be avoided. The same restraint applies to the use of a pure white background. On the other hand, the use of neutral grey has much virtue.

Not only does it lend itself to fine tonal distinctions with changes in lighting; it is equally effective for any skin color and the various shades of red found in most lesions, thus obviating the delay in background changes.

The totality of the background describes both its completeness and the fact that it is uninterrupted. The area covered should be sufficiently large to extend safely beyond the periphery of the photographic field. In this connection, the meeting place of floor and background bottom is notoriously ignored. These two peripheries should be made to merge imperceptibly by attaching a section of curved metal to the bottom of the background frame. This metal and the adjacent section of floor are both painted to match the background color.

The Legal Release Form

One important necessity in clinical photography which is usually left for the last moment, or may be entirely overlooked, is the acquisition of a signed release from the patient The easiest way to solve this problem is to include a permissive paragraph in the general operative release signed by the patient. If a specific photographic release must be signed, the following may serve as a model for most applications:

STATEMENT OF RELEASE

In order to assist in improving medical diagnosis and treatment, I hereby authorize the (insert name of hospital) and its **staff** to use medical illustrations made of me in any manner they may consider proper

Signature of Patient or of Guardian Consenting for Incompetent Patient

Signature of Witness

234, 235

Left, equipment in working arrangement for photographing any specimen either by transmitted light or by an incident source Incorporated in the lens assembly is an arrangement for accurately centering the Micro Summar or Tessar in use Right, same setup, but equipped with extension tubes and conventional lens.

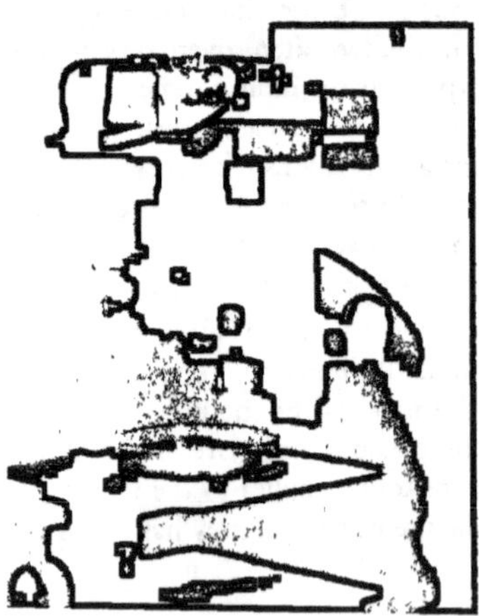
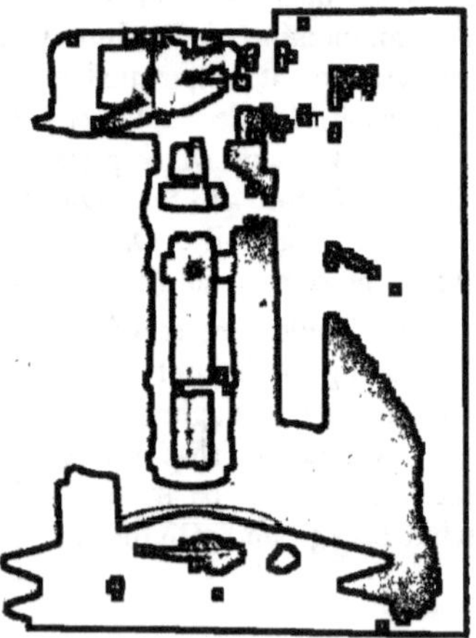

Photographing the Gross Specimen

After the clinical photographs are made, the next important function of the medical photographer is the reproduction of the gross specimen. The photography of organs removed in the operating room or at autopsy has been greatly influenced by the advent of inexpensive color film The advantages of recording the surface detail of the subject in lifelike color is easily recognized. Obviously, this is best accomplished if the specimen is photographed immediately after surgery, before fixation and post-mortem reaction have begun to produce their deadly artifacts. Moreover, we have come to appreciate the value of the esthetic and psychological considerations in medical photography.

Less obvious perhaps but much more important, is the fact that along with other vital information this photograph of the fresh lesion is available for comparison study and teaching long after the original specimen itself has been subtly or considerably changed by immersion in formalin, alchohol or other preservative reagent In fact, with few exceptions, the modern method permits most tissue specimens to be discarded shortly after the photograph has been taken

Arrangement of Unit Specimen

The unit for specimen photography should be so arranged that

1. Specular highlights can be controlled
2. Backgrounds can be textureless
3 Color backgrounds and change in background contrast can be made

In order to obtain these specifications we can proceed as follows

1. We may control highlights in a number of ways. Complete elimination is possible only by using Polaroid screens over the lens and lamp. These screens must be handled judiciously to avoid giving the specimen the waxy appearance caused by elimination of all highlights The Polaroid screen also acts as a filter which can cause a slight color shift in the photograph, a property which may be useful in photomicrography, but is deleterious in specimen work All other methods attempt to subdue the highlights by dealing with the lamps themselves. The size and distribution of the reflections depend upon the size of the radiant lamp area and the number of lamps used If the luminous source is small (or decreased in size by being kept far away from the subject) the tissue highlights will be correspondingly small. Therefore large frosted lamps and photofloods will extend the lighted areas while projection filament lamps with their smaller radiant sources will diminish these reflections. Increasing the number of lamps used to illuminate the specimen will increase the highlights. The specularity is also lessened as the lamps are set at a greater distance from the specimen.

When the fresh surgical specimen is very wet, the more extreme reflections may be toned down somewhat by carefully patting the surface with an absorbent lintless cloth.

It is essential that the technician photograph each specimen as though he were illustrating a text. He should insist upon having the tissue cleaned, trimmed and sponged. The specimen should be laid out with great care; dry spots, if any, should be wetted, and pointers and probes, if used, should be arranged so as not to cover important parts or interfere with anatomy. The specimen can be supported by drilled lucite rods, themselves set into lucite bases, capped with rubber.

2. *The background for the gross specimen* The excellence of the gross specimen background should provide more than the mere exclusion of undesirable detail; it should also permit increase in contrast between the subject and the dominant feature being recorded. This may be accomplished esthetically through the use of carefully chosen color. Again, however, regardless of the type of background used—opaque or transilluminated—the important requirement is that it be textureless. A textureless background is obtained by placing the specimen holder at a sufficient distance to keep the background itself out of focus. In this manner, any solid color opaque material can be used, and its color reproduction will be controlled by the intensity and the intervening distance from the lamps which illuminate the specimen.

Most technicians prefer to place the specimen on a sheet of clear glass

236, 237 *The marked improvement in the rendering of detail when using a condenser in the light path of low-magnification photography instead of a ground glass (left) is clearly indicated in these illustrations.*

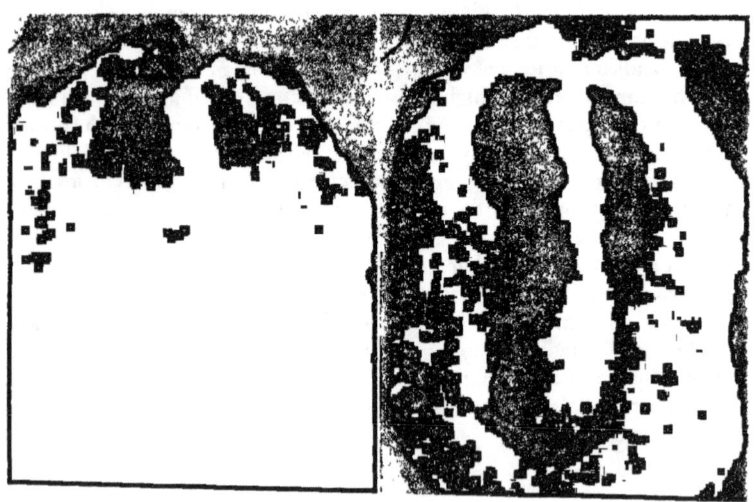

and arrange the lamps to produce minimum reflection. With the use of trans-illuminated light, background colors can be changed by the introduction of colored glass or plastic sheets. In order to avoid overexposing the periphery of the specimen (especially a light one), the intensity of the transilluminated background should be determined by previous tests and kept to a proper level in relation to the overall exposure. The restrictions which apply to the use of bright white in clinical photographic backgrounds are of even greater moment where the gross specimen is concerned. Some serious workers prefer the use of dead black as having least interference with the reproduction of any specimen color.

An apparatus where the specimen platform is transparent and not opaque therefore provides the greatest versatility. It consists of a box containing a number of lamps mounted in the base. Above these lamps are positioned one or more plates of ground or opal glass. Small ventilating holes are angle-drilled all around the box. A shelf is built five or six inches above the diffusing glass to hold the specimen If it is possible to make the holder adjustable in height, such a feature can prove very advantageous. When transilluminated backgrounds are used, the light reading for exposure determination should always be made with the background lights off.

After the photography of the gross specimen is completed and the tissue is returned to the pathological laboratory for histological processing, we can then describe the techniques which are employed when the finished sections are returned This involves the microscope and its special apparatus and brings us to one of the most fascinating aspects of our work. However, before we discuss photomicrography, let us see what happens to the tissue itself and renew our acquaintance with the histological technique.

Preparation of the Microscopical Specimen

Immediately after the surgical specimen has been photographed, it is available for processing by the histology laboratory. Here are brought into action the techniques which result in the finished slide for microscope exam-ination. In order to understand the necessity for the procedures used, it is essential to recall the fundamental problem faced by the microscopist. This consists of the following:

1. The tissue must be fixed so that all the characteristics which appear during life are retained intact.

2. The specimen must be thin enough so that light can pass through it.

3. The various components of the cells must be differentiated in some manner, preferably with dyes

4. The specimen must be made permanent for future review or study.

174

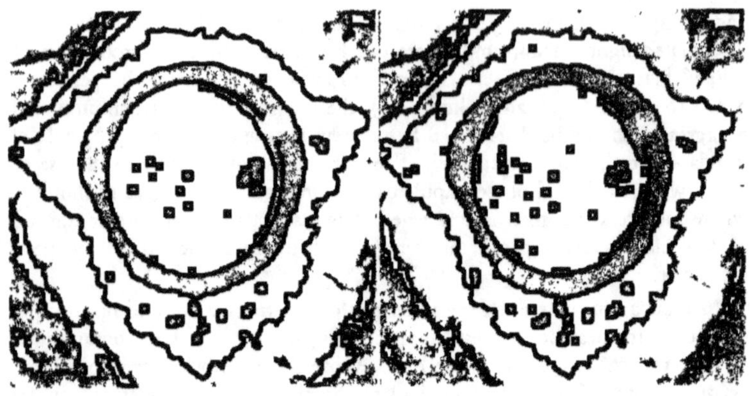

238, 239

The choice of a microscope lens can make a considerable difference in the clarity of image detail, as these illustrations demonstrate. This picture of the human ovum (Graafian follicle) was taken at left with an achromat lens; at right, with the more highly corrected apochromat

In order to accomplish this, the histologist is faced with the following course of action:

Killing and fixing the specimen. The techniques which apply here depend somewhat upon the tissue itself. This is especially true of the fixative, which in all cases, consists of a solution of chemicals that is used to kill and fix the cells. The reagent may include formaldehyde, one of the alcohols, glacial acetic acid, potassium bichromate, or picric acid. If very fine cellular detail is necessary and small bits of tissue are used, cytological fixatives which contain osmic acid in combination with some of the above reagents are employed. The function of the fixative is to kill and fix the cells in a state as close as possible to their living form. Since some ingredients of the solution may shrink the cell and others swell the cell part, the chemicals are combined so that the action of one is minimized by the counterbalancing action of another of the solution components.

The fixation of the tissue may take from an hour to twenty-four, depending upon the nature of the specimen and its size. When fixation is accomplished, the fixative is washed out with a proper solvent—either water or alcohol. The specimen is now ready to begin its journey to the next stage where the second criterion is attained. This consists of making it sufficiently thin for light transmission. To accomplish this state, the tissue is brought into successive alcohols of increasing concentration beginning with 35% and ending finally in absolute alcohol. In this way, the water in the specimen is removed and the "dehydrated tissue" is now ready for immersion in oil.

The alcohol is replaced by a paraffin or collodion solvent. When paraffin is used, such a solvent is xylol or benzol. With collodion, ether or chloroform is necessary. The xylol or benzol or toluol penetrates throughout the tissue and as it does so, the tissue "clears" and is ready for the wax. The paraffin is kept just melted at 68 to 70 degrees and the tissue is brought into the liquid wax and kept in the paraffin oven until the wax has replaced the oil. The specimen is then removed, placed in fresh molten paraffin and rapidly hardened in a block of wax. This block is attached to a proper microtome holder and is cut with that instrument across a wedge knife of very great sharpness to a thickness of one to ten microns. The microtome knife itself must be honed not only to great sharpness but it must have no surface irregularities, for these will appear as tears, ridges or nicks in the tissue. As the section is cut, it comes off the microtome blade in ribbon form. Portions of this ribbon are adhered to a slide with egg albumen and when the section has dried, the preparation is ready to be carried to the third stage—where the cells can be stained The process now proceeds in reverse.

The paraffin is first removed by placing the slide in xylol. The oil is then replaced with successively decreasing concentration of alcohol and brought down to water. Now the cells are stained by immersing the slide in a solution of hematoxylin which dyes the nuclei The excess stain is removed in running water and the slide is again advanced into stronger alcohol to a solution of eosin in 70% alcohol. Here the cytoplasm is stained pink, the tissue is now completely dehydrated and cleared once more in xylol. At this point, a thin cover glass is cemented to the slide with a drop of xylol-balsam solution. When this dries, the three factors which can cause destruction of the specimen have been eliminated. The first is the presence of water, the second the presence

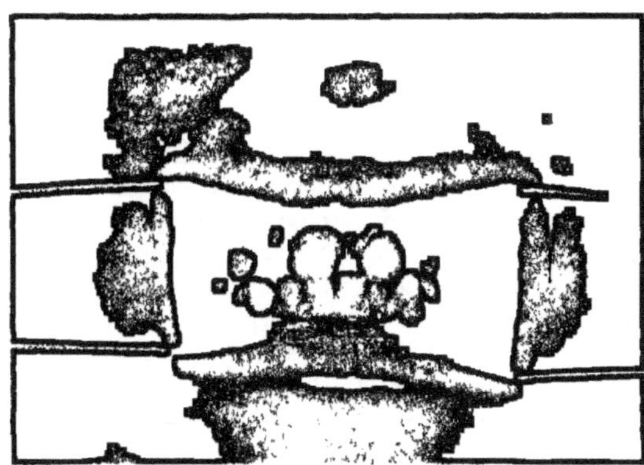

240

A typical example of dental photography, using extension tubes and illuminating the subject evenly by using an electronic flash lamp on each side of the camera Retractors are used to keep the mouth wide open during the exposure to expose without interference the area being photographed

241, 242 *The bounce-light flash technique (see Chap. 11) with electronic flash was used to photograph these examples of bladder stones (those shown at right are appropriately called "gravel") The lights were shielded to produce soft illumination. This is straight photography, with extension tubes*

of air, and third, the presence of bacteria. With these removed, the only remaining problem is the fading of the stain.

For photomicrography the important features of the slide are the thickness of the cover glass and of the specimen, and the nature of the particular dyes used In color photomicrography corrective color compensating filters may be needed to enhance the color values with a particular color film, but in black-and-white negatives filters to obtain proper contrast are almost always desirable

Photomicrography

Probably no aspect of medical photography has profited as greatly from the perfection of inexpensive color film as has reproduction for research and teaching in the microscopical sciences. Consider the problems faced by the lecturer previous to the coming of the "age of color." The alternative of projecting the valuable slide itself with a carbon arc lamp (which is so hot it melts the balsam and fades the stain) is thus always a very expensive procedure, but small tissue biopsies which rarely yield more than one or two slides makes this impossible Although black-and-white lantern slides were available, such material was totally inadequate when it was essential to reproduce varying shades of color Such color differentiation is present in Giemsa and Wright

177

stained blood cells, and are considered very valuable in interpreting differences in the chemical structure of the cell constituents.

Teaching hematology with 35mm film is another good example of the tremendous value of color photomicrography for projection. Since the majority of such cells are magnified with the oil immersion objective, much time is wasted if the lecturer must find a single cell with the tissue slide microprojector. The image flashing by on the screen while the operator searches for a particular place is not only distracting to the audience, but conducive to a quick headache. All this is completely changed by 35mm film and the present fine film slide projectors.

The reflex camera is almost a necessity where moving objects are being photographed or where, for example, constantly changing conditions such as in crystal growth, the subject must be observed to the instant of exposure.

No matter what we are studying or what lighting technique is being used, four important principles should be considered when working with the microscope.

1. All lenses, mirrors and prisms in the system must be positioned in exact optical alignment.

2. The image of the light source must be properly focused as carefully as the specimen itself.

3. Iris diaphragm and other apertures are regulated only in accordance with strict optical laws.

4. Although vibration cannot be eliminated entirely, it is essential to arrange all parts of the apparatus so that this factor is kept to a minimum.

We realize then that in order to get the best results it is not sufficient simply to attach the Exakta directly to the microscope, turn on the lamp and make the exposure. To organize the components of the photomicrographic stand, we must consider the importance of the factors just described.

Limited space demands that we be specifically concerned here with the best means of utilizing the Exakta for general microscope photography. Most photomicrographers are best served by a simply arranged stand which can be modified by the technician to suit his personal requirements. This consists of a solid wood or metal base into which an upright rod or tube pillar is firmly anchored. The microscope and its illuminant are bolted down a proper distance apart at either end of the base. The camera is attached to a separate rider which can be moved up and down the pillar and clamped tight anywhere along its length. The entire unit is then set on a solid table at a height which is most comfortable for the operator.

Not only should the microscope be permanently fixed to its end of the

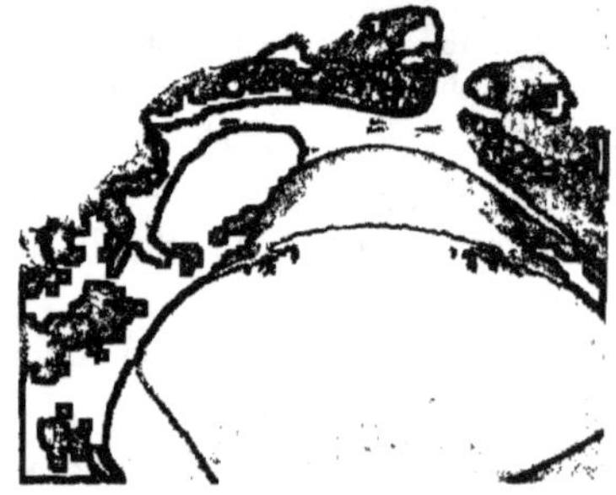

243-245

Suiting the lens to the subject. Below is section of normal human eye showing cornea, lens and optic nerve, taken with a 100mm Micro Summar Bottom right (dark spot is a growing tumor on the cornea of the human eye) was taken with a 35mm Micro Summar The corneal transplant in a rabbit's eye, top right, was photographed with a 135mm lens and extension tubes

base, but the substage mirror should be replaced by a front surface mirror mounted at a $45°$ angle on a plate permanently attached to the photomicrographic base and in the center of the microscope base fork This will obviate the recentering difficulties which invariably arise whenever the mirror is cleaned or is inadvertently disturbed The distance from the microscope mirror to the lamp will depend upon the size and type of lamp chosen and the focal length of the condensers necessary for that illuminant. Usually this distance is not more than 10 inches. The lamp housing, too, should be bolted down to the base so that its alignment will also be stable at all times

The Exakta may be fastened to a bellows extension which is itself attached to the pillar rider At the end of the bellows is inserted an adapter which is moved over and fits into a similar adapter positioned at the eyepiece. This interlocking but non-touching, system provides a vibration-free, light-tight connection. The bellows permits small changes in magnification and, even more important, greater freedom in limiting the subject field The pillar should be anchored where it does not interfere with the microscope movements. The camera is positioned correctly when it is in optical alignment with the eyepoint center and turned to enable the observer to look directly into the camera field lens.

The Choice of Illuminant

The essential role of the light source in microscopy and photomicrography and the importance of the proper use of the lamp and its condensing system frequently has been emphasized. In fact, it can be stated that most image faults arise from the use of a poor illuminant or the employment of improper illumination techniques. This is especially true when we consider the significant improvements in the microscope and its auxiliary apparatus which have become available in recent times, many of which demand much greater care in the use of the instrument. Some of these important contributions include phase contrast optics; reflecting and quartz objectives for ultraviolet research, and microdensitometer accessories for cell component investigation. In all microscope study, whether visual or photographic, careful attention should be paid to the proper collimation of the light beam.

The choice of illuminant depends as much on the technician's budget as it does on the photographic requirements. The preferred source can be chosen with more certainty if we study a description of the good and bad properties of each type available. Theoretically all lamps can be used for both monochrome and color photomicrography. However, in actual practice a particular color emulsion may require such extensive filter balancing that the intensity may be cut severely in the process. Such a light loss emasculates the speed of the entire system. Unfortunately, our concern for light intensity must remain a very basic one. Under the exigencies of the present optical laws (which are not likely to be materially changed in the very near future) we dare not permit any circumstance to squander even a fraction of this valuable commodity. In fact, in spite of our best efforts, we are bound to lose much of what we start off with. Indeed, we have only to turn to the higher magnifications to see how essential a feature the lamp intensity can be.

We must remember too that it is not the entire lamp output but the luminosity per unit emissive area that is the most important factor in photomicrography. For this reason, it is possible to obtain more useful light from the smaller emissive area in a 100-watt zirconium lamp than from a 150-watt projection filament with its much greater luminous area. It is interesting to note that the problem of collimating the light beam from the source to the microscope becomes more complicated and difficult as the size of the emissive area is either greatly increased or very diminished in size. This is the reason why the optics for the zirconium lamp, which has a very small emissive area, has a complicated construction and is quite expensive, while the optics design development for the very much larger gaseous discharge tube is still incomplete for some systems, despite the expenditures of much money and research.

246

Value of Low and High Magnification.
This photograph of a portion of a tape-worm, which can grow in the human body up to 30 feet long, was taken at low magnification in order to include the head and the hooklets, which hang on to the intestine while the segments keep adding up The 100mm Micro Summar lens was used

247

To reveal more detail than was possible with the 100mm lens, a 35mm Micro Summar was substituted to take this much smaller section. In both cases, the illumination was appropriately condensed for the lens in use Neither picture could have been made as readily with extension tubes and conventional photographic lenses.

Features of a Good Lamp

When the Exakta is used in photomicrography, the camera will rarely be more than 8 inches away from the microscope ocular. We can anticipate far less light loss than would be true if a larger film size and longer bellows extension were used Therefore, unless phase microscopy, polarization or dark-field techniques are used, the more powerful lamps which are vital elsewhere are not quite as crucial for the Exakta. Although many microscope lamps are available, some are more advantageous than others; a few are designed for special purposes. The desirable features of a good lamp are:

1. A small luminous source.
2. The source should be textureless.

3. The infrared component (heat) should be minimal.

4. The special sensitivity should permit ready filter correction for color film without too great light loss.

The lamps which answer some of these criteria are as follows:

1. Projection filament lamp 110-volt or low voltage.

2. Coil filament lamp 6v. 5 amps.

3. Ribbon filament lamp 6v. 18 amps.

4. Carbon arc lamp.

5. Zirconium arc lamp.

In all the above lamps, suitable condensers are necessary to collimate the light. Filters are available from both Eastman Kodak and Ansco to balance any deficiencies in the spectral characteristics of the sources. A series of tests should be made with the particular histological stains used in the laboratory to determine the best exposure and filters. Since all physicians may not agree upon the finished character of a particular color photomicrographic transparency, this test will also enable the technician to become acquainted with the personal factors which may be just as important as the other photo-technical aspects of the procedure.

Aligning the Apparatus and Taking the Photomicrograph

1. After all mirrors and lenses have been cleaned, open all apertures and turn on lamp

2. Center lamp beam on microscope mirror

3. Using 16mm objective and 10x eyepiece, center mirror to microscope.

4. Recenter lamp beam to mirror, if necessary. Note: it is a good idea when setting up an optical system to retrace one's steps, each time accomplishing a more careful, more exact positioning of the component parts.

5. Close iris diaphragm of substage condenser and center to microscope objective.

6. Focus microscope illuminant on substage iris diaphragm and recheck all centering.

7. Position slide on stage, focus on proper specimen area and lower Exakta light-tight adapter over eyepiece.

8. Close iris diaphragm of substage condenser and make sure camera is centered to the iris diaphragm image.

9 Open iris, take light reading for exposure evaluation Read the light transmission at the focusing glass of the Exakta with specimen in sharp focus. No filter should be used in taking this reading. The calculation

248, 249

Very high magnification photomicrographs taken with the oil immersion objective to obtain the greatest detail in the illustration of two stages of the process of cell division (mitosis).

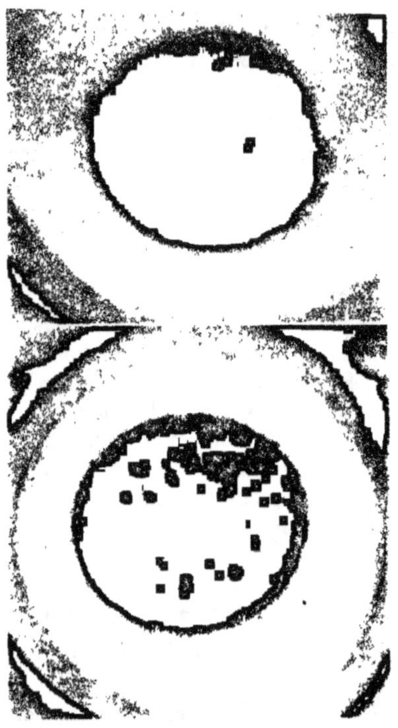

250, 251

These low power microphotographs were needed to show the field of which the details above are a very tiny part The cancer cell is known to divide abnormally, fragmenting into innumerable bits and spreading irregularly in all directions The picture at left shows the normal gland formation of the tissue At right, the normal cells are shown replaced by a disorderly tumor growth, resulting in the loss of the organ's functioning

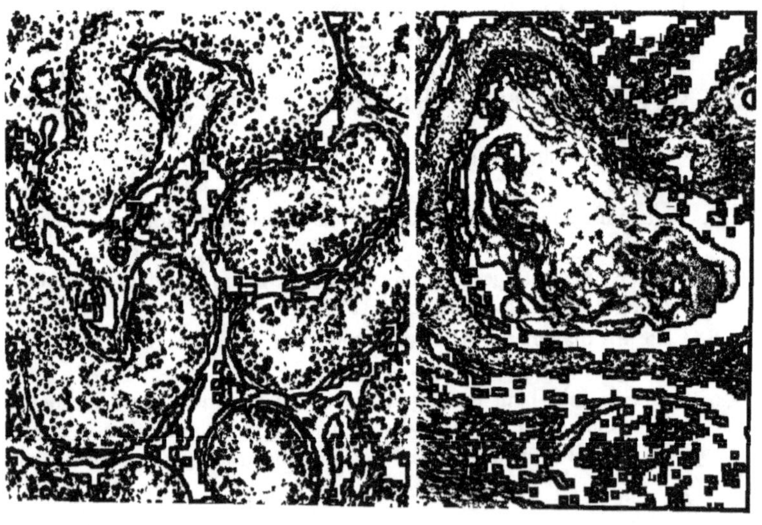

for filters, if needed, is made after taking the reading

10. Expose film for required time.

Timing the Exposure

The constant need for minimizing vibration predicates the use of an isolated shutter apart from the camera. This separate shutter should be mounted with anti-vibration cushions on the photomicrographic base, wherever the light beam narrows to less than 1 inch. The camera is set for time and the separate shutter operated independently The exposures for use with color film are described later in the comparison timing setup for the Weston and G.E. meters. The meter is read by holding it at the camera after the specimen is focused but without filters in the light path

Time-Duration Photomicrographs With the Exakta

The technique of time lapse may be accomplished with the still as well as with the movie camera. Indeed, time-duration still photomicrographs must be made if the series is contemplated for publication. Important uses are to depict growth of crystals or cells or, in fact, any change which produces marked differences over a period of time. The technician should endeavor to safeguard the stability of all photographic conditions and keep a photographic, as well as optical record, to insure repetition of these conditions for future needs

Photomacrography (Low Magnification Photography)

The previous discussion concerned itself with photomicrography However, satisfactory reproduction of large specimen areas is often a difficult problem even for the experienced technician In fact, the uninitiated microscopist and photomicrographer may be surprised to hear that the very highest magnifications are not necessarily the most difficult images to record. The very lowest powers or "survey fields" may, on the contrary, very often be even more arduous to prepare. One of the chief reasons why this is so stems from the difficulty in properly illuminating such a larger specimen area with transmitted light. The primary value of the low power photomicrograph is designed to show tissue relationship. We may consider all magnifications from 1 to 30x to fall into this category. Either one of two optical systems are available to obtain such low powers.

1. Conventional objective and ocular; both of low magnification. These objectives are available from 2.5x to 8x; the oculars from 2x to 10x.

2. Short focal length special microphotographic objectives which are used by themselves. Many manufacturers have computed such a series from 10mm to 120mm focal length.

The great advantage of the first method lies in the continued use of the

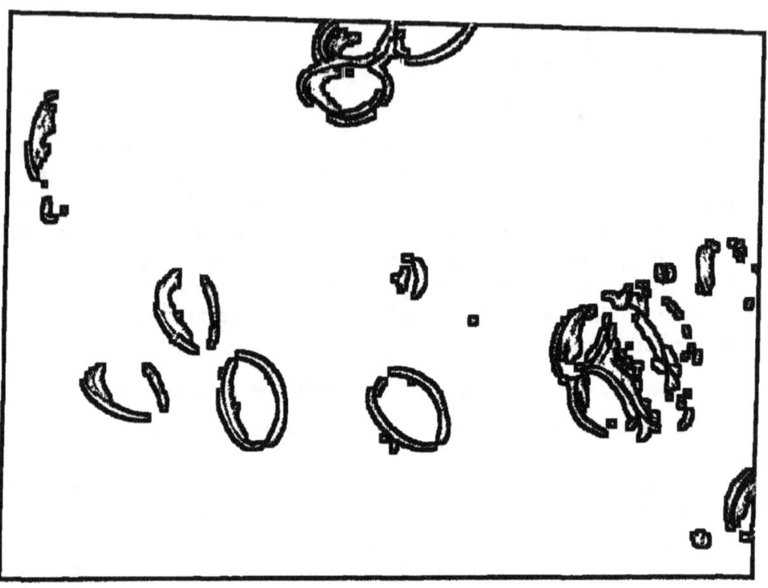

252

A striking example (parasite eggs) of the new field of phase contrast microscopy, in which very small differences in refraction show tremendous differences in contrast. This increase in contrast permits the study of living cells without the aid of staining and the introduction of artifacts which are part of the staining procedure

microscope stand and the fine focusing which it affords However, the conventional low power objective-ocular combination does not offer the extended range of magnification which is possible with the special photographic objectives Another important advantage of these photographic objectives lies in the greater flatness of field, the better color correction and the more satisfactory angle of view of these specially designed lenses.

Illumination of the Specimen In Low Magnification Photography

The conventional microscope condenser is specifically designed to collimate the light properly when objectives ranging from oil immersion 1.9mm (100x magnification) to 16mm (10x magnification) are used with it. However, objectives of lesser magnification demand increased coverage of the light area because of their increased angle of view In the conventional set-up we can obtain this increased coverage only by racking down the condenser to such a level that there is actual interference with the numerical aperture and therefore a lowering of the resolving power of the entire optical system. We may avoid such an unhappy situation with its subsequent aberrations by completely replacing the research condenser with a special condenser computed for use with low-power objectives. This will insure matching the numerical aperture of the objectives without sacrificing the resolving power. Some of the modern research condensers, however, have provision for splitting the lens system to accomplish this.

The Contrast of the Photomacrograph

The overall contrast of the specimen is a very important consideration in low-magnification photography. Although this original contrast will influence the photographic result the following factors are also important in the production of the final contrast:

1. Section thickness, the stain and the freshness of the stain.
2. The filters used, the type of film, the film processing.
3. The accuracy of exposure, the exposure-processing relationship.
4. The processing paper and the paper developer contrast.

Other factors include the age of the film, the age of the processing solution. We can therefore see the danger of losing contrast. It is especially important that the section not be cut too thin. In fact, the low micron tolerance so necessary for detailed study at higher powers may prove to be disadvantageous for low magnification photography. As the magnification level is lowered, the section thickness should be raised; thus if 5 mu is a suitable thickness for 100x magnification, 10 mu is a better thickness if the same area is photographed at 25x, and 20 mu may be preferable when that area is photographed at only 5x magnification.

Cavity Illumination in Endoscopic Photography

All technicians who enjoy the added zest which the challenge of greater than ordinary difficulties offers, can interest themselves in the special problem which endoscopic photography affords. The inner anatomy of such organs as the mouth, naso-pharynx, ears, vagina, rectum, although accessible, are especially difficult to photograph for two reasons. The first is the presence of sphincters or other tight-closing muscles which necessitate the introduction of retractors to keep the orifice open; the second and real challenge is the need for proper illumination: very bright, cool, and short, to allow for rapid photography. We are aided greatly in the choice of retractors by the availability of many specialized surgical instruments suitably designed for specific cavities. The problem here is to minimize the specular highlights reflected by the metal by blackening or otherwise dulling the surface reflectivity of these retractors

The problem of illumination, however, is not so readily solved. Unfortunately, common bedfellows of disease are increased sensitivity and pain. Therefore, we must keep basic irritants, such as manipulation and heat, minimal. This we can do if we make the apparatus instantly adaptable and we keep the lamp both cool and bright.

Depending upon the funds available, either one of two systems may be used. In the first, conventional projection filament or coil filament lamps are set at either side of the camera to spot directly into the orifice. The heat from these lamps may be minimized by designing the circuitry to include relays which provide for rapid lamp sparking just before exposure. However, this arrangement, though often convenient for oral cavity photographs, is not usually suitable for intravaginal and cervical record The speculum necessary for the female genital tract is best illuminated by a single lamp. Another way of reducing the heat would be to arrange the illuminants so that the rays are first directed to preset mirrors. The reflected light is then passed through heat absorbing glass into the orifice However, one must guard against a substantial light loss which often results from this technique.

253

Typical arrangement of electronic flash lamps in closeup photography of living laboratory animals Such an instantaneous light source is imperative in this type of work because of subject movement.

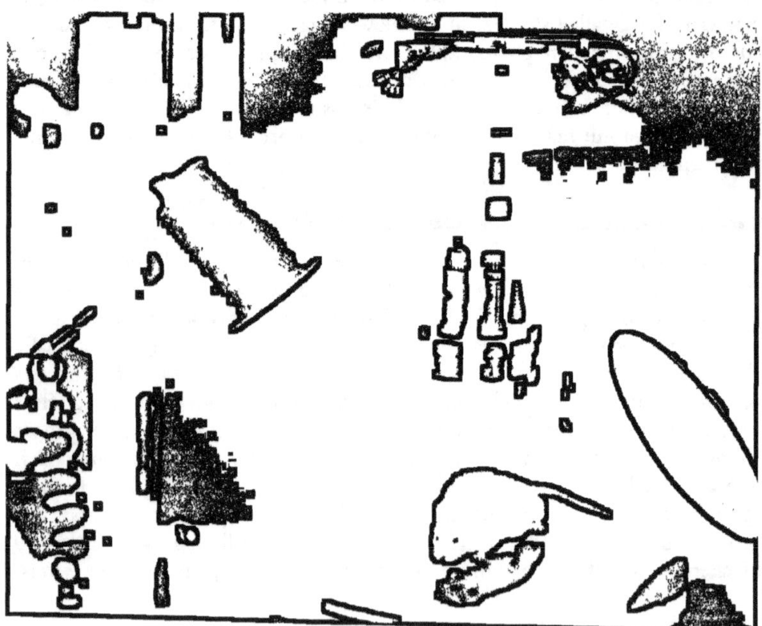

Wherever possible, all mirrors should be front-surface coated. Optical parts should be so designed to perform best at very short distances. In this respect, it may help keep the photographic lens closer if a hole is cut in the mirror through which the camera lens may pick up the image Of necessity, the lamps used for most endoscopic work should be small, projection type with tightly wound coil filaments. These may be normal 110v. or low voltage. For greatest efficiency condensers should be used with these lamps. Some technicians have ingeniously mounted suitably small, very bright, low-voltage lamps directly into the speculum or other retractor. The efficiency of such lamps is limited by the size of the orifice diameter and the distance of the surface photographed to the camera lens. If conventional flash lamps are used at the close range demanded in endoscopic photography, the glass envelope should be dipped or otherwise shatterproofed.

The second system is the use of the spot-shaped coil or ring-wound gaseous discharge tube. The two great advantages of this type of illumination lie, of course, in the great speed of the actual exposure and the very high-brilliance, low-heat flash.

The choice of optimum focal length is dependent upon the particular cavity to be covered and the working distances available Very rapid exposure, imperative to avoid vibration blurring, is so crucial that it is often necessary for other factors to be compromised. If the brightness of the lamp is less than desired, the lens aperture should be opened to compensate. This will demand more critical focus, but fortunately only a single surface plane is usually required.

Exposure Evaluation and Timing

No description of preferred working methods in medical photography is complete without a discussion of a logical way of evaluating exposure and timing. The suggestions given here are applicable to every aspect of medical photography from clinical to reproduction of X-rays and the taking of photomicrographs.

What is the proper exposure for any given subject? How is the best way to obtain this information? Both these questions, which must be answered before any photograph is taken, demand even more careful attention when the photographs must be such accurate reproductions as are usually required in scientific photography The problem may be more complicated than merely measuring the transmitted or incident light and then converting this reading directly into an exposure. Actually, we must consider all possible factors which relate to the finished photograph. Perhaps we may later compromise with some features in order to obtain more desirable effects in others. Naturally

254

An advanced type of photographic apparatus, which permits viewing the specimen separately from the camera, thereby providing a critically precise means of focusing and placement of the specimen.

the evaluation of all lighting conditions and specimen features to select desirable exposure is greatly simplified if the intensity of the illumination is raised sufficiently to obtain a reading with a conventional exposure meter.

Indeed, the choice of proper timing becomes complicated when the distance between subject and lens decreases steadily beyond the minimum three feet. As we move the lens closer to the subject, tubes or bellows extension must be made part of the optical system. It is the introduction of these new variables no less than the need to concentrate the light upon the smaller areas being recorded, which necessitates the more careful interpretation of all the information regarding the conditions involved.

It is possible of course, to prepare a chart precalculating the extra exposure necessary to balance the changes incurred in optical conditions. Many technicians have done this for their own setups. Very often the Kodak grey reflection card can be very helpful where circumstances permit its use. When light intensity permits, the best method utilizes a direct reading from the Exakta ground glass for here we have the advantage of working with the reflected image intensity at the film plane distance, so all of the optic factors are automatically taken into account. Since we are not reading the object brightness but the intensity of the image on the ground glass, we cannot use the exposure directly indicated by the meter.

The table below gives exposure times (determined experimentally) for color film ASA 10 when the ground glass reading is as indicated. The data can be readily translated into exposure times for films of different speed, or exposures at lens apertures other than that at which the reading was taken.

Weston Reading	G. E. Reading (Hood Removed)	Norwood Reading	Exposure Time
2	—	—	1 sec
4	—	—	½ sec
8	2	4	¼ sec
16	3	8	1/8 sec
—	4	—	1/20 sec
32	5	16	1/30 sec
—	6	24	1/40 sec
65	10	32	1/60 sec
13	—	—	1/100 sec

It will be found that these exposures hold well for closeups, low magnification photographs and photomicrographs. If the light is too bright, the intensity should be controlled with neutral density filters. A series of experiments recently completed has shown the deleterious effects of closing down the iris beyond the optimum value for any individual lens. We wrote previously of compromises. This is a case in point. The iris of the microscope substage condenser should be closed down judiciously only when the need for depth of field is paramount.

Timing the Exposure

In order to minimize vibration, all exposures longer than 1/50th second should be accomplished by turning the light on and off. This is true regardless of the camera being used, and is one of the important reasons why I prefer electronic flash. The speed of the exposure puts it beyond the danger of vibration interference.

190

Index

TO 134